THE WAYS OF BLACK FOLKS

THE WAYS OF BLACK FOLKS

A Year in the Life of a People

LAWRENCE C. ROSS, Jr.

Dafina Books

KENSINGTON PUBLISHING CORP.

http://www.kensingtonbooks.com

DAFINA BOOKS are published by

Kensington Publishing Corp.
850 Third Avenue
New York, NY 10022

All Kensington titles, imprints, and distributed lines are available at special quantity discounts for bulk purchases for sales promotion, premiums, fund-raising, educational or institutional use.

Special book excerpts or customized printings can also be created to fit specific needs. For details, write or phone the office of the Kensington Special Sales Manager: Kensington Publishing Corp., 850 Third Avenue, New York, NY 10022, Attn. Special Sales Department. Phone: 1-800-221-2647.

Dafina Books and the Dafina logo Reg. U.S. Pat. & TM Off.

Library of Congress Card Catalogue Number: 2002103433
ISBN 0-7582-0057-9

First Printing: January 2003
10 9 8 7 6 5 4 3 2 1

Printed in the United States of America

The book is dedicated to my son, Langston,
who's always had a warm smile and
big hug for his oft-traveling daddy.

CONTENTS

ACKNOWLEDGMENTS

When writing a book like *The Ways,* literally hundreds of people help you along the way. Unfortunately, no matter how determined you are to keep track of everyone you want to thank, you inevitably forget some people. So in advance, I say thank you. But I would like to thank specifically, my wife, April, for enduring the trials and tribulations of having an absentee husband. I would like to thank my son, Langston, who if I'm lucky, will barely remember that his father was gone for almost a year. Also, I would like to thank my agent, Deidre Knight, and my editor, Karen Thomas. Both are shining lights in the publishing industry. I would be remiss to forget about my tiger at Kensington, Jessica McLean, who looks after her author's interest like no other. And also I must thank my booking agent, Kimberly Branch, who skillfully coordinated my hectic schedule.

I would also like to thank Nikki Giovanni, Ginney Fowler, Michael Gordon, Boyd Tinsley, Rebecca Wright, Oona King, David Lammy, Dr. Preston King, Christian Mann, Allyson Carson, the Wilson family, Salome Thomas El, Maria Manning, Lileth and Ed Pottinger, Blanche Richardson and the staff of

Marcus Books, Ralph Gilles, Elisabeth Epps, Ainsley Burrows, Deborah Harris, Danielle Carr, Zakiya Carr, Marcio "Kibe" Macedo, Jose Marmo, Rosangela Valle, Mother Beatrice, Adailton Moreira Costa, Susan Taylor, Diane Weathers, Victoria Cooper, Tamice Parnell, Ronald Gordon, Paul Sekyere, Natalie Gill, Okofo and Imokus Robinson, Dr. Michael Williams, the staff of the Golden Tulip hotel in Ghana, Linda Horton, Ayaba Akofa Adaobi, Grace Cameron, Rob Evans, Congressman Chaka Fattah, Guru, Ronald Anthony Mills, Eric Stephens, Natalie Byrdsong, Bill Campbell, Frank Ski, and Sarah Honda.

INTRODUCTION

As a fourteen-year-old high school freshman, I began developing my personal philosophy. It was then that I, like other African-American teenagers, read *The Autobiography of Malcolm X*, by Alex Haley. Through those words of Malcolm X I first realized that I was not simply a person unto myself. I was a member of a race, a participant in a culture, and the carrier of a rich legacy. I knew other African Americans, people that I would never meet, depended upon my contributions for our collective survival. It was then that I decided to become a writer. And I've made it my life to write about my people, the African-American people.

Black people in general have always fascinated me. As an African-American writer, I have observed how a people so often portrayed as an amorphous group is so often exceedingly diverse.

We are remarkably wealthy yet numbingly impoverished. There has never been a time when more black people have been educated, yet in some countries, the educational system has failed us and our children are either dropping out of school early or graduating from high school illiterate.

We are complex yet simple, different but the same. No matter what religion, black people tend to be more religious than any other ethnic group, yet are also more liberal in our politics than any other ethnic group.

We are virtuous and imperfect. Black people volunteer in their community at a high percentage, yet the prison system is filled with black faces convicted of crimes.

African Diasporan communities around the world or just one black person may often mirror all of these attributes and vices!

The genesis of *The Ways of Black Folks: A Year in the Life of a People* began when I was in the process of writing my previous book, *The Divine Nine: The History of African American Fraternities and Sororities.* In that book, I interviewed African Americans from different African-American fraternal organizations, different regions of the United States, with different experiences and different outlooks on life. These were just ordinary people leading ordinary lives. Each had a unique story to tell that helped illuminate a piece of the puzzle which explained what it meant to be an African-American fraternal member.

As I finished *The Divine Nine,* I began to wonder if we as African Americans were connected by our stories. And because I have always felt an intimate kinship exists among all the people throughout the African Diaspora, I began to wonder about the stories of peoples I had not yet met, such as black people in Brazil, Jamaica, Canada, and Europe. Are we connected beyond the obvious bond of our ancestors having been in slavery? Do we retain elements of Africa that could provide the sinew for our commonality? And how do African Diasporans view life in other countries, and how do they think others view them, particularly in Mother Africa, a land that so often carries the hopes and dreams of our people?

The Ways of Black Folks: A Year in the Life of a People is about—people. Ordinary stories by ordinary people. It is that simple. Some subjects were specifically chosen for the book, while other subjects were picked at random. Their stories, however positive and negative, are their own as individuals. No story is more important than another; however, collectively, all of these stories tell us something about who we are as African Americans, Afro-Brazilians, Afro-Caribbeans, and West Indians in Britain.

For fourteen months, I traveled nearly 150,000 miles searching for those stories. From the frigid cold of Toronto to the rainy streets of London, the smoggy skies of São Paulo, and the warm beaches of Ghana, black people had stories to tell.

While writing *The Ways of Black Folks* I had a conversation with a young black woman. She adamantly refused to be called African American because she believed that she had no connection with the African continent or its people. She just wanted to be known as a black woman, no more and no less. Her argument was that she couldn't point out where she came from on the African continent, and that she was now an American. She thought that the term *African American* was *politically correct*, but that if people were being true to themselves, they would realize that they were just Americans. And while this is a view heard from a lot of African Americans—and Africans—I respectfully disagree.

Malcolm X once stated that if kittens were born in an oven, no one would call them brownies. And the same analogy applies for Africans born in America, Brazil, Canada, the Caribbean, Europe, or anywhere else that we are born and live. The essence of being an African doesn't change because of different locales or circumstances. The African-ness of our being remains in our speech, our manner of worship, our food, and millions of small and large traits that continue to make us who we are. In my opinion, to think of oneself as being *just* a black man or black woman needlessly limits one. In fact, it is exceedingly important for all Africans within the Diaspora to constantly reassert their African roots for a number of reasons.

First, it is a cultural inheritance that was paid for in blood. I can't imagine that my African ancestors, brutally ripped from the land of their birth, wanted those of us who survive today to forget where we came from. To forget or disassociate is to allow those who stole us to ultimately succeed in separating our people from our humanity. Our unique circumstances in coming to our new countries mean that these additional New World experiences add to our African base experience. In other words, the

American experience adds American traits to my African heritage. The same goes for the African in Brazil, the Caribbean, and Europe. As one person stated during my travels, those of us in the African Diaspora are members of the largest African tribe in the world.

Second, to think as an African Diasporan is a way for black people to leave the boundaries of their own political borders and cooperate with black people in like situations. If you are an African American interested in reparation, which is more powerful: to include only the forty million African Americans who live in America, or to include the millions of Africans living throughout the Caribbean and South America? Only if you can see beyond your small world can you see the ways in which we are connected.

Read each story within *The Ways of Black Folks* and listen to the people. You will agree with some, disagree with others, but all of their experiences are legitimate. Then go out and add your own experience to the Ways of Black Folks.

Lawrence C. Ross, Jr.

THE WAYS OF BLACK FOLKS

1

The Execution of Wanda Jean Allen
McAlester, Oklahoma

You're not only in my prayers; you're also in most of my confessions. You're everything I ever wanted. I'm very happy with your love. You're my everything. P.S. I'm the type of person who will hunt someone down I love and kill them. Do I make myself clear, Gloria? Jean.

—A letter from Wanda Jean Allen to Gloria Leathers

The January snow still lingers on the patchy brown Oklahoma earth, as if an involuntary reminder of a recent winter storm. But this is the old Indian Territory, and the ground, which is more accustomed to a constant baking sun, rebels, mocking the dirty, discolored snow. With the rolling gray skies soon bringing California storms from a thousand miles away, the weather brings a sense of impending gloom. Today someone will die. It's in the atmosphere and you can feel it in your bones.

Ruby Wilson's home, in Edmond, Oklahoma, is the typical home of a proud matriarch. Although her children have long ago moved away, she has covered every wall in her small apartment with photographic memories. As if she is trying to wrap herself in a warm familial embrace, each of these framed images chronicles the lives of her children, grandchildren, nieces, and nephews. Weddings, graduations, enlistments in the military: one can track the lives of her beloved simply by looking at the stair-stepped photos.

A quiet and modest woman, Ms. Wilson relies on her faith in God to get her through the days. A well-worn family Bible, complete with color depictions of Jesus' life, sits on the coffee table. It lies open, ready for comfort in times of crisis. In the past twelve years, she has used that Bible more than once.

On December 2, 1988, Gloria J. Leathers, 29, was shot in front of the village police department in Oklahoma City. Wanda Jean Allen killed Gloria Leathers. The two had originally met in jail, Leathers in for shoplifting, Allen serving time for manslaughter. After their release, the two had become lovers. Lovers, until things turned violent at home. After enduring years of domestic violence, Leathers had had enough. It was time to get a restraining order against Allen. However, as she stood in front of the police station steps, minutes from filling out the papers for the order, she was gunned down. Leathers's mother, Ruby Wilson, had accompanied her daughter to the police house that day to file the order, and witnessed her daughter's murder.

Allen had been convicted and sentenced to death by lethal injection. After twelve years of delays, false starts, and last-minute appeals, Allen was finally scheduled to die. Tonight she will be the first woman executed in Oklahoma since 1907.

For Leathers's family, this night is not about revenge; it is about closure. Even Ms. Wilson, who saw her daughter die, has come to terms with her murder.

"Some people say an eye for an eye, a tooth for a tooth. I don't believe that. Just because you hit me, I don't have to hit you," she says, her eyes never lifting from the floor.

But an execution is scheduled, and the state is going to hit back. As the family prepares, an unanswerable question remains: how do you prepare for an execution? How do you act? Who do you invite to see it? What emotions course through your body?

Gloria Leathers's brothers, Gregory Wilson and Robert Ferguson Jr., sit patiently in their mother's living room. It's noon, and the execution is set for 9 P.M. Wilson, the older brother, is military through and through. His bearing and presence speak of twenty years of being a staff sergeant in the U.S. Army as he commands respect—even in his civvies. Although quiet, his demeanor is one of a man who is used to dealing with stress, but you get a sense that this is one event that he's not quite sure how to resolve. So thinking about his sister, whom his family affectionately called Kee-Kee, helps take the edge off.

"My sister Kee-Kee would always send me a care package for Christmas, no matter where she was," Wilson said wistfully, leaning forward in his chair as he spoke. "She could be in prison and I could be assured of a CARE package. It would consist of sausage and cheeses. To this day, it still mystifies the hell out of me how she was able to send those things, even when she was in prison. That's the one thing that I miss the most about her. Being in the military, I didn't get to see her a lot, but I realized that she was dead when I didn't get those Christmas presents."

Wilson doesn't necessarily think that executing Allen is the solution, but he is not saying he's against the death penalty. He just wonders if letting her live could provide clues to why people murder others.

"Personally, I don't want this lady to die," he said. "It's not going to solve the problem. You can eliminate it but you didn't solve it. I think that we do society an injustice if we didn't get someone to go inside this woman's head and find out what made her do what she did. If you kill her, then the answer goes with her. If we get the answer out of her, then we prevent someone from getting killed down the road."

Wilson actually liked Allen, and when Allen and Leathers were together, he thought that it was one of the happiest times the family had seen their sister having. But they didn't know Allen had a dark side. They didn't know that the reason Allen had been in jail the first time was because of manslaughter. She had killed her previous lover, Detra Pettus, in 1981.

Ferguson is a postal worker in Jefferson City, Missouri. Young, outgoing, and on track for a new promotion, he has been the main spokesperson for the family during this ordeal.

Although he tries to maintain his emotions, Ferguson's eyes betray feelings of anger and resentment toward the killer of his sister. For him, when his sister was murdered, the most valuable thing taken away was time. Time was needed to resolve long-standing issues with his sister.

"Kee-Kee and I were the ones that always fought," he said. "Personally, I don't think that we had a chance to bond and make that part up. I resent that. We never got that chance to heal."

As for his views on Allen's execution, Ferguson is short and to the point.

"I say that if the evidence is cut and dry, then execute her," he said unblinkingly.

In an extraordinary set of circumstances, the state of Oklahoma is scheduled to execute a prisoner each Tuesday and Thursday during the month of January. And like most capital-punishment cases, Allen's case has sparked international outrage by capital-punishment opponents from around the world.

Allen has said that she is a changed woman and that she has turned her life over to God. Her attorneys have claimed that Allen is mentally retarded, with an IQ of sixty-nine. The front pages of Oklahoma newspapers have carried Allen's statements to the Oklahoma Pardon and Parole Board, eliciting sympathy from the public.

"Please let me live," she pleaded. "Please let me live."

The parole board rejected her pleas.

"She's really harping on that she turned her life over to God," said Wilson. "Well, if she turned her life over to God, then she shouldn't have any problem with accepting the sentence. Jesus Christ was executed; so let it be if she is true to what she says. Talk is cheap and actions speak louder than words."

"People say that she's sorry and that she's changed," Ferguson added. "But this happened twelve years ago, and only after they set the execution date did everyone want to come forward [telling us this]. My mother's been in the same location for these past twelve years, and no one has come and apologized or said anything. Now all of the sudden, everyone is so sorry."

What particularly galls the two brothers is the presence of the Reverend Jesse Jackson in Oklahoma. Jackson has been lobbying the governor for clemency in Allen's case and has been leading prayer vigils in Allen's name. When Wilson and Ferguson woke up this morning, they saw television images of Jackson being arrested for civil disobedience and spending a night in the Oklahoma County jail. Although they recognize that Jackson was protesting the institution of capital punishment, they resent the fact that he has made no efforts to get their side of the story. They feel that he has ignored the victim in the case of their sister.

"My problem with Jesse is that he is only for the poor and the inmate," says Ferguson angrily. "You need to be for everybody. I'm not taking anything from them, but you need to be for everybody."

The door opens to the apartment, and two white filmmakers burst in. For the past two months, Liz Garber has been chronicling the lives of both the Allen and Wilson families for an HBO documentary titled "The Execution of Wanda Jean," and today is the endgame. Although they have gotten to know the family, their presence rings of an unnecessary intrusion. They are trying too hard to prove to themselves and the family that they care, so they are overly exuberant in their greetings and salutations. Gregory flashes a glance of annoyance in their direction.

It's now three o'clock and it is time to drive to the Oklahoma State Penitentiary in McAlester, Oklahoma. It's a two-hour drive from Edmond, and the bulk of the family will be waiting at the prison when they arrive. The family, including Leathers's daughter and her children, all begin the sober journey.

The drive is nondescript. The caravan of cars snakes its way through the Oklahoma highways, entering and leaving old Indian territories long ago stolen from Native Americans. Finally the prison is within sight. At the main gate, television crews have set up their operations, and across the street from the prison, capital-punishment opponents silently hold signs protesting the coming of death.

When you look at the Oklahoma State Penitentiary at first, second, and third glance, you realize that this is one frightening place. It is a massive white castlelike structure whose job is to intimidate and overwhelm anyone who unfortunately passes through its gate, and it does its job extremely well. One glance tells you that it is nearly impossible to escape from this fortress.

After passing through security checkpoints, the family makes its way into the prison. For the next few hours, a small anteroom will be the gathering point for both the Gloria Leathers family and the Pettus family as well. The Pettus family is there to see what they believe is final justice done for the murder of their loved one, Detra. The two families greet each other with warmth and love, as three little children rip and run through the room.

"We've got to stop meeting for negative occasions," Ferguson says to the group with a smile.

It's five o'clock and there are four hours to burn before the execution. After thirty minutes, the warden and other prison representatives make their way to the family room and begin explaining to the family what is going to happen in the coming hours. First, they note that the Tenth Circuit Court of Appeals, in Denver, Colorado, has rejected Allen's appeal. There is an audible sigh of relief. In the past, the families had gathered for a scheduled execution only to have a last-minute appeal grant Allen another chance at life. That had proved agonizing to the family, as it meant that they would have yet another day to relive Kee-Kee's death.

Allen is down to her last two appeals this evening: one before the United States Supreme Court, and the other before Governor Keating, who cannot grant clemency but only a stay of execution.

Surprisingly, the atmosphere in this room is not one of doom and gloom but of a light, easy banter, and it contrasts sharply with the warden's sober tone. Maybe it is the children, who blissfully play hide-and-go-seek with each other. Maybe the feeling that when this execution occurs, this long nightmare will soon be over. Or maybe it is a little simpler than that, and maybe no one quite knows how to act at an execution. Again, how do you act at an execution?

The warden announces that the family will have an opportunity to tour both death row and the execution chamber. Everyone in the family wants to see where the killer of their loved one lives, and where, in a few hours, she will die.

The families make their way to the other side of the prison, where they are taken on the tour. Death row, where about fourteen prisoners live, is nothing extraordinary. Large steel doors with little slits for windows, not the stereotypical iron bars of the Hollywood movies, lock the prisoners in their cells.

"The Death Row inmates are in their cells for twenty-three hours a day and are only let out for one hour of exercise," says the prison guide.

The prisoners are allowed to exercise in a bleak concrete area that is fully secured. At all times, they are wearing handcuffs and leg irons, and they are not allowed any human contact. During the weekends, they are on twenty-four hour lockdown.

A large tarp has been placed around the death cell of Wanda Jean Allen, so she can meet with her family in privacy. Her cell is a short walk to the execution chamber, where the prison officials take the family next.

"At the time of the execution, the family will come into the chamber first and sit behind this smoke-covered glass," says the warden, who has joined the family for this part of the tour. "No one can see you behind this glass, but the room is not soundproof. You will then leave last, so that no one will be able to see you."

The execution chamber is a surprisingly small room divided into two areas. In the witness area, the victim's family watches the execution behind tinted glass windows. In front of them the press sits, while in front of the press sit the representatives of Wanda Jean Allen. All face the execution room.

The execution room looks like any doctor's office in America, with one exception: none of the patients strapped to these gurneys ever walk out of this office alive. A lone telephone stands a silent vigil for any last-minute reprieves.

For the first time at the prison, the family members are very quiet and reflective. There is a definite nervousness that invades their souls. It seems to dawn on them that this is where someone is going to be killed. No one has any questions for the warden.

Twelve family members are allowed to witness the execution live, while the rest have the option of watching on live closed-circuit television in another room. All of the family members, except for the children, who are not allowed, would choose to watch Allen die in one form or another.

The family members make their way back to the family room, and there are some tears. A couple of people have got lightheaded from the experience, and the easygoing nature of before has disappeared. The minutes and hours begin to drone on inexorably. The face of Ruby Wilson, Gloria's mother, shows the stress. She has said little in these hours.

Prison officials pass out notepads so that the family can write out a press statement about the execution. About fifty newspaper and television press representatives, including journalists from Europe, are covering this execution. They are in a separate building, and the family will have to face them after Allen has died. They relish the opportunity.

"I can't wait to tell Jesse Jackson about himself," says Ferguson, as he writes furiously.

It's now 7:30 P.M. The United States Supreme Court has rejected Wanda Jean Allen's appeal. It is now in the hands of the governor, and he has already gone on record saying that he will let the execution go through.

Pizza arrives for the family, but no one is really hungry. An aunt has a diabetic seizure. The prison paramedics come rushing to her aid, but she is okay. The room grows more and more quiet as the pressure begins to mount. Suddenly, the warden's assistant comes into the room.

"It's time," he says.

The families quietly make their way to the execution chamber and the closed-circuit room. Everyone goes except for one girl who is under 18, and the children. It's 8:20 P.M.

The children continue to play and sing *Sesame Street* songs as the minutes tick on.

"La la la, it's Elmo's World!" sings one and the others join in.

It's now 9 P.M. Wanda Jean Allen will be strapped to the execution gurney and given a fatal drug combination of sodium thiopental, a fast-acting barbiturate that causes unconsciousness, pancuronium bromide, a muscle relaxant that paralyzes the diaphragm and thus arrests breathing, and potassium chloride, which causes cardiac arrest. The process is designed to kill the prisoner in about fifteen minutes.

At 9:21 P.M., a prison representative comes into the family room and announces that it's over. Wanda Jean Allen, murderer of Debra Pettus and Gloria Leathers, is dead.

As the families slowly walked back into the family room, Gregory Wilson felt no sense of pity for the condemned, even though he wanted to, even at the moment of her death.

"I wanted to feel sympathy for her but I couldn't," he reflected his face ashen. "She gave her last statement, which was "Lord forgive them; they know not what they do" and then stuck her tongue out at us. It sounds like to me that she's still not accepting responsibility. She didn't show any remorse for what she'd done."

He walks away as family members hug and console each other. When you look into the faces of each of the two families, it seems as though they are seeking to understand what they just witnessed. And inevitably, they ask themselves, will this be enough for them to put their Leathers and their Pettus to rest?

The last order of business for the family was to meet the press. The Oklahoma prison officials had pressed the family to make their statements and not take questions, and the family agreed. They walked into the pressroom, heads held high, with a dignity that quietly reaffirmed the reason that they were there. They were there for Gloria Leathers.

Katina Wilson, Gloria's niece, read a statement that represented the family's feelings.

"We, the family of Gloria Leathers, feel that justice has been served," she read. "We can now go on with our lives and put all of this behind us. We can never put the memory of Kee-Kee behind, but we put the hatred and the question why didn't she [Allen] let her live behind. What society doesn't know is that the family of Gloria had nothing to do with the decision that the judge and the jury made. You guys feel sorry for Wanda Jean, but your concerns should be about the effect this has had on the Leathers family and the Pettus family. We are the victims."

As the family members filed out of the pressroom to make

their way home, Robert Ferguson was asked if he remembered Wanda Jean Allen begging the parole board, "Please don't kill me, please don't kill me."

Ferguson looked at back and stated, "My sister wasn't given a choice about life."

He then hugged his mother and walked off into the cool Oklahoma night.

2

Sex and the Sisters

Somewhere in San Fernando Valley, California

The desire of a man for a woman is not directed at her because she is a human being, but because she is a woman. That she is a human being is of no concern to him.

—Immanuel Kant

Okay, here is the premise of the new movie, *Open House.* A couple is trying to lease a condo. There's some dialogue, more dialogue, and even more dialogue. Finally, the couple leases the condo at the end of the movie. *The End.* Oh, and there's one more thing. In between all of the dialogue, the couple leasing the condo has sex with each other, with their "clients," and with everyone else in the cast. Welcome to the strange world of pornography, African-American style. It is a world where African-American actors and actresses, some who've only met minutes before, have sex on camera for money. Each actor, actress, director, and mere functionary has a different story, reason, and philosophy that guide their lives within this business. But one thing unites them: they all have an exit strategy to leave the porn industry. Unfortunately it is never implemented.

In a nondescript warehouse in the San Fernando Valley, about twenty-five miles north of Hollywood, California, "Mom" is cooking up a feast of bacon and eggs for the movie crew. A motley collection of scruffy twenty-something's, the crew of *Open House* has a camaraderie that comes from having worked together on porn film after porn film. As they dig into Mom's fixings, they joke easily, generally accusing one another of being secretly gay. There's a feeling of family as they prep for a sixteen-hour day of filming.

They get their easygoing attitude from their director, Jay, whose doppelganger must be actor Steve Martin. He is a non-stop dynamo, one minute talking with the crew and in the next making changes to the script. After passing out the scripts, he retreats to his office to go over the day's shoot with his writer and assistant director.

In a makeup room just off the lounge area, actress Nickki Fairchild is getting ready for her day's work. Like most of the women in today's film, she is a very pretty woman. Small of stature, almost delicate, Fairchild stares into the wall mirror as she prepares for her day. She's alone in the room, nearly invisible, since she hasn't spoken to anyone outside this area. She silently tussles with her hair until her makeup woman makes her entrance. As she sits in the chair, ready to become a celluloid star, you can see a mental and physical transformation begin.

"I grew up in Albuquerque, New Mexico, and I came out here [to Los Angeles] in 1998 to do acting and modeling," says the 22-year-old. "I was supposed to be in *Baywatch* but I wasn't able to learn how to swim fast enough. So I started dancing and eventually got into the movies.

"I got into the industry when I met a woman named Dee at LA Erotica [an adult strip club in Los Angeles]. Dee and her husband asked me if I would be interested in making a movie, and I said sure."

Fairchild says that most African-American women in the pornography industry are recruits from Los Angeles adult strip clubs. With a payout of $600 to $800 per sex scene, adult films are very attractive to some young women looking to make easy money. But before they get into the sex industry, most adult actresses had ordinary, mundane occupations.

"I was a preschool teacher before I got into movies, and this is far on the other side of that," Fairchild laughs. "But it is still my favorite job that I ever had."

Fairchild has done "quite a few movies, although I couldn't

honestly say how many" in the year that she's been in the adult-film business. She talks about the good and bad points of the movies.

"I'm a very sexual person, so I get to let out my frustrations a lot more than the average person, which is a good thing," she says revealingly. "And it is a lot safer than dating, 'cause everyone in the industry is tested, and always gets tested. That's unlike going out and dating strange people where you never know. It's also a lot of fun as you get to travel and meet a lot of people, some who are in-the-closet freaks, or just freaks in general."

Just entering the building and telling jokes as he walks, is the main male star of today's shoot. His name is Evan Stone, a white actor who has just won best-actor honors at the Adult Video News Awards Show in Las Vegas, which is the Oscars of the Adult Movie Industry. Nickki will be having sex with Stone on this shoot, although she has never met Stone before today.

"I'm a little nervous about this scene, but it should be pretty fun," Fairchild says. In the adult film industry, women often have the power to pick and choose their partners, but since Fairchild is so new to the industry, she doesn't yet have that power. But she is given a little bit of choice.

"I have my favorites," says Fairchild, speaking about various actors. "Sometimes the studio will give you a list of three people, and I can choose my favorite from that list. In my perfect world, I have a small crew that I would work with, because when we work together, we work together well."

Danny, Jay's assistant, comes into the room now and talks about a confidential memo that is floating around the industry. It shows that even porn isn't immune to racism.

"I first thought it was a joke," he tells Fairchild, "but it wasn't."

The memo in question comes from one of the adult-film industry leaders, a company known for promoting its female stars more than any other company.

"They have a list of rules, and one of the last rules is that the white female stars cannot have sex with black male actors," Danny says incredulously. "Can you believe it?"

Reminiscent of the unwritten codes that prohibited movies with interracial love relationships from playing in the South, the adult industry has its own, until recently unwritten codes. One is that a black male actor having sex with a white actress is taboo. Many of the companies feel that a black male having sex with a white female is degrading to the white actress. Also, a lot of white adult actresses refuse to work with black male actors because they feel that their fan base will feel that they are somehow "despoiled" by the act. However, there are no rules against white male actors having sex with black females. Apparently no one is "despoiled" in this interracial sexual relationship dynamic.

"The companies also feel that they won't be able to sell their movies to hotels or cable companies if they have black men having sex with white women," Danny explained.

Danny is a youthful-looking 38-year-old brother from the Westside of Chicago who got into the industry accidentally. A few years ago he helped out Jay with some computer issues and was offered a job. He had been a claims adjuster for an insurance company for ten years prior, and honestly, he still looks like he's a claims adjuster. He is Jay's "guy Friday," who, when he is not taking care of the books, sometimes travels as a bodyguard when actresses dance at adult strip clubs. He ultimately wants to do computer networking when he gets out of the industry.

"When I first started working here, I was like 'Wow!' but you try to act cool about it," he says, speaking about the sex that happens in front of him each day. "But now, after having been in the industry this long, it's more like, 'Are we done yet?'" It gets old pretty quick, and it destroys the fantasy."

Actors and actresses in the adult industry are known for having short careers, but what is not often talked about is the high turnover among adult film crews. These crews watch sex acts all day and night and eventually begin to have a nonchalant attitude about the whole thing. And this becomes troubling.

"If you are filming sex acts, but you are not getting aroused by it, people begin to really get worried," says Danny. "They're afraid that this will cross over into their personal life, so they leave the business."

Soon, other actresses arrive. Obsession, a beautiful sister with long, curly hair, makes her way to the makeup room. Originally from Lexington, Kentucky, Obsession moved to Los Angeles in 1988. She had myriad retail jobs before answering an ad for nude photos. After a year of posing nude, a photographer got her into adult movies. She has made about 200 films since her beginnings in 1995.

"I hadn't had a lot of sexual experiences when I first started, so I was uncomfortable having a man put me in the doggie [a sexual position]," she says as the makeup artist works on her face. "But something just clicked in me. My pride went away as far as moaning. I used to think that if I moaned, I thought it let a guy know that he was doing me good, and I don't really believe in that. But now I moan."

Obsession feels that people mistakenly assume that actresses who have a lot of sex have a lot of sexual partners.

"I've had sex every day during the last year, but in reality I've only had sex with about ten partners," she explains. "People don't realize that. They think that she's in a porno so she's fucking everybody. It's not really like that."

Enter Tracy, or Dic Tracy, as he's known in the industry. Everyone in the adult-film industry, especially actors and actresses, goes by some sort of pseudonym. Normally the actors go for names that exude a strong masculine appeal, such as "Rock" or "Stone," while actresses use names that sound alluring or sensual.

Tracy is not an actor but an assistant director, and on this shoot, Jay is giving him the chance to direct some scenes. He is a large brother probably close to three hundred pounds. He got into the adult-film industry via an ex-girlfriend. He had been an actor, a bodyguard, and now he was learning how to direct. Good-natured, he goes over the outfits for both Fairchild and Obsession.

"I want you," he says, speaking to Fairchild in the dressing room, "to wear this purple dress in the first scene." Fairchild is now standing topless, and no one notices. Tracy hands Fairchild the purple dress, while he chooses a black ensemble for Obsession to wear.

"Perfect," he says.

Tracy will direct Fairchild and Obsession in the first sex scene of the day, a girl-girl scene.

Twenty minutes later, Evan Stone, Obsession, and Fairchild are downstairs on the set. This warehouse contains a number of different ready-made sets that can meet the needs of any adult-film situation. There is a fake bedroom, a fake kitchen, a fake bar, and a fake recording studio.

In scene one, Stone and Fairchild will meet Obsession in a fake leasing office. Obsession needs her condominium leased, and Stone and Fairchild are leasing agents.

On the set, Stone is hamming it up as the eight-man crew constantly razzes him about winning the AVN best-actor award. A big white guy with stringy dirty-blond hair pulled into a ponytail, his job in this scene is basically to read some simple lines and open the door. He does it perfectly. Flushing says her lines just fine, so Tracy is ready to shoot.

The cameraman is a guy named Matt, a young man who looks like he just stepped out of the skateboard park and picked up a camera. His job is to film from different angles so that when the shoot is done, they will have enough film to edit. He also has to shoot for two versions of adult film. But that comes later.

After the dialogue scene ends, Tracy calls for the girl-girl scene to begin. As with most films, this scene is filmed out of sequence. This is the ending scene of the film, where Obsession "thanks" Fairchild for leasing her condo.

But before they can start the girl-girl scene, Obsession must douche.

"It's important to stay clean, because you don't want to be embarrassed," Fairchild whispers.

While Obsession goes to the bathroom to douche, Fairchild opens a box containing about ten sex toys, including a water-filled dildo.

"This is my favorite," says Fairchild as she lists some of the many toys that she has acquired over the years.

"I've gotten most of my toys from other movies," she says with a smile, holding some for the crew.

Obsession returns and everything is set for the scene.

"So how many positions are we going to have for this scene?" the film editor asks Tracy.

"Why don't we have three different positions?" says Tracy.

"So slurpy-slurpy, and then toys?" says the film editor, who times the scene via a monitor. "Slurpy" refers to Obsession and Fairchild taking turns performing cunnilingus on each other. "Toys" refers to the various dildos Fairchild has brought along.

"That sounds good to me," says Tracy. "Let's begin in the chair."

Tracy retreats out of camera range, yells "Action!" and after a brief bit of dialogue, Fairchild and Obsession are naked, with Obsession performing cunnilingus on Fairchild. Fairchild begins to moan loudly as Obsession concentrates and begins to really get into her work. Standing directly over the two, Matt is holding the camera, filming at different angles. A member of the crew holds a boom mike over them, while a gaffer holds a handheld light to better light Obsession's actions.

In the meantime, Tracy is yelling instructions to Obsession. He wants Obsession to "open her up," meaning he wants Obsession to spread Fairchild's labia for the camera. Obsession does this, but there is a problem. Fairchild has begun to bleed. She is on her menstrual period.

"I'm sorry, I've got to go to the bathroom," Fairchild says as she runs off.

"[Her being on her period] wasn't a problem for me," Obsession says as she waits for Fairchild to come back.

Since time is money, Tracy tells Obsession that it is time for "pretty girls," a term for when a still photographer takes sexy photos of the women. These are the still photos seen on box covers, and which are sold to various magazines. Periodically during each sexual act, the still photographer will stop the action to take more photos. This process reminds you of the old farmer's adage about everything on a pig being sold, from the "rooter to the tooter." This feels the same, as though everything about these women would eventually be sold.

Fairchild returns, and the scene continues. The two move to the desk, when they move into a position commonly called "sixty-nine," in which each woman faces the other's vagina. Matt is ordered to shoot in two different ways; one is for the soft-core market, which cannot show any penetration. This version will go to cable channels and hotels. The other is for the hard-core market, which will be sold as videotapes and DVDs.

As the sex action continues, what immediately strikes you as you watch people having sex live is how unnatural it is for non-participants to be there. The presence of the crew and staff allows no intimacy, and part of the essence of sex is its intimacy.

The only sounds in the room come from Obsession and Fairchild, and instead of being erotic or sexual, their moans become the same white noise that is heard during any workplace activity. There is no fantasy in this room, and the reality is somehow too unpleasant to watch.

After orgasms, their scene is over. Obsession and Fairchild dress, and the crew quickly get ready for another scene. They move the camera equipment about twenty feet to the right and make their way to the fake-bedroom set. It is another sex scene, but this time it will involve Evan Stone and another African-American actress, Vanessa Blue.

"I was a stripper and a bondage model before I got into movies," says Blue. "A friend of mine asked me to do a girl-girl movie, I did it, and I went on from there. I did about seventeen scenes, and then I retired. I came back to the films because I want to write and direct adult films."

Blue, who has recently had her breasts enlarged dramatically, describes herself as being "sexually aggressive" and doesn't feel that she has to have any feeling for the person she's having sex with.

"I can fuck you and then not care if you get hit with a car right afterward," she says coldly, eyes unblinking.

Stone, who briefly disappeared while Obsession and Fairchild were doing their scene, is back now. Stone and Vanessa Blue make their way to the fake-bedroom set. This scene has even less dialogue than Obsession and Fairchild's.

After a brief rehearsal, Tracy tells Stone and Blue to go for it. Stone undresses, and even the jaded crew are amazed by the size of his penis. One crew member makes the sound *"boing"* as Stone begins to masturbate to remain erect, or, as the adult industry calls it, keep "wood."

Stone keeps wood throughout the session. In an amazing bit of skill, Stone is able to consistently keep wood while telling jokes to the crew, walking around during "pretty girls," and drinking a bottle of water. Apparently there is a reason Stone won the best male actor award at the AVN. Where other men may have fallen short, Stone is a professional in more ways than one.

The formula for this scene goes like this: Stone performs cunnilingus on Blue, who then goes over the top in her groans. Blue reciprocates by performing fellatio on Stone. Her signature move is to swallow Stone's sizable penis whole and then gag on it. This action brings appreciative cheers from the crew. Finally, intercourse is about to begin, and Stone asks for "magnum" condoms. He's not bragging.

Safe sex has come slowly to the adult-film industry, and condoms are a hit-and-miss proposition. Some companies demand their use, but others don't. Some fans complain that it takes away from the fantasy. This particular set and film uses them.

Before any of the actors are allowed to work, they must possess a current HIV test. This test must be updated every thirty days, and gives the actors a sense of protection. But since a lot of these actors work frequently within that thirty-day period, and many have partners outside the industry, theoretically someone could be working with HIV.

"I think that they should be checking for a lot more diseases than HIV," Danny whispers as he gets the test results from the fax machine prior to the shooting.

This scene will take about forty-five minutes total time, and it is Stone's job to stay erect for about twelve minutes of sexual action. In between this, he will be interrupted numerous times to take photos, change camera tape, and to give Blue a break.

Their sex is very rigorous, with both of them playing off each other like dance partners. Stone mounts Blue in the missionary position, puts her feet in the air, and begins rapidly penetrating Blue. Even though Blue is screaming, you get the sense that she is nonplussed, with an almost "been-there-done-that" attitude. Suddenly, during a slight break in the action, Blue slaps Stone hard in the face and then pleads for him to give her more.

"Fuck Me!" she demands.

Stone complies.

Matt, the cameraman, is standing directly over them now, and he and Tracy are giving constant directions. This is not a job for the easily distracted. Stone and Blue move around the bed trying various positions, and at one point, Stone's condom comes off inside Blue. The action stops as Stone retrieves the condom, but no one seems concerned.

After about forty-five minutes, it is now time for the climax of this scene, or othewise known as the "money" shot. Jay asks if Blue has a problem with Stone ejaculating into her mouth. She doesn't have a problem with it, but she's afraid that when he ejaculates, it will get in her hair, and it will be impossible to get out before her next scene.

"She's got to like having cum in her mouth or we'll just have him cum on her breasts," Jay says to Tracy.

Blue agrees to do the mouth shot.

"It's just something that our hard-core fans like to see," Tracy explains.

Again, there are two different versions of this event filmed. For the soft-core version, there is the "fip" or fake internal pop, with *pop* being the porn slang for ejaculation.

Stone and Blue have more intercourse, and upon a prompting from Tracy, fake an orgasm.

For the hardcore shot, Stone begins to masturbate. As if trying to let Stone concentrate, the crew is quiet until he finally ejaculates into Blue's mouth. End of the scene, and Tracy is happy.

"Lunch!" someone yells.

The crew breaks down the equipment and begins making their way up the stairs, where Mom has prepared burgers for lunch.

As you watch Vanessa Blue sitting alone on this set, something strikes you about all of the people in this film. Though they talk about either being happy or content with working in this industry, there's a hollowness, not in their words but in their eyes. If the eyes are the windows to the soul, then those eyes are saying that the soul is troubled. Each person's eyes reflect a sort of dying light, as if their souls are reminding them of the truth of what they do for a living. Blue condenses it into one all-encompassing statement.

"I don't care if you call yourself an actress or stripper," she says as she wiped Stone's semen from her mouth and breasts with baby wipes, a required item on every adult-film set. "The reality is that we fuck for money. And that is all you do and that is all we are."

The eyes of Fairchild, Obsession, Blue, Danny, and Tracy betray the fact that each one knows this fact all too well.

3

The Crowning Glory

The Upper East Side of New York City

Do your work with your whole heart, and you will succeed. There's so little competition.

—Elbert Hubbard

The sinks are ready. The clear domes of the blow-dryers wait like royal sentinels, each lifted to attention and awaiting its master. It is raining outside, but four of the five ceiling fans are rotating anyway, providing a gentle breeze. Cesar has ordered tea. It is time to let the first ones in.

On the Upper East Side of New York, they come early and often. Wearing scarves, head wraps, baseball caps, and other means of disguise, they all ring the buzzer for entrance, eventually making their way upstairs. At Manning Hair Designs, each Saturday morning means that for black women all across America, as one sister succinctly states it, "It's time to get your hair did."

Two women, Madame C. J. Walker and Marjorie Joyner, revolutionized African-American hair care in the twentieth century.

In order to supplement her income as a washwoman, Madame C. J. Walker began selling homemade beauty products door to door. Eventually, Madame Walker's products formed the basis of a thriving national corporation employing at one point over 3,000 people. Her Walker System, which included a broad offering of cosmetics, licensed Walker Agents, and Walker Schools, offered meaningful employment and personal growth to thousands of black women. Madame Walker's aggressive marketing strategy, combined with relentless ambition, led her to be labeled as the first known African-American woman to become a self-made millionaire.

An employee of Madame Walker's empire, Marjorie Joyner, invented a permanent-wave machine. This device, patented in 1928, curled or "permed" women's hair for a relatively lengthy period of time. The wave machine was popular among women white and black, allowing for longer-lasting wavy hairstyles. Joyner went on to become a prominent figure in Walker's industry, though she never profited directly from her invention, for it was the assigned property of the Walker Company.

Today, the legacy of Walker and Joyner is now in this New York City shop. And there are few things in a black woman's life that elicits more passion than her hair. Husbands, boyfriends, and, in some cases, girlfriends may come and go, but for the average sister, hair is eternal. It is embraced and loved right after a visit to a salon; while it will be reviled and cursed a week after the roots should have been done. A black woman's hair is her crowning glory, and its care is paramount not only to a black woman's well-being, but also to her sense of confidence as she tackles the world. And key to making sure things look just right is a black women's hair salon.

"We try to make our customers feel comfortable," says Maria Manning, owner of Manning Hair Designs.

A stylish young woman, Manning has owned her salon for seven years, three of those in her current East 62nd location. After building this salon from the ground up, she knows the formula for success.

"It's important to make the client feel as though this is a place that they can relax and talk about anything," she says.

The hair salon is the sanctuary away from all things that storm a black woman's citadel each day. She relies on a sort of steadiness, a familiarity in her hair salon. Yes, she may have a devotion to her stylist that will make her travel forty-five minutes from Jersey to the Upper East Side (that would be a Rutgers graduate student on this particular Saturday), but it's got to have something else. The salon's got to feel just right in her psyche and her soul.

Manning has been able to position her salon as one that is able to do any type of hair. From natural styles such as dreadlocks, twists, and Afros to perms, hair extensions, and weaves, she has tried to adapt to every whim. Manning is proud that her stylists can even do nonblack hair.

"You can't go to a lot of salons and find nonblack people who can do black hair," she says. "But our stylists are good enough that we have a nice-sized clientele of non-Black women."

In the vision of the stylists at this salon, the current icons of great celebrity hair range from women as different as Julia Roberts, Jennifer Lopez, and New York native Mary J. Blige. Even Hillary Clinton gets the thumbs-up for her current hairstyle.

"It makes her look a lot younger," hairstylist Felicia says.

Any topic can provide a cornucopia of opinions for both the clients and the hairstylists at Manning Hair Design. As they sit down to talk, their first conversation of the day immediately encompasses everything women like to talk about on a lazy Saturday: men, sex, baby's daddy, and the plight of black women. Today the topic is Jesse Jackson, who has just announced two days ago that he is the father of a twenty-month-old out-of-wedlock baby.

"Well, I don't understand why he couldn't just use a condom," Desiree said to no one in particular. Desiree is getting her hair permed. "I think that he was creeping for a long time, and he just got caught."

While their hands are in the constant motion of shampooing, coloring, blow-drying, flipping, twisting, and scrimping, Maria, Felicia, and the other stylists must also be the all-knowing ear. This ear knows when to propel the conversation forward and when the client wants to reflect in her own thoughts.

"I mean, he could have used a condom," one says.

"Well, you know how men are," says the stylist.

"When I first heard about it, I thought the baby would be twenty *years* old, not twenty *months* old," another says.

Laughter sweeps the room.

"Well, I think that all men are not faithful in the first place," says another stylist.

"How about the fact that he was counseling Clinton at the same time?" a client says. "I bet that Clinton is saying that at least he didn't get Monica pregnant!"

The "uh-huh's" and "nah-uh's" fill the room as every woman in every chair is now engaged and invested in the conversation. Personal experiences are recounted. Jesus' name is brought forth in response to Jesse's reverend status. And most of all, everyone's opinion is heard.

All the while, Maria Manning is listening. Not for idle gossip and opinion, but for key information that may have an impact on her future as a businesswoman. One bit comes from an innocuous comment stemming from a conversation about Harlem.

"They are renovating those brownstones in Harlem, and there is one woman who is about to open up a spa. I can't wait for that to open," Marsha says.

With those words, Maria's eyes open a little wider. Marsha is one of her most loyal customers. She hasn't missed an appointment for over two years and is completely happy with Manning Hair Designs ("Maria knows that I'm going to be in this chair every two weeks," says Marsha), but is now openly saying that she can't wait to go to Maria's competition.

"See, that hurts because that is what I want to do," Maria says when Marsha leaves. "I moved here three years ago to expand, but I need even more room to open a spa. But to get one of those brownstones in Harlem costs about $300,000, and with that you only get a shell. She [the future spa owner] must have some capital behind her."

Although Marsha has assured her that she will always be a loyal client, Maria knows that this spa is a threat. As she continues greeting her clients, working on the hair of others, the conversations continue, but this time you get the impression that Maria's not listening.

"Boy, that hurts," she mutters to no one in particular as she tends to her customer's head of hair. "Boy, that hurts."

The hair dryers, clients, and hairdressers drone on.

4

The Mr. Chips of the North Philly

North Philadelphia, Pennsylvania

It is in fact, a part of the function of education to help us escape, not from our own time, for we are bound by that but from the intellectual and emotional limitations of our own time.

—T. S. Eliot

The first thought that enters your mind when you visit Twenty-fourth and Jefferson is, why? Why must people have to live this way? Why must row after row of boarded-up, abandoned brick buildings exist on these streets? Why must children dodge bullets as they try to go to school? Why must ghostlike silhouettes of unemployed black men populate block after block of this neighborhood? Why can't someone take notice and, more importantly, take some action to make changes here?

But take a closer look at this North Philadelphia neighborhood. Look past the towering forty-story Norman Blumber public housing project. Look past Mr. Leo's corner market, a store whose outside wall is plastered with photos of the neighborhood's dead, some from natural causes and others from not-so-natural causes. Look past the only art in the neighborhood, a small billboard of Philadelphia native Kobe Bryant, advertising the latest $200 basketball shoes in a community that has one of the lowest income levels in Philadelphia. Ignore the green, graffiti-scarred wall it is posted on. Look past the irony of the "one way" street sign that has been placed directly underneath the billboard. It's a sign that sends a subliminal message to the residents of this community that sport, specifically basketball, is the only way out of here. Maybe it is; maybe it isn't.

But does anyone take the time to notice John Reynolds Elementary School? It sits unassumingly on the corner of Twenty-fourth and Jefferson, yet this one-hundred-year-old building is the center of the universe for this community. Within its walls are people, people who care about the future of this desperate community. About 350 children, ranging in ages from five to eleven, are waiting for the tools that will allow them to escape their prescribed destiny. For anyone who cares, anyone who wants better, Reynolds is a daily factory of hope for children, parents, and community members. Its only mandate is that it cannot fail in its mission.

Principal Salome Thomas-El walks into his office at 8:30 A.M. A combination of long work hours, night classes at Lehigh as he worked for his Ph.D., and a newborn baby have conspired to makes him blurry-eyed. Although he didn't get to sleep until two in the morning, he doesn't lack energy, because he knows that his day is a continuous stream of challenges. Parents will be summoned about their children. Maintenance will be dispatched to repair the crumbling building. Teachers will request meetings. Everyone will want something from him. He has to be ready.

Unbeknownst to him, his receptionist has been hazing him mercilessly to arriving teachers for the past thirty minutes. You know this receptionist because she worked at your school. She's cranky but always exhibits a kind heart. She's an older woman who somehow moves as fast as the fifth-graders.

"Do you want to know the real Mr. Thomas-El?" she asks everyone who walks into the reception area. Her mischievous grin gives away her affection for the principal.

"Because we'll tell you the truth, not the propaganda!"

Thomas-El just smiles because he knows it is all in good nature. He knows that the receptionist and all of the other teachers want him at the school; in fact, they need him at the school.

The 36-year-old Thomas-El wants to make a difference in the lives of the children of North Philadelphia, and he is. He is currently writing a book called *I Choose To Stay,* which tells the story about how he was able to make a difference with children who don't often find opportunity knocking at their door.

"I was working at a middle school about a block away from here, and I turned down a raise because I wanted to stay in the neighborhood," he recalled. "I wanted to stay close to these kids because [often when] so many brothers are able to advance [in their profession], it pulls them away from the community."

What makes Thomas-El special is not just the fact that he stayed in the community in spite of the money, but how he is able to make an impact.

He was working as a vice-principal at Vaux Middle School when he read that the school had once had a great chess team. Thinking that the children needed something that expanded their sense not only of themselves but also of their place in this world, Thomas-El decided to revive the team. It was an immediate success.

"The kids became good right away," he said. "They were beating middle school kids and high school kids, and eventually, they beat students from Bucknell [University]. And what was most surprising is that we immediately won a national title. Some schools have been playing for ten and fifteen years and haven't won a title, and they come from the suburban schools. We won it in our second national tournament."

People began noticing the success of the chess club, and a chance visit from actor Arnold Schwarzenegger helped Thomas-El begin a collaboration that would benefit his small group of children.

Schwarzenegger, who was visiting the Philadelphia schools through his nonprofit foundation, spent some time playing with the Vaux chess team during his visit. He was so impressed with their play, he committed to providing scholarship money for the school.

"I found out that he was a big chess player and that during downtime on his movie sets, he constantly has chess games in progress," Thomas-El said.

Other schools in Philadelphia noticed the success of the Vaux chess club and began offering Thomas-El incentives to come to their school. They wanted him to replicate his chess club success, and they were willing to pay for it.

"I was offered a $25,000 boost in salary to move to other schools," he said. "But I wanted to wait until a position opened up in the neighborhood."

That opportunity landed Thomas-El at Reynolds two years ago. Reynolds, which contains students from kindergarten through fifth grade, was noted as one of the low-achieving schools in the Philadelphia school district when Thomas-El arrived. Recognizing the inherent challenges that exist for urban schools, Thomas-El is trying to change the mindset of the students, parents, and teachers at Reynolds.

Here, the students wear uniforms, not just because it helps control clothing costs and erase socioeconomic distinctions, but also for safety reasons.

"One of the great benefits of uniforms is that if there is a truant on the campus, he is easily identified," he says. "You can identify your children because they all look the same."

Disadvantages surround Reynolds. Whether it is the poor neighborhood surrounding it, or the centralized school bureaucracy that prevents local schools from truly succeeding, the obstacles sometimes appear to be daunting. One critical challenge is the fact that Philadelphia principals don't have local control of their schools, yet they are all judged by the same yardstick in terms of results.

In the Philadelphia urban district where Reynolds is located, the city spends about $6,000 per pupil, whereas in suburban districts, the city spends about $14,000 per pupil. However, despite this disparity in funding, all schools are mandated to get results from the same standardized tests.

"We have excellent teachers in Philadelphia, but it is difficult to attract those teachers to urban areas, because the suburban schools pay so much more," he says while sipping tea.

Combine this situation with the fact that school principals in Philadelphia do not have the power to hire or fire teachers, it becomes very frustrating for anyone trying to create an excellent school.

"The schools are centrally controlled, and there needs to be more school-based management, because principals here in Philadelphia are paid on school performance," Thomas-El says.

As a result, urban schools are presented with younger, less experienced teachers, while suburban schools are the benefactors of more experienced teachers who have either transferred into their schools or have had long tenure. If Thomas-El ran the district, he would have beginning teachers come into an urban district, and have them learn to stick it out in the less than optimal circumstances that he has to deal with on an everyday basis.

"My dream is to go into a class of about to graduate teachers and explain to them the rewards of working with urban children," he says emphatically. "Because when you work here, you see everything."

Thomas-El is quick to note that the teachers at Reynolds are dedicated, and his first task of the day demonstrates the results of their efforts. If it is 10 A.M., it must mean that it is medal time, and the children are waiting.

"When I arrived here, at least three-fourths of our kids were reading below grade level," he says as he reaches for a manila packet of shiny golden medals. "We had to really restructure our reading program. We implemented an early-reading program, and I was able to recruit some really talented staff to go along with the great staff that we already have at the school. From there, we got them the materials that they needed to really motivate the students. As a result, we just received an award from the school district as one of the top 49 schools out of 250 to meet their literacy target."

As part of their process of motivating their students, Thomas-El and the teachers instituted a program that awarded medals to students who read 100 to 400 chapters of books.

"The kids really get on me if I don't pass out these medals," he says with a smile.

The walls of Reynolds are plastered with the names of children who have excelled at reading, and each paper cutout lists their current "book" total. The teachers and students define a read chapter as being one book. As Thomas-El makes his way into one of the classrooms, the children immediately begin yelling out the number of chapters they have read. Thomas-El checks their numbers with the teachers and awards medals accordingly.

"Mr. El, Mr. El, I read 300 books," says one fourth-grader.

"Okay, okay, here is your medal," Mr. Thomas-El says as he checks the official "books" log.

As Thomas-El continues distributing medals in each classroom, he stops to acknowledge the parents who are volunteering at Reynolds. It seems as if each classroom has at least one parent hard at work.

"Parents get a bad rap," he noted as he walked out of the third-grade class. "We have some parents that really like to volunteer. The participation is not as high as I would like it to be, but that's because some of these parents are working two or three jobs. But we find that we still have parental involvement from those parents because when these children come home from school, these parents make sure that their homework gets done. That's parental involvement."

The push-pull of being a principal is constant throughout the day. Within the first four hours of the day, Thomas-El will have to deal with lack of heat in the cafeteria. A leak has been found and maintenance can't work on it because of the asbestos in the walls. He'll have to placate an angry parent in the hallway. She's angry because her child has been fighting yet again, and she's also angry because this is the third time that she's had to leave work early to deal with it. He's got sick teachers, sick children, and a student who is destroying books.

"We know that this is a symptom of something that is going on at home, and I've scheduled a meeting with her parents," he says about the destructive student.

And at the end of the day, he has to train teachers on the intricacies of identifying schoolyard bullies.

"It never ends," he says.

But he and the other teachers at Reynolds are making a difference. When you look into the classrooms, the children are attentive. The teachers are caring but demanding. It is evident that the children are learning concepts at Reynolds. Whether it is the kindergarten-aged Head Start children learning to play with blocks, or the third-grade students acquainting themselves with the intricacies of math, the teachers at Reynolds are stimulating these children to ultimately succeed.

What keeps these teachers in this school going are the smiles of the children as they receive their reading medals. What keeps these teachers in this school is the triumph of having two Reynolds alumni graduate from nearby Cheyney State University. And what makes Salome Thomas-El "choose to stay" is his love for these diamonds in the rough. He knows that they deserve more than what America has designated for them, and he is determined that they succeed.

"I'm hoping to continue to add grades to Reynolds so that when they leave here, they go immediately to high school," Thomas-El says as the bell rings for the end of the day. "These are my kids, and I would love to be able to track them after they leave here. I think that we provide them with a good enough foundation so that we could get them either into a private school or a magnet school. And from there, it would be off to college."

Suddenly, the custodian comes to Thomas-El's door. A teacher has been the victim of a hit-and-run driver. Although the teacher is unhurt, Thomas-El is needed to talk with folks in the neighborhood about a description of the hit-and-run driver. Even outside this little schoolhouse, Thomas-El is needed.

5

Of Canada, Codfish, and the Caribbean

Toronto, Canada

One cannot think well, love well, and sleep well, if one has not dined well.

—Virginia Woolf

Lileth Pottinger runs up the forty or so steps to the second floor with the grace of a ballerina. Carrying hot plates of roti, jerk chicken, and rice and peas, she traverses the stairs quickly, but she's not rushed in her actions. Her movements are elegant and measured, and after about twenty trips back and forth, she seems no worse for the wear.

"It keeps you in great shape," she says, smiling. She's only a little bit out of breath.

This is Sunday, and Sunday is supposed to be a slow night at The Real Jerk. But the thirty or so party patrons upstairs, combined with the rapidly filling first floor, are contradicting that notion. It's supposed to be her husband, Ed's, rare day off, but even he's supposed to come into the restaurant a little later. Enough with the brief respite; it's time that Lileth glide back into the kitchen. The staff has another tray of food ready.

Jamaican natives Ed and Lileth Pottinger are the owners of the best Jamaican restaurant in Toronto, The Real Jerk. Seventeen years ago, they decided to open this restaurant, and just like Lileth's trips up and down the stairs, they've seen the highs and lows of the restaurant industry. But through it all, they've had each other, and that's what has made them a success.

Their story begins in Jamaica, in 1979. Ed, who was born in Jamaica but grew up in England, returned to Jamaica to work for his uncle. He had just finished college when he met Lileth, who had just finished high school. Ed had always wanted to open a restaurant, and since Lileth had studied the culinary arts, it seemed to be a natural match.

"He always loved jerk chicken and jerk pork, so we opened up a restaurant in Jamaica," she said.

For a couple of years things were going well, but Ed had to move to Canada in order to take care of some family business. Lileth soon followed him. After her move to the Great White North came marriage, a baby, and a second child on the way. They were island people living in a cold climate.

Ed was working steadily at General Motors, but he wasn't happy.

"Ed had taken a year off because of an injury, and when he returned to GM, he realized that he didn't belong there. So he quit his job," Lileth recalled.

Initially, this decision didn't please Lileth. They had a mortgage to pay and children to feed. Ed knew that he had to be independent, but he also knew that he had to make it happen as soon as possible. So every day after he quit his General Motors job, he left the house.

"For a week and a half he would leave the house each morning, and then come back without telling me. He did this until one day he came to me and said that he had found a restaurant," Lileth said.

Skeptical of leaving her new cashier job to open another restaurant, Lileth reluctantly agreed to look at the restaurant. That day, they agreed on a lease. One day after signing the lease, they cleaned it up and opened.

"We used paper plates and plastic utensils," she laughed.

It was rough in the beginning, and Ed and Lileth learned various skills about how to keep a business going. In the beginning, Ed would have to walk out into the street and talk people into trying out the restaurant. Soon these new customers would become The Real Jerk's regular customers.

"And that's how we built it, one customer at a time," she said.

"We couldn't pay our bills on time for about three years, and we'd only pay them when the person came to turn things off," she reminisced.

Those days are long gone, and today the walls are covered with awards and citations from various Toronto newspapers and magazines showing that their efforts have paid off. They all proclaim The Real Jerk as being the number one Jamaican restaurant, year after year.

Today is Ed's day off, but he's decided to come to the restaurant around closing time. Until then Lileth holds down the fort. The staff that she manages all speak with the gentle, lilting patois of the West Indies. Whether they are from Trinidad or Jamaica, there is a kinship. But the clientele is even more global than the staff.

On this night, French Canadians mingle with Jamaican expats. In fact, as Lileth and Ed grew The Real Jerk business, they found that their most loyal customers were not local West Indians, but white and Asian customers who were attracted to this different cuisine.

"This area of downtown Toronto doesn't have a lot of West Indian people," she said. "It was predominantly whites and Asians in this area. So there were no black people around."

When selling Jamaican food to their early non-West Indian customers, Ed and Lileth pretty much had to make people try different things such as curried goat. Now, since a lot have made trips to Jamaica and other islands, many of their customers are much more adventurous.

"They now come into the restaurant with a more open mind," she remarked. "In fact, I think that our curried dishes may be the most popular."

Lileth goes about tending to her upstairs dinner party while Stacey McKenzie, a waitress from Jamaica, works the bottom floor. In comes a new dinner party. After being seated, a rather large man from Jamaica announces to Stacey that he is here with his friends from Trinidad.

"The Trinidadian restaurant was closed, so I thought that I would take them to a proper Jamaican restaurant," he says haughtily.

He then begins to interrogate Stacey about every item on the menu.

"Do you have jerked fish tonight?"

"Do you have curried goat?"

"Are the oxtails good tonight?"

"Do you have akee?"

And so the conversation went. As Stacey patiently answers each question, the large man makes not-so-polite under-his-breath comments to his Trinidadian friends about the wait staff.

"I don't know about the waiters here," he grumbles.

Lileth sighs when told about the customer. It doesn't surprise her.

"My greatest problems are customers being unreasonable," she says. "If I have to go the extra mile for the customer, I will go the extra mile. But if I think that they are wrong, I'll tell them that they are wrong. I'm sorry, but I have to do that."

Surprisingly, Lileth says that the most difficult customers are not her white Canadian customers but her West Indian ones.

"Sometimes, because we are all from the islands, they are very hard to deal with," she recounts. "You can take a dish right off the stove, serve it, and have people tell you that it's stale.

"I'm just appalled at the behavior of some people," she continues. "We were all poor when we grew up in the Caribbean. And our moms, for example, made codfish fritters. So we would go to the store and buy a quarter pound of codfish and they would make a big pot of it. You would barely be able to taste the codfish. Even with the fritters, you'd slap it between bread and take it to school for lunch. And you were satisfied. Now I have people come [into the restaurant] and look at their codfish fritters and say, "There's no codfish in here," like they were born with codfish in their mouth! I mean this really pisses me off! Codfish is a luxury item; it's the national dish of Jamaica. It's an expensive dish and I don't make any money from it. So when you see it on your plate, be happy about it."

The occasional rude customer aside, Lileth says that her customers are generally loyal and dedicated customers. And even while thinking about those difficult customers, her smile never leaves her face. She knows that they come with the territory of serving the public.

Though they have been successful at their current location, they did have a rough period when they made a fateful decision to open a second restaurant in the heart of Toronto about ten years ago.

"We've had our ups and downs," she said, with her eyes cast downward. "We bought this building and then lost it when we expanded with another restaurant in the heart of downtown Toronto."

The second restaurant held 300 people, and it was a nightclub/restaurant. It actually did very well, but the old restaurant had to be left to inexperienced managers.

They hired managers that didn't understand how to manage the staff and how to treat the customers. As a result, the original restaurant suffered. Plus, the financial strain of running two businesses began to take its toll. Added to that strain, Lileth was pregnant with their third child.

"We closed the nightclub and decided to go back to basics," she said.

The basics now include lines outside the door during various festivals, as people throughout the Toronto area make a pilgrimage to The Real Jerk. The basics now include working from "can't see in the morning" to "can't see at night." The basics now include working hard so that Lileth and Ed's three children have opportunities their parents never had. The basics now include producing food that brings smiles to the faces of their customers.

But right now, at this moment, the basics include making sure that the party of thirty upstairs gets thirty desserts.

"Well, it's back to work," Lileth says with a smile.

For Lileth, this Sunday night is just getting started.

6

Books, Books, and More Books

Oakland, California

The worth of a book is to be measured by what you can carry away from it.

—James Bryce

Blanche Richardson has a popular author, whom she has nicknamed Mr. Ten Chairs, scheduled for a book-signing in a couple of weeks, and she is not looking forward to his appearance. A popular writer of black male-and-female relationship fiction, Mr. Ten Chairs is known within the Black book industry as having an ego a lot larger than his writing ability. But why does Blanche call him Mr. Ten Chairs?

"You see, we received a frantic call from his publisher a while back," Blanche explains. "The publicists said that the author was concerned about doing a book-signing at Marcus Books because he thought that we could only fit ten chairs in our store! So he has become known as Mr. Ten Chairs in the store."

Blanche laughs because that's the only thing that one can do in the face of such absurdity. Marcus Books, perhaps the oldest African-American bookstore in America, has feted thousands of authors, most of them more prominent than Mr. Ten Chairs. And it is more than able to accommodate as many people as make their way to the Oakland store. But that's life as an African-American bookseller, so Blanche laughs.

African Americans have always needed a sanctuary in America. This sanctuary, whether it is inside the barbershop, beauty salon, or church, is a space that allows us to be our true selves. We can talk in the way we like to talk, and about the subjects we like to talk about. We can believe in the way we like to believe, in the manner we find appropriate. We can laugh in the way we like to laugh, loud and boisterous. And in our sanctuaries, we can do it all without the interference of the white people that so dominate the rest of our lives. Those sanctuaries are important to our survival as a community and as a people. In Oakland, Marcus Books acts as that urban sanctuary.

You walk into Marcus Books and you are immediately surrounded by your heritage. Posters of W. E. B. DuBois, Frederick Douglass, and Malcolm X vie for brick wall space alongside a large red, black, and green African-American flag. Rows of shelving hold hundreds of books, journals, pamphlets, and postcards. Some of the authors are well known, like Iyanla Vanzant and Terri McMillan, while others are self-published authors known only to their family members and local readers. A new point-of-purchase display for E. Lynn Harris is sitting next to the front counter. Mood music could be playing Bob Marley, Miles Davis, Mutabaruka, or Marvin Gaye. Either way, you know you are home. You've found a place that is completely yours, even though you don't literally own it.

"I think that people get a different vibe from our store versus a Barnes and Noble," said Cherysse, Blanche's daughter. "It's not like the [African American section] is stuck in a corner with a little table. At Marcus, we've read their book or we know what other people thought about it. They are surrounded, when they come into our store, by people and things that look like us."

"Marcus Bookstore was founded in 1960 by my parents, Drs. Raye and Julian Richardson," said Blanche. "They had met and fell in love at Tuskegee Institute, where my mother was a student and my dad taught. They moved out here (San Francisco Bay Area) in the 1940s and my father started a printing business while my mother worked in the post office.

"The first printing business was in the Fillmore district of San Francisco, and he did a lot of printing for the Black community that lived in the Fillmore back then. And both of them were also politically active. He was drafted (during World War II), and he said that it was the worst thing that ever happened to him in his entire life. He didn't like fighting for the white man's cause. He came back from the army and restarted the business. Both my parents liked to read a lot and had a difficult time finding books. And when they did, they would loan them to their friends and not get them back. So they would begin ordering two and three books at a time and eventually began putting the books in the windows of the printing business. And I guess that we started with those two or three books and now we have twenty thousand books in our inventory."

Initially the printing press and the bookstore were housed in the same building, but Marcus Bookstore would branch out in 1960 with a new San Francisco store. After that, the Oakland branch was opened, and over the next forty years, Marcus Bookstore has seen a cavalcade of African-American authors pass through its doorway.

"Some of the first authors we had in the store were both Nikki Giovanni and Sonia Sanchez," Blanche recalls. "They also came to my father to see if he would print their poetry for them as well. We also had Claude Brown, who wrote *Manchild in the Promised Land,* LeRoi Jones, otherwise known as Amiri Baraka, and also James Baldwin came into the store, but he didn't read. All of the African-American writers eventually came through the store."

And what about today's authors?

"Most of the authors that come into the store are fun," says Blanche. "Eric Jerome Dickey is great, and he's pretty much a one-man show. He has such a nice manner about him. Each time he comes into the store, I always pull out a tape measure to see if his head has grown any bigger. But it never is. He's very grounded."

As a local African-American institution, Marcus Bookstore is also inherently political. The inclusion of leftist, nationalistic, and Afrocentric reading material in its inventory is a direct reflection of the consciousness provided by Blanche's parents.

"My parents have been politically active since grade school," Blanche laughs. "Both sets of parents were Garveyites and they learned politics from the cradle."

Blanche, who manages both the Oakland and San Francisco Marcus Bookstores, is part of a multigenerational team of employees. She has worked in both stores for over twenty-five years, but all sons, daughters, grandchildren, great grandchildren, and in-laws—have worked in the store at one time. Blanche's pregnant daughter, Cherysse Calhoun, is manning the register today. From the youngest to the oldest, they all know their African-American books.

"I think that we've done a lot to promote black literature and also help a lot of authors get published, which is great for us because the more that black authors write, the more books we have to sell," Blanche notes. "We stay very politically motivated here, and this gives authors a forum to bring issues to the community.

"There is much more African-American literature out here now, and I think that we are on a much more equal level as white folks in terms of being published in all different areas. I would say that we used to see a lot of books that specifically dealt with race. The fiction was usually written in some depressing manner, i.e., Richard Wright-type stuff. Because at that time, that was what could get published, although that wasn't all we had to say as a community. But that's what the publishers would pay for.

"And then all of the nonfiction dealt with race," she continues. "Race or religion either—one of those things was always sent to us. But now we've actually got some 'happy' literature.

"I can't say that the quality of African-American literature has changed over the years, because a good book is still a good book, and a so-so book is still a so-so book. But I can say that we have a lot more so-so books. We have a lot more 'I can write and I can publish myself, or I can go to Simon and Schuster and they'll publish it,' and I think that they have less concern for the quality than I personally do. I think that some of the stuff that major publishing houses publish is insulting to black people. I would rather see someone writing that is well educated, rather than see material where someone obviously said that 'this is okay for black folks; they'll read anything.' "

Blanche laughs easily when she talks, but the laugh doesn't mask the fact that selling books in the African-American community is still challenging, to say the least. Marcus customers still have a propensity for window-shopping at the Marcus Bookstore while purchasing the book at a chain bookstore.

"We can't fight the chain stores in terms of the clout they have, so there is no point in going at it that way," Blanche reflects wistfully. "We would certainly like to change the minds of black people who don't understand the meaning of "buying black." Those are the Black people who don't understand what a loss it would be if Marcus Bookstore went under because they saved a quarter on a book at one of the chains. People will tell you in the same breath about how wonderful you are and how they bought the book at Borders. Some people don't see the conflict there. It really used to tick me off, but I'm learning to roll with the punches on things like that.

"When I hear things like that," Cherysse says, "I try to gauge the customer's personality and let them know that as a black business, they are actually insulting us when they say things like that.

"We are definitely feeling the pressure of the chain stores, especially since African-American literature is become very popular. The hype for African-American authors is incredible now. Chain bookstores don't just have an African-American section in their stores anymore; they now have the books in all parts of the stores. Instead of two or three shelves of books, we are now all throughout the store."

Any independent business has to try to outfox its larger competition, and Marcus is no different. Marcus tries to cultivate its place in the community in a number of ways.

"We have a large book club here that has been going longer than Oprah's book club," Blanche said. "It started out with about three hundred members, and over the years we've had about one hundred regular members.

"We also sponsor readings, along with private receptions or luncheons with authors. Our regular customers get discounts on books, and they get preferred seating when our authors come to town. That's good for them, because we tend to have about one hundred and fifty authors in Marcus per year.

"I see us having more stores in the future, and not just here in the Bay Area. We would like to have one in Kingston, Jamaica. That's something that we've always discussed among others is—having a store somewhere in the Caribbean. Through our travels, we know that they do not have one. Also, our store has not only national appeal, but also international appeal. We are a 'must' stop for authors, so it would be nice within two years to have a presence internationally."

But not all authors have decided to make Marcus a stop on their tour. These authors don't want to be "stigmatized" as a black author.

"Oh, yes, we get those authors that don't want to be here," Blanche said. "You hear that 'I don't want to be called a black writer; I just want to be called a writer.' So their thinking must be 'Let me let the white guy make all of the money on the book tour.' For example, Colin Powell drove right past us and didn't stop in. And we get those publishers that market their black writers as being colorblind. This is 'just an author,' they will say."

But generally Blanche and Marcus Bookstore don't have problems with publishers. As she stated earlier, the bookstore is a must stop for most authors, but it took time for that reputation to develop.

"It took us a very long time to establish a relationship, because generally they didn't know that we were here, and when they did find out they didn't care that we were here. But after a while, they began sending us letters thanking us for our work with their authors. Plus, we get testimonials from authors. We just had to keep beating the doors down to the publishers until they had no choice.

"We try to return as few books as possible, and we give the author a very long shelf life here. Some things on our shelves, such as Sister Souljah's *Coldest Winter Ever,* have remained out there a long time after they have been published, and it has been a best-seller for us. And we also stay ahead of other stores when books come in new. Plus, there are certain books that I think are jewels, so I keep them on the shelves. It allows me to show it to customers and turn them on to new voices."

Watching Cherysse work behind the counter, it is easy to see that the Richardsons must be a living reference source for every customer that comes in. For over four hours, Cherysse has had this same conversation with almost every customer who purchased a book during that time:

Customer: "You know, I'm looking for a book that I heard about on the radio. . . ."

Cherysse (smiling): "Yes."

Customer: "But I can't remember the name of it. But I do know that the author was a woman."

Cherysse (mentally narrowing the possibilities in half): "Well, was she a new author?"

Customer: "Yes, she was a brand-new published author. I think that the book was named after a jazz musician."

Cherysse (nodding knowingly): "Look on the third shelf and pick up Jenoyne Adams's book, *Resurrecting Mingus.* It was just released last month."

Customer: "That's the name of it! How did you know?"

Cherysse: "We try to know as much as possible about every book that we stock."

And so it goes with every customer. Yes, it may get monotonous, but Blanche says that it is that close attention to their customers that helps Marcus Bookstore to survive.

"We listen to what the customers have read recently and try to give them as large a variety of possible other books from which to choose. Things that don't sell well in other bookstores, such as poetry, will sell well here. Especially things like spoken-word CD's, and the older stuff like the Countee Cullen and Langston Hughes really sells."

It's now time to get ready for tonight's author, Alice Randall, author of the controversial book *The Wind Done Gone.* After a successful court fight against the estate of *Gone With The Wind* author Margaret Mitchell, Randall's presentation of the classic Civil War drama has sparked enormous interest and has already propelled her book onto the various best-seller lists. She's arriving in about an hour, and the store gets a call from her security people saying that she was threatened during an early-morning radio interview. But no worries, they've had plenty of controversial authors in the past, and even death threats are not new.

Soon, after the chairs have been set out and the readers have been jockeying for prime space, Randall comes into the bookstore. A very vivacious woman, she moves easily through the crowd and sits down at the head of the table. Soon, Marcus bookstore owner Dr. Raye Richardson, now a long-time professor at San Francisco State and the interviewer for this book-signing, enters. The respect she commands is palpable by the way the assembling crowd murmurs around her.

As she sits down next to Randall, they begin a discussion that goes over the recently concluded court trial, and Randall explains how this book was cathartic for her to write. All in all, this is your typical book-signing and reading.

As Cherysse continues to sell books during the lecture, and it looks as though they should sell around two hundred during this evening, Blanche is gently surveying the room to see if everything is going okay and if the customers are happy. From their faces, it appears as though they are. This look of satisfaction on the staff's and customers' faces recalls something that Cherysse noted earlier in the day.

"I feel blessed that I was able to work here all of my life," she said. "I don't know if I would have loved black people as much as I do now if I hadn't had this opportunity."

Indeed.

7

The Designer to the Cars

Detroit, Michigan

Always design a thing by considering it in its next larger context such as a chair in a room, a room in a house, a house in an environment, an environment in a city plan.

—Eliel Saarinen

Car guys are different from the rest of the population. A car guy sees a mundane vehicle like say, a minivan—and in his eyes, it's not just a kiddie hauler but a potential hotrod. A car guy will put a powerful 3.8-liter V8 engine in the soccermombile, replacing the all-too-mundane engine it once had. They'll do things such as replace the cushy driver seat with a seat more appropriately found in a Ferrari sports car. Simple hubcaps for this new twelve-passenger mean machine? You've got to be kidding! A car guy takes those hubcaps off and puts on shiny 18-inch alloy wheels. Hey, while you're at it, how about some brakes from a Dodge Viper, the supercar of all supercars?

Ralph Gilles is a car guy, and the aforementioned minivan is his creation. It's what he uses to drive his family around. But what separates Gilles from the rest of his car-guy brethren in America is not that he has a hopped-up van. The difference is that Gilles gets paid big bucks to be a car guy. Ralph Gilles is senior design manager at Daimler Chrysler in Detroit.

Sitting at his desk, right in the heart of the Daimler Chrysler design studio, Gilles's job is to fantasize, sketch, and then oversee the actual three-dimensional clay design of future Daimler

Chrysler cars. The office walls are filled with futuristic full-color car interior designs, while the floor is littered with plastic parts, all which have a secret, experimental look to them.

"I've been sketching cars since I was five years old," said Gilles, a Montreal native of Haitian descent. "I know that there was something latent [working with cars]. The [desire] was underneath there, but I didn't know quite how to tap into it. I thought I wanted to be an engineer, but it wasn't until I was sixteen that I knew that there was a career called car design."

Gilles's older brother was able to investigate the profession for Ralph, and after conducting some research on design schools, Ralph decided to go to the Center for Creative Studies School in Michigan. Once he was at the Center, Chrysler recognized Gilles's skills and decided to offer him a job in the design department, even before his graduation in 1992. And the thirty-one-year-old has been designing the interiors and exteriors of Dodge and Chrysler cars ever since.

"I specialize in interiors mainly," Gilles said. "I've had some opportunities to do some exteriors, but for the most part, I've done interiors. I always loved interiors in school because I had so much control over so many products and where they were placed. Usually in [designing] interiors, people leave you alone. There's not as much passion because not that many people want ownership of the interior, being able to say, 'I designed this,' versus the exterior. I could care less about the notoriety; I just want to design stuff. And interiors are loaded with stuff."

Beginning with the Chrysler LH and Dodge Intrepid models, Gilles has put his stamp on most of the Chrysler line, including work on the company's uber-sports car, the Dodge Viper.

The design center where Gilles works is a large room filled with designers behind desks, and a variety of full-sized cardboard, clay, and metal models of future Chrysler cars.

A short tour of Chrysler's design studio reveals the full-scale passenger car models for the 2004 year that Gilles has been working on. Every so often during the day, various Chrysler vice presidents ask for Gilles's advice about certain elements of their clay car models. Mostly, the conversation centers on moving elements such as headlights a quarter of an inch, or broadening the front grille, or even small things like added bows in the design.

"One of the things that is real important is trying to manage the brand and make it instantly recognizable versus the other carmakers," Gilles says while walking through the studio.

There is a science to the art of car design. Gilles can't just decide to put knobs and controls wherever he would like to put them. The car industry has rules that are at least thirty years old governing where things should be in a car.

"We work day to day with resident engineers in our studio that constantly watchdog us and make sure that we are meeting all of our requirements," he said. "We have to have the right zones, the correct distances, and the right knob diameters. If you don't do this, the car just won't feel right. It will feel screwed up."

But these restrictions don't mean that Gilles isn't inspired by odd design. He may look at other industrial design elements and see if he can put them into a car.

"You try to get as much exposure as possible," he says. "The auto industry is so limited by rules and regulations that you tend to get trapped into these paths because you have to meet so-and-so requirement. So if you look at what, say for example, what furniture is doing, where they have virtually no rules, you get kind of inspired by default. They are off doing something different. So I look at their work, and that may inspire a finish that I use in a car interior I'm designing. In the end, people have to sit in the car and use it, and enjoy it."

In his wildest imagination, where cost and safety issues don't rule, Gilles has a fantasy of creating a car with design elements never seen before.

"To do something for the sultan of Brunei, I would love to use things like granite, marble, and polished rare metals," he says. "A lot of times we try to simulate those textures with fake things or plastics, but I would love doing it in the real stuff."

In real life, perception of quality is one of the most important design elements that designers must use.

"When someone opens the door of a car, it has to look like it is worth more than it really is," he notes. "It has to exceed the expectations of the customer."

Gilles also says that customers have to feel comfortable with a car interior soon after they take a seat.

"It has to be intuitive," he continues. "You should be able to sit down in the car and, within about ten minutes, understand the car very well. You shouldn't have to guess at what stuff does; it should be obvious as to what function a button has. And lastly, it has to be relaxing. It should settle you down."

There are, of course, things that can make a design a failure. They are simple things.

"The one thing that can make a car a failure is if it doesn't fulfill its expectations," he says. "The car is promising more than it delivers, it's slightly overpriced for the amount of content, or it's answering a question that no one asked. You may have a car that's great and all, but there is no need for it."

In this vein, Gilles is most proud of his most recent project, the new Jeep Liberty. The Liberty is the replacement of the venerable Jeep Cherokee.

"The reason I'm very proud of it is because it was a very cost-restrictive project," he says. "If you know the Cherokee, the interior was very spartan. What I love about our Liberty interior is that in the end, we were able to do something that looked very expensive and tailored, without it costing any more than the old car."

Looking around the studio, there is a noticeable dearth of black faces. Gilles believes that it is not that the auto industry doesn't want to hire more minorities, but that the schools are not doing a good job in letting potential designers know about the opportunities.

"The numbers of black people [in design] are low, but they also come into the design schools at a low rate," he says. "For some reason, there is a huge interest in car design from the Asian community, and the black community is just starting to get there. When you go back to the high schools, you see a handful of potential candidates, but you also know that a lot don't have the means to go to college, or they lack the knowledge about the opportunities in car design.

"That certainly was my case," he continues. "My counselor had no clue that car design was even an option."

Gilles's interest in art didn't go well with his late father, who believed that he should study to be a lawyer or a doctor like his brother. It was only when his father saw one of his design creations in a car that he realized the significance of his son's work.

"Once he saw a car interior that I had worked on, he then understood. My brother had a plaque made for his car that said, 'Made by Ralph Gilles,'" Gilles laughs.

Gilles is a designer on the way up. He's on track to become a director, yet he's trying to become the best he can be by pursuing a master's in business administration.

"I want to be able to walk into a meeting and not only know about design, but also the business side of the car industry," he said. "You've got to be as versatile as possible in order to succeed in this business."

Obviously, Gilles knew what he was talking about, because about three months after making that statement, he was promoted to director.

8

Elisabeth in Her Own Words

Charlotte, North Carolina

Speak what you think to-day in words as hard as cannon-balls and to-morrow speak what to-morrow thinks in hard words again, though it contradict every thing you said today.

—Ralph Waldo Emerson

From Elisabeth's Journal:

This morning in physics class there was a lady (girl? woman?) in the back of the room with a very fussy baby- I can't remember her ever having brought the child before. Actually I'm not even sure who she was, because I was sitting in the front row and didn't want to be rude enough to turn around and look like all of the folks around me were doing. At some point Dr. Tyson interrupted himself and admonished her, "Madeline, you're going to have to do something back there"- at which point she excused herself. But she came back, and the kid still cried and fidgeted and fussed- and I felt so bad for both of them. Eventually they just left, which was probably best because she certainly couldn't have been getting any real notes taken.

When she left that time she left for good, but if she had been there at the end of class I would have spoken to her. I would have told her not to be embarrassed, and I would've told her that last semester I had to bring A. J. with me to this same class one day when he was sick and couldn't go to school. I would have told her that I understand how it feels to not have a sitter, but to not be able to miss class either. I would have told her that I know how crucial class notes are, not to mention the fact that Dr. Tyson is infamous for the pop quizzes. I would have told her that if it happens again not to worry, that I'll copy my notes for her. I would have told her that I'm a single mother too, that I know all too well about the demands of balancing motherhood and education. I would have told her, but by the time class was over she had gone.

She walks and talks with a self-assuredness that tells you that she has no time for frivolity. Yes, she can have fun, but she knows where her priorities are. She's a full-time college student at the University of North Carolina Charlotte campus and a full-time single mother of a six-year-old son. She has trials and tribulations about relationships with boyfriends, and her relationship with her not-often-there-for-her father is still evolving. She has goals, plans, and ambitions. She doesn't want to be, she doesn't hope to be, she is a sister who knows that she will be a doctor. Through all of it, she keeps a steady relationship with God. In other words, Elisabeth Epps is your typical uncomplicated-complicated sister.

But Elisabeth does something a little different in her life. She shares it all, the good, the bad, and the ugly of her life with strangers and friends from around the world. Elisabeth is the author of a continuing online journal called a Web log. In her variously named journals, Elisabeth speaks to any who log on about her daily life. It is all there, raw and riveting for all to see.

"The first online journal entry that I published publicly on the Internet was the E-Spot, in the fall of 1998," Elisabeth says. "It wasn't a 'Web log,' in the sense that it wasn't updated daily, and it didn't use publishing software but was instead coded and uploaded manually. I had been keeping a journal on the computer (offline) since fall of 1995, when I matriculated at North Carolina School of Science and Math (high school). I decided in 1998 to make the journal public because there were a few journals I read on the Web that had intrigued and excited me, and I guess I kind of thought 'Hey, I can do this too. . . .' Plus, I've always been quite a computer nerd, and I have always kept journals (I have them from the time I could write), so the online journal was a natural melding of two existing passions."

In her journal, Elisabeth is brutally honest about her life and the lives of others. No topic is too touchy or too personal. While the average person may bottle up her experiences, no matter how minor or major, Elisabeth lets them flow out onto the screen. Often her words reflect what it means to be a woman, African American, or both.

From Elisabeth's Journal:

It's common knowledge that when a party spot in Charlotte gets too hype (i.e. when too many black kids start coming) that it shuts down. If it's a black establishment, it manages to get itself closed entirely or gets renamed under new management; we've seen it happen at more places than I can remember: BB Jams, Vintage on the Boulevard, The Arena, Club Outrageous, FX, and many more.

If it's a "white" place that we black kids "take over," they then under the guise of preventing one of the two previous fates, do all that they can to keep us from coming back. In my short party-going tenure it's happened at City Grille, then Salamandria's and now at Fat Tuesday's. When I say "white" place, I mean it is not a club marketed to the black youth, nor is it advertised on the black radio stations or other such mediums. Instead, it's a regular old bar that through word of mouth we all find out has a college night (over twenty-one free with college ID), and we all somehow congregate at to chill once a week. Inevitably, some mischief occurs that is blamed on us, and we are systematically deterred from coming back.

I use "we" to mean myself and other young blacks, but what these establishments really use are blatantly offensive tactics to keep the black men from coming back at least, and by doing that they know damn well they've gotten rid of most of the Black girls too. Call me what I am- but I paid five dollars last night to chill with some brothers, and that's not what I got. There is no room to misconstrue what was happening last night. It was racism.

A few months back some college kids begin frequenting this local Latin club- not our usual spot- and by this time a month ago, Wednesday night at Salamandria's was the spot. Everybody who was anybody, and a whole lot of us who weren't, was trying to be up in there.

By last week- there was a required "Membership" fee in addition to the cover charge. Though I won't here go into the politics of their actions and how I know them to be attempts to keep young (blacks) out, the tactics last night at Fat Tuesday's aren't so ambiguous.

Apparently three weeks ago there was a shooting outside Fat Tuesday's. In an effort to bring a better "crowd" in, they revised their dress and age requirements for men. Young men now have to be twenty-one to get in (for women it's eighteen), and they have to have shirts tucked in, non-baggy shorts or jeans, no sneakers or sandals, and no "words" on their shirts. I have my issues with the dress code itself, but my issue is how it wasn't applied universally.

Melissa and I sat outside, waiting for our friend Kesha to show up, and watched as black guy after black guy- who'd been in there last week without incident, mind you- were turned away for one of the dress code violations. Even one in loose-fitting khakis was told they were too baggy, along with more than I can count who were actually dressed up in a shirt brandishing the "Sean John" or "Roc-A-Wear" labels apparently too prominently for the bouncers' liking. Meanwhile, white boys one after the other strolled in pants just as baggy (two even in sweatpants!), and more than I can count with huge ass "Abercrombie and Fitch" plastered across their chest. (Don't let me get started on the white dude in the baggy-ass surfer shorts, tank top not tucked in, and J. Crew thong flip-flops!)

What the hell? You know I had to say something, so I did. I was already pissed because pseudo-cops on bikes were trying to get us to stop "loitering" on the boardwalk that we'd hung out at for some ten years. (How the hell do you loiter on a boardwalk anyway? That's what the shit is there for!) So I carried my little "trouble-making ass" up to the bouncers and asked someone to please explain the lack of consistency in the implementation of the dress code to me. My jaw almost dropped when one of the bouncers- a black dude no less- told Melissa that they had been instructed to "screen carefully", and try to keep the black guys who "looked like they might cause trouble" out!

For all their concerns about age, attire and apparently race- guess who the fool that started shooting a few weeks ago was? A white dude over twenty-one. Isn't that some shit? He wasn't even one of us and he ruined it for all of us. Now we've got to find a new place to hang on Wednesday nights- or my friends do rather, 'cause I only go out about once a month any damn way. It's a damn shame for Fat Tuesday's, after the shit they pulled last night- next week is going to be as dry as ever, and whether they realize it or not, young black money is just as good as any other. Our power as an economic force is underused; this is one instance where it really mustn't go untapped.

"The journal is indeed very cathartic, borderline therapeutic. It's always good to be able to get emotions out and analyze them," she says. "It keeps me honest and really forces me to look hard at my thoughts and actions. I write about happy, silly, and incidental things, too, ones that don't need analysis!"

Obviously, keeping an online journal for all to see is not without its drawbacks. People anywhere can see what is happening in your life. Students on her University of North Carolina Charlotte campus have confronted Elisabeth about some of her remarks, and recently she has had to think about what she is writing. But even if she scrutinizes her words more closely in order not to offend some people, the value of the online journal outweighs any negatives.

"The single best thing [about writing the online journal] without a doubt is having it as a reference," she says. "It is an easily accessible glance at where I was (emotionally, physically, academically, spiritually) a month, year, years ago—and I can use it as a ruler by which to measure personal growth. In addition to that, I have always adored writing, and though I still write through school, between my psychology major, philosophy minor, and premed concentration, all of my writing is pretty academic and stoic; the journal provides me an outlet to kind of keep my mind and fingers nimble.

"Thirdly, though it has always overwhelmed and surprised me, one awesome thing is the people I have met through this journal or through their own journals. Sometimes it's a random or anonymous note that mentions a shared experience; on a rarer occasion it might be a long letter that sparks a 'real' friendship. The interaction with others, some who are like me and some who are not, both online and off, and my own exposure to them has been wonderful."

"The downsides of keeping the public online journal are several," she continues. "The worst has been that people have had a tendency to overestimate their relative importance in my life. I have had 'real' friends offended because I didn't mention them in some circumstances, and of course I always run the risk of a stranger stumbling upon a lone random entry and taking it out of context, assuming that I am as crazy/depressed/emotional/mean/silly or whatever emotion might be highlighted in one entry. It has been difficult to remind people that this is a glimpse of my life, not a play-by-play account.

"Lastly, there have been times where I have felt obligated to write, where it has taken over more of a time commitment that it ought to. It is these times when I have just put publishing the journal on hold altogether (although whether I choose to make the entries public or not, I still write every day)."

From Elisabeth's Journal:

Today, well, yesterday actually (if I started going to bed at a reasonable hour I'd know what day it was) was Kenneth's and my one-year anniversary. We both acknowledged the date, exchanged congratulations and all- but we didn't celebrate. No flowers, no cards, no celebratory dinner , , , and none of that really would've been appropriate- since we aren't actually together anymore anyway. I broke up with him three weeks ago, but very little has changed. Broken up or not, I've taken him to and picked him up from the airport each of these past two weekends when he went for his recruiting visits at Dayton and JMU.

Broken up or not he went with A. J. and I to Virginia to spend this past Easter weekend with my Grandmother. Broken up or not he hasn't stopped meeting me at my classes, kissing me, hugging me and holding my hand- and I haven't stopped him. I don't know when I will, and I don't know if I want to.

The stereotype of the single mother is one that she is somehow a burden on society, someone destined not to get an education or advance very far economically. But Elisabeth debunks that myth.

"There are many misconceptions [about single mothers]. That we are 'easy,' uneducated, that we tried to 'trap' someone. Supposedly all we are after is a support check; we have to depend on welfare," Elisabeth says. "I suppose the notion that disturbs me most is the one that somehow my age or marital status at pregnancy compromises my worth as a mother or woman. True, I had a lot of quick growing up to do when I got pregnant, but I did it. Frankly, I am a pretty awesome mother; my son is happy and healthy and wants for nothing, physically or otherwise. Getting pregnant at a young age wasn't the end of my life like others seemed to predict; rather, it was really quite the beginning."

But things have not gone so well in Elisabeth's relationship with her son's father. While their initial years were stormy and filled with angst, Elisabeth has come to peace with how she must deal with a relationship that will continue for the rest of her life.

"I think that if I would have considered him as a potential father of my children instead of just as a boyfriend at the time we consummated our relationship, we never would have consummated!" Elisabeth laughs. "The fact is, though, of those few indiscretions of youth, if I 'had' to get pregnant, he's not the worst one I could have been pregnant by.

"He doesn't frustrate me as much as he once did," Elisabeth continues. "I ask nothing of him, and at the risk of sounding immodest, I realize that he has it made. I don't 'bother'him; he knows that my family and I will carry this load and let him come through when and if he decides too. I pray for him daily, for his salvation, for his growth as a father. But when it comes down to it, I don't stress much over his shortcomings as a father because, well, I picked him. I feel like he has to answer to our son and to his God for his actions (or lack thereof), and not to me. As for our relationship, although we did somehow manage to produce an exquisitely beautiful, happy, healthy child, I know we will never be together intimately again. One thing we are doing, which we might not have done when we were together, is learning to move past civility and into peace. We have both left all the 'drama' behind, and it is both my prayer and my expectation that we are now moving from a peaceful phase to something more akin to friendship, and certainly to being partners as parents."

In the end, this sister with an "old soul" wants simple things, and her online journal reflects that. Each daily entry shows a black woman taking one step at a time toward multiple goals: mother, student, lover, doctor, and human being.

"I want to be happy and healthy," Elisabeth says. "I want to live an honest and examined life, to live without regrets and without hesitation. I am trying to raise a son that will do all the same. If I can ever make A. J. a tenth as joyous as he has made me, then I will have succeeded as a mother. Those are abstract ideas, but more concretely, ten years from now I'd love to be married, practicing medicine, and if not pregnant, then soon to be pregnant. As much as I know I was destined to be a doctor, I know that my first calling is to my eventual husband and children."

And will she still be writing her online journal?

"I will always keep a journal. I always have, and as best I can surmise, I might like to keep the online version as long as it is relevant and viable," Elisabeth concludes. "I certainly expect to keep it through undergrad, and maybe beyond, although of course I won't devote as much time to it as I have in months past once I enter medical school!"

9

Radical Rhymes with an English Accent

Kensington, London, U.K.

A poet is a bird of unearthly excellence, who escapes from his celestial realm arrives in this world warbling. If we do not cherish him, he spreads his wings and flies back into his homeland.

—Kahlil Gibran

I'm not a poet, but I love the expression and feeling that the poets bring. I just love it," said Sherrie as she settles into her seat. "I come out to listen at least once every two weeks. It's much more refreshing than watching the telly. When I come to these events, I like to hear as much contrast as possible, so I don't hear the same thing. I've always been interested in poetry; it's a natural expression of myself."

There has been a revolution happening in the United States and the United Kingdom. People, particularly black people, are turning off their televisions, the radio, and the internet and are making their way to various coffee houses, libraries, and storefronts. They are there to listen to poetry. But this is not just poetry but the performance poetry, otherwise known as the spoken word. It is a nascent movement that takes over from earlier poetry movements such as the Beat poets of the 1950s. Amateur and professional poets vie to tell their stories in such a way as to capture the vocal appreciation of their audience.

Like any art, the spoken word is fraught with inconsistency. Not every poet and every bit of poetry is good. At any given performance, you can be sure to find poets that are introspective, insightful, and disciplined poets, while there will be others who hide the shallowness of their poetry through eccentric quirks. Either way, whether the poetry is good or bad, people are listening. And often, the reaction to the poets depends on what the audience is looking for on any particular night.

Tonight, young, hip black British are meeting in the small auditorium at Kensington Library in London. The poets who surround the tiny stage are members of the Farrago Radical Rhymes, a London based poetry collective that brings together poets from throughout England and the world. Part workshop, part performance art, Farrago provides a comfortable atmosphere for new and established poets to demonstrate their work.

The auditorium soon fills with nearly one hundred people, who all look like they're dressed to go to a trendy London nightclub but chose an evening of poetry instead. The poets begin performing. Each poet gets about two minutes on stage, and all inevitably run over their allotted time. But no one in the audience seems to care. They are having a great time.

Gemma Weekes, from the Hackney area of London, gets up to read and rocks the auditorium with her poem, "What the Time, Mr. Wolf?"

With toothy smilelike sunshine
spiked with darkness he
slice me into eclipses,
his hands stretch long shadows
coloured licorice

He lather me into bubbles
I born and burst into pearl scent swirls

I rounded by his beauty
my tongue shiver into stutters when
I ask him for the time

But he doesn't know
what time it is
He "don't know sorry."

While his clock-face
reflects the lie and
the dying seconds
and damn.
I missed the train again.

Then I read:
Crude swallowswallow
breathe you in and die
float and die I drown and die
covered dyed by you I
die and born and die

you spread for miles
pure crude oil spread for miles
break sunshine heat into
mirrors blacken horizon with
gorgeous, dirty iridescence
rot gently beneath your
layers

no air time space or breath or life or me
only dark things live here
they float face-up
they cannot fly
swimming, my mouth
full of you
Eyes sticky and sightless nostrils clogged
with the stench of your perfection
Gently I rot beneath your
opaque layers

slippery with danger
how gorgeously iridescent
you smolder in daytime

infinitely opaque you imply
the depth of pastels in
your delicious black

only dark things
live here

slide silken and fatal over
my skin like heat
you stick like
heat you cling

like dirt and sweat
and cobwebs
like semen these
sticky fantasies

ecstasies of cruelty
drizzle against my inner thighs
you spread for miles

how smooth your torture
your blackness close around
my throat slipping flammable
poison over my tongue

I swallow swallow
breathe you in and die
float and
die I
drown and die
covered dyed
by you I
die

and born and die
you spread for miles of
layers rotting gently
beneath the stench of
your perfection only

dark things live
here they too
heavy to fly

"I've been writing for about three years now. Basically I just try to condense my experiences into something that I can transmit to people. I use whatever affects me, really," says Weekes as she basks in the praise from the crowd. "Sometimes being a black female poet, we have a lot of cultural baggage, but I realize that being a black woman is not the only part of me. I'm also five foot nine, I also live in Hackney, and I also wear glasses. I'm also a [college] graduate, so there are a lot of things for me to express. I try not to limit myself. I also write fiction, as well, and I'm trying to record a CD as well."

The poets who follow Weekes are of varying stages of development. Kat Francois, the reigning Farrago U.K. SLAM! champion reads her poem "Essence of a Woman." She is a standout, but a few of the newer poets lose their nerve as they try to express on stage what sounded so eloquent in the privacy of their homes. After about an hour, it is clear that it is time to bring some professional poets to the stage.

"Let's bring up some New York poets to the stage," says Farrago organizer and fellow poet John Paul, after a lull in the action. "Let's see what they're about, shall we? Let's see if they match that London talent we've seen tonight."

In the midst of a "poetic renaissance," Ainsley Burrows, a self-published poet, spoken-word artist, and musician, stands up and makes his way to the stage. At twenty-five years old, Burrows has established himself as an accomplished spoken-word artist, a universal poet, and a talented musician in the New York area. He is currently on a European tour called Babylon by Foot, and over the next few weeks, their travels will take them the length of England and throughout Germany.

"The Babylon by Foot tour started because I wanted to create a solid foundation for touring poets," Burrows said. "I wanted to establish a touring route through which up-and-coming poets and spoken-word artist could take their work to the world. The name itself came from an album that Bob Marley put out called Babylon by Bus. On tour with me are poets Osagyefo, Greg Purnell, and Simone Felice."

Before becoming a poet, Ainsley pursued a career in the financial industry and received a bachelor's degree in accounting. Later, he began graduate work in an MBA program, but it was in his first year of graduate school that Burrows decided he could no longer deny his passion for writing.

While studying for his MBA, Ainsley began writing for the university newspaper, performing some of his early works of poetry, and he also formed a band named Vertical 8. His performances became popular, and Ainsley soon found himself touring the local area colleges. After an almost-fatal car accident, Burrows realized that writing was his calling, and he decided to leave business school to pursue writing full-time. The energy put into his literary career gave birth to a self-published book of poetry entitled, *Black Angels with Sky Blue Feathers,* and a debut album of spoken word called *Cataclysm.*

Black Angels with Sky Blue Feathers is a collection of poems that embraces the soul; it is expressed in an articulate fashion that true poetry lovers can appreciate. The book begins its literary genesis with a poem entitled, "A Rose in Harlem," depicting a woman with a soul and spirit as deep as Harlem itself, and concludes with a piece called "Notes on my piano," giving insight into Burrows's philosophy on life.

"I am a mere chronicler of the stories that I see in the eyes of these victims of time. I see their hurt. I write about them and their pain in order to understand myself and my pain," he said.

"I am inspired by beauty and contradictions, life, struggle, and exploitation. I write about women a lot and I write about the state of humanity. Sometimes I write about myself in third person."

Derived from *Black Angels with Sky Blue Feathers,* his debut album, *Cataclysm,* is a combination of spoken word and musical artistry. It gives poetry and music lovers a feeling of having their cake and eating it, too, as one listens to the poetry that is fluid, passionate, and complex, enhanced with music that strengthens its delivery. Each song takes you on a musical, inspirational journey that allows you to bear witness to the depth of Ainsley Burrows's spoken word.

"My greatest struggle as a poet was trying to get a major

publishing house to take on my work," reflects Burrows. "It seems they are only interested in established writers. Many of these publishers are not about poetry as they are about sales. One of my greatest successes has been publishing two books of my own work, one of a fellow poet, and touring all over Europe and North America without any help from a poetry house."

The poem Burrows is reciting tonight is called "Uneven Dreams."

I stood
in the scorpion of her
lost in the memories of her inertia
deep in the wet of her soft
moving flesh
flushed against mine
eyes filled with emotions
tears intact
I'm sorry
but I cannot love you
still moving deep
into the delicate
of this swan's purple
fingers whispering
teething the flesh
from my back
like candles looking for excuses
she
the medicine . . . woman
with juniper hands
and at the moment of orgasm
she promised me
that when she die
she would will her womb
to give birth to me
in the next life
so she could love me
unconditionally

and that was 17,000 years ago
when we existed as echoes
in a windstorm
on an imploding planet.

Two universes
overembracing
the thread of her is
I danced with illusions
embroidered in mystery
murdered by many men
she too was alone
searching, torpid, unaware
walking into walls
dragging her broken heart
around in a steel cage
this daughter of a blacksmith
laying atop my easel
like a parable
interwoven into the paper of my being
bleeding
I read her two chapters
from a book of zebras
she stopped me
and said
she spent the past 400 years
giving out eyes
at the gate of a city.

Looking for you
which strangely explained
the first three years of my life
caught my breath drowning
woke up in a coffin
cotton stuffed in my nostrils
insides empty
eyes removed
she was gone

and the silence
tasted like embalming fluid on my lips.
A tender knocking
at the door of my conscience
it was an old woman
wrinkled and waxy
in a red shawl
white-haired beaming transfixed.

I was Buddha.
She handed me a liquid marble
that emitted so much heat
I broke out in tears
crying for no reason,
just crying,
crying because I understood
crying because I didn't understand.
Cried so hard it became 1920.
She now a jazz singer
under red lights
dancing with strands of cigar smoke
winked
it became 1828
she now my wet nurse smiling
I screaming . . .
brought forward
broke her heart at the prom
brought back broke her heart before I met her
just so she would keep her distance
died twice as a child avoiding her
she aborted me once
moved to China
changed her race
running
just so our paths wouldn't cross
just so our crosses wouldn't path.

Until one London evening . . .

I got a card in the post
pictured a slim Asian woman
with stolen eyes
in a red robe
old but timeless
eyes stolen from a lover . . .
me
she drawing circles
on the foreheads of the dust-quilted children
knitted from ether
blowing around in circle
at the gate of the city
and in her left shoulder burning bright blue
a black candle waxed with tears
forever frozen black
she pulled me into the photo
the photo fell
falling into another slice
of the universe
where she sat burning.
Ember floating like bubbles above her head.

Pulling pins from her aura
each pin a lifetime wasted
each lifetime in the form of a song
each song an ember
blazed singing
emitting so much light
I blinked . . .
and in that flash
seventeen faces
of this same woman
eons ago
centuries ago
years ago
futures ago
and before I could say

"What is your name?" she vanished.

And I find myself in this diner
and she is serving
black coffee
and donuts
to a trucker
with a white beard
wearing a red cap
tagged "made in China"
she walked over to my table
and gently placed a plate with two eggs
bleeding
like eyes
looking up at me
I looked up at her
"Have I seen you some place before . . . ?"

She said "No"
and walked out of the diner.
Like a wet nurse
like a jazz singer
like the daughter of a blacksmith
and left me with my heart chained to her pillow
"I am sorry but I can't love you"

Chants of "Booyaka! Booyaka!" ring out the audience's approval as Burrows finishes his first poem. It is quite obvious that Burrows has that something that sets him apart from the rest. With his serious but approachable style, along with his disheveled Afro, Burrows even looks the part of a serious poet.

"I love London," says Burrows. "The scene is not as developed as New York, but with that you get real, honest poetry. A lot of the topics are similar, which shows that as Black people we face the same problems or similar problems worldwide. One major difference was that many of the U.K. poets were not as expressive as the American poets.

"I am not sure how my poetry is translated in the heads of

the readers. I have never really inquired for fear of seeming too self-absorbed. Anyway, I think written poetry has a stronger impact in that it allows the readers to create their own interpretation of the words."

"We've just heard some of London's finest poets tonight," John Paul concludes. "We proved that it doesn't matter if you are from New York or London or anywhere else. It's about whether you like the poetry. It's about whether you have good spirit. It's about whether you believe in the words that you say up here onstage."

"I think that spoken word is beginning to develop its own place in the art word," says Burrows as he and the rest of the poets sell their books and CDs to the audience after the show. "I think the popularity can only help spoken word as an art form in that we will have means of getting the words to the public and not just sharing it among ourselves."

10

Of Rain, Spain, and Niggers Everywhere

Notting Hill Gate, London, U.K.

Racism is a refuge for the ignorant.
It seeks to divide and to destroy.
It is the enemy of freedom, and
deserves to be met head-on and stamped out.

—Pierre Berton

"Have you talked with any of the black people here?" asks Eric. He pours me a Guinness as he talks. "They are different from blacks in the States."

A good pour of Guinness means that you have to pour it about three quarters full, let it settle a bit, and then continue to fill it. I mentally do the same thing in digesting his words.

He leans forward from his side of the bar, as if to tell me a secret. I draw closer.

"And they are not very friendly," he says in a conspirator's whisper. "You know how when you see a brother walking the streets in the States that he'll give you that nod . . ."

Eric motions with a practiced flick of the acknowledgment. Every brother or sister in America knows that nod, that nonverbal communication that tells their opposite that even if others don't see you, I see you. You are important to me.

"Well, they don't do that here," he says while picking up empty beer glasses from the bar. "They'll walk right by you. They are more interested in what island you come from, you know: 'Are you from Jamaica or Trinidad?' versus just recognizing that we are all black."

He walks to the other side of the bar.

The Devonshire Arms is not at all what it seems. A traditional pub that sits in the Kensington and Chelsea borough of London, it attracts English regulars and American tourists in equal measure. The English patrons feign an interest in their American cousins while watching English football matches on the television. Meanwhile, the American tourists try to soak up a bit of English atmosphere by saying typically English comments such as "cheers, mate!" and such non-English sayings such as "G'day!" ("That's Australian, mate!" says one bemused Englishman.)

Eric is a brother from Long Beach, California, and he tends bar here with his white, dreadlocked girlfriend. It's a pretty good gig in that they get free room and board and a small salary. In exchange, they get free brew and time to explore Europe. In the past year, they've seen pretty much everything. Everything except for what will happen tonight.

About thirty minutes after that initial Guinness pour, an older, white married couple from Georgia sidles up to the bar, whiling a little time as they wait for a theater show to begin. The husband stands slightly disengaged while the wife nurses . . . well, maybe she doesn't nurse perhaps as much as she delicately guzzles, her three beers in twenty minutes. She overhears the conversation between Eric and myself and becomes excited by the sound of American accents. It is obvious that her pleading face is waiting for an opening, any opening, that would allow her to enter the discussion. She's full of questions. Questions that she somehow forgot to ask during her fifty or so years of living in America but she now feels comfortable asking in England.

"I would like to ask you a question," she drawls with an eager, bright smile.

I make a bet with myself that the question will deal with some black person she knows.

"We have friends that lives in our neighborhood. They are black . . ."

No! I never would have guessed! I think to myself.

"And our neighborhood is all white," she continues.

I sip a little bit more of my Guinness while her husband shifts uncomfortably in his chair.

"Now, their daughter went to college and found out that she wasn't accepted by either the white students or the black students. She really had a hard time."

There is a quiet rolling of the eyes by the young Americans overhearing the conversation. Zephyr, a white art student from Santa Cruz, turns to her sketches and Bacardi and Coke. Eric moves to handle the order of a patron, while Michael, a white American technology executive, tries to become as small as possible.

As I brace myself to answer this ubiquitous race question, probably the eight thousand, nine hundred and sixty-third time that I've been asked a race question in my lifetime, but hey who's counting? As I prepare to speak I silently promise to keep the answer simple and short.

"Well," I begin, "what your friend is going through is reflective of a general dilemma a lot of African Americans have to go through."

I take another sip of my Guinness and continue.

"It is my opinion that if an African American grows up in a white community, they can get a false sense of full acceptance because the local white people in their area may either accept or at least tolerate them in their midst."

I knew that the next part was the kicker and that she probably wouldn't like what I had to say.

"But as you note in her experience, she was not accepted by the white community when she got to college. What you've just seen is the reflection of real racism in America. White people who didn't know her didn't accept her. She thought, because of her experience growing up, that white people would fully accept her, that they would "transcend her race" and get to know her. But of course that didn't happen."

The husband looks at his watch and is again shifting even more uncomfortably in his chair, and the woman's eager smile slowly disappears as she mentally calculates my answer. I know that she needs to demonstrate that white people are not alone in their ignorance.

"But the black people didn't accept her, too," she stutters nervously.

"That doesn't surprise me," I retort. "I'm pretty sure that they thought it strange to find a black woman who probably had little or no connection to the black community. And she probably didn't, and I'm generalizing here, I'm sure she didn't know anything about being black in America. So it becomes a shock to both when they meet. But eventually the black community will accept her. We always do."

With that, the husband got up and made a motion to his wife.

"Why, thank you very much for your time," she drawls as she rises to leave.

"Absolutely, no problem," I lied.

They leave. The conversation among the Americans and English continues. The drinks flow. The hours roll on. I mention why I'm in London, and people begin to offer suggestions for possible topics.

"You know, I traveled through Spain and I was struck by the African influence in the country," says Michael, the white executive. "Have you ever been interested in writing about that?"

"Sure," I say. Can't be too hard on the guy; he's just trying to be helpful.

From about ten feet away, a Scotsman makes his way to our group. He's been drinking ale for the past six hours. His face, redder than a Macintosh apple, is looking directly my way. His mouth is forming words that I can't hear over the murmur of the pub crowd. But as he notices that I missed his statement, he decides to yell it at the top of his lungs.

"If you can find niggers in Spain, I guess you can find niggers everywhere!" he slurs.

The conversation in the pub stops. Eric comes sliding to our side of the bar. Zephyr and Michael, along with the English patrons, all bow their heads in shame. But I don't really notice all that, because it is all in the periphery. I just realize that, as those words float into the atmosphere, I am going to have to go to an English jail for assault on this man.

I rise slowly, bringing my nose within an inch of his beer-soaked nose. I contemplate throwing a straight right and dropping him in his tracks. I really contemplate that. But then I think, "Why should I be deported and he live to sit here another day?"

"Let me tell you something," I say in my most menacing, psychotic, threatening, this-black-man-is-crazy monotone voice. "I come here to London and I respect your country. But if you ever say that word again, I will knock you the fuck out."

For the first time in probably twenty years, the Scotsman finds immediate sobriety. His face becomes pasty white, and he takes three steps back. Eric comes around the bar, and the Scot begins to plead for forgiveness.

"I don't know what got into me, mate," he says as Eric begins backing him to the door. "I'm sorry if I offended you."

Those are his last words as the pub door closes behind him. Soon, the previously invisible patrons of the Devonshire Arms begin to rise and walk toward me.

"Don't mind him, mate," one says.

"We apologize for him; I hope you have a better time here in London," another says.

But I don't really hear them. I just pick up my Guinness and begin thinking of a lyric from a reggae song by a dub poet named Mutabaruka:

"It no good, to stay in a white-man country too long!"

Eric comes walking up with a white towel.

"Another Guinness?" Eric asks as he wipes the counter.

"Yes, please," I reply.

Zephyr keeps sketching on her now-full pad, and the Devonshire Arms goes back to normal.

11

The House of UnCommons

Westminster, London, U.K.

If people had been aware that by the new millennium, London, our capital, would have over 25 per cent of its population from ethnic minorities and that forecasts expect that by 2014 over half of the city will be non-Anglo-Saxon, that Leicester and Birmingham would be vying as to which city would have a black majority first, Enoch Powell would have been prime minister.

—Tory MP John Townsend

The first meeting of the day is officially called the Standing Committee on the International Criminal Court Bill, but really, it is another chance for the opposing political parties to clash over the United Kingdom's growing integration with Europe. The Tories, or Conservative party of the U.K., want to limit their country's participation in Europe while the Labour party wants to embrace the New Europe. Either way, this group of about twenty members of Parliament are debating, trading insults, and laughing together as they work out the various amendments and clauses to the bill.

Sitting on the Labour side of the room are two black members of Parliament, or MPs, Oona King and David Lammy. They sit listening intently to the arguments on both sides, intermittently standing to make a point. When a lunch break is called, the two make their way to the MPs' dining hall.

Technically, the thirty-five-year-old King represents Bethnal Green and Bow section of East London, while Lammy, twenty-eight years old, represents the Tottenham section of London. But in reality, as two of only ten blacks of the 659-member British

Parliament, they represent black people throughout the United Kingdom, no matter the location.

"One of the biggest challenges is balancing your responsibilities to your constituency and those that elected you, and your responsibility as a black MP for the black community, in a country where we do not have a representative democracy," said King.

Lammy concurred.

"If an MP in Newcastle has a question about black youth and wants my opinion or expertise, then I'm not going to turn him down because this is not in Tottenham. I have that responsibility to deal with those issues."

"Since I am only the second black woman ever elected to Parliament," King continued, "every black women's organization in Britain is writing to me to look at their cause. In theory, I'm quite entitled to say no, but of course, I don't."

King, whose mother is from a working-class Jewish family in Newcastle, and whose father, Prof. Preston King, is an African American from Georgia, was educated at both York University in England and the University of California at Berkeley in the United States. She is the second black woman elected to Parliament and has been in office since 1997.

The Harvard Law-educated Lammy is the son of Afro-Caribbean parents. One of the young hot politicians in the New Labour party, Lammy grew up in the same London area that he now represents.

In Great Britain, the term *black* can mean a couple of things: *Black* can be defined in a macro way, including all dark-skinned minorities—Asians and people of African descent—or in a micro way, defining only the Afro-Caribbean population.

By most appearances, national black political power in Great Britain is still in its infancy. The first Afro-Caribbean members of Parliament, Bernie Grant, Paul Boateng and Dianne Abbott, were elected in 1987. And the black and immigrant presence in England has long been met with resistance from some whites in England.

In April 1968, Tory MP Enoch Powell read his infamous

"rivers of blood" speech, in which he said that Britain was "literally mad" to allow large-scale immigration of blacks into England. Even as recently as 2001, Tory MP John Townsend declared that Britain's "homogeneous Anglo-Saxon society" had been "seriously undermined" by mass immigration. Both men were denounced, with Powell being fired for his remarks, but their remarks opened up a dialogue on race in England that had been swept under the carpet for a long period of time.

"You've always had a perpetual discussion about race in America," said Lammy. "We've only had it in fits and starts [in England]. We'll discuss race after a riot, after a murder, but not consistently."

Today, King and Lammy represent the second generation of Afro-Caribbean members of Parliament, and while they are wielding more influence on a national level, they still have to fight a seemingly apathetic black British population. But Lammy doesn't think that apathy adequately describes how the Afro-Caribbean population views politics in Great Britain. A lot of the lack of political participation in the black community could be attributed to a missing connection between British government and minority communities.

"We have had what are consistently described as low [voter] turnout at our elections," said Lammy. "But what concerns me about the blanket discussion about black voters is that it is so simplistic. It focuses on apathy without getting behind what I believe are two central reasons for that. One is that the journalists don't seem to understand that in London areas like Oona's and mine that there is a tremendous amount of mobility. People are poor and they live in council housing, and they live in poor, run-down private-landlord accommodation . . . and the last thing they are thinking about is voting. Sixty percent of my constituency moves about, and this never comes up.

"The second thing, and I say this very passionately," Lammy continues, "is that we have come into this country as poor people, and certainly as black ethnic minority people we have come to expect very little of government. And to be honest, there isn't a great deal of examination [by the black community] as to who is in power. There is a lack of faith in government, and the challenge of our party is to connect to black ethnic minorities in a language that they can understand. After four years [of Labour being in power], we are not there yet."

Under Prime Minister Tony Blair, King and Lammy are a part of the so-called "New Labour," a refashioning of the Labour party as a moderate centrist party on the model of former U.S. President Clinton's new Democratic Party. In fact, Tony Blair, as the head of the Labour Party, has been admired and mocked as a Clinton soundalike.

"New Labour is about marrying social justice and economic growth," King said. "And we say that the two are not enemies of each other, and that you need to create one to sustain the other."

"In a way, New Labour is a response to the twenty-first century," Lammy continued. "The tribal camps that have tried to rule this country [in the past] have been overwhelming Tory. They ruled based on class, and that is difficult to defend in the twenty-first century. New Labour is an attempt to govern for everybody, rather than a faction of the country."

While this "New Labour" is now dominating Parliament, black MPs like King and Lammy still face challenges. One of the most daunting is the fact that more than half of their constituents don't vote; however, those same constituents often need their help. That stress can be overwhelming.

"I have about 150,000 people in my area but only 70,000 electorates," King said. "In an area like mine, the ones you deal with the most, paradoxically, are the ones that don't vote. These are the ones that I try to help the most, and I never get a vote in return. They may have immigration problems, or they just arrived from the Congo, they are not going to be able to vote.

"Compared to the average white MP, we as black MPs have a higher need from our constituency, and on top of that you've got an extra level of need from the black community," King noted.

Lammy thinks that this burden is so overwhelming, it quite possibly killed his predecessor, Bernie Grant.

The Guyanan-born Grant was one of the first black members of Parliament. A hard-driving muckraker who cut his teeth as a hard-left trade union leader, Grant began his political career in Tottenham after having been elected to a local council seat via the Labour Party. He built a loyal following among the unemployed, the black community, and the left by championing their rights when it was exceedingly unpopular to do so. For example, Grant opposed rent hikes for people who lived in subsidized housing, eventually winning a battle within his own Labour party.

Suspicious of the police, Grant was unsympathetic to their plight after a 1985 riot. After a police officer was killed in the riot, Grant expressed no regret.

"What the police got was a bloody good hiding," he said.

And although the Labour party condemned him for those remarks, Grant remained a hero to the disenfranchised. Whether it was wearing a traditional African robe made of Ghanaian cotton at the opening of Parliament, or asking that Rastafarians be exempt from paying a poll tax because of their religion, Grant was often the face of black England. He died at the young age of fifty-six.

"Bernie Grant has tremendous respect in both this country and this House," Lammy said. "The single issue that he worked on—and I don't think that Bernie would mind me saying this—was the issue of race. And I'm glad he was single-minded on this. He took the view that any black person in this country was his constituent. Now, I don't mind being on the record as saying that I think, as honorable, noble, and gracious as that was, the fact is that that responsibility killed Bernie. And he's not here today because of the amount of work that that generated. And I think that we lose out for that. That's why I feel very strongly about having more people in this place that look like us."

Looking forward, Lammy thinks that this generation of black Britons needs to make a greater effort to be properly educated if it hopes to benefit from any prosperity generated.

"One of our huge challenges for our community is in the area of education," he said. "Ironically, many of our parents coming from the Caribbean and Africa were very educated people. They had to take lower-paying jobs and unskilled jobs to pay their way in a country where they were newly arrived immigrants. But they were educated people. Something went terribly wrong during the eighties in this country in terms of mainstream, or what you in America would call public education. That affects employment prospects and quality of life. I'm not saying that all blacks are not educated, but we do have generations that are lost."

"Some of the most shocking results are when you look at the exclusion rate of young blacks," King added, talking about those disenfranchised. "There is a combination of low expectations and racism which has created an education underclass."

Lunchtime is now over. It's back to work for both King and Lammy, and that means attending the foreign minister's questions. As they get up to make their way to the chambers, King makes one last comment.

"The next stage is for us to reach into the institutions that have been controlling us," she said.

King and Lammy hope that in the future, others will join them in doing just that.

12

The Lady Harris in Paris

Paris, France

Of the gladdest moments in human life, methinks, is the departure upon a distant journey into unknown lands. Shaking off with one mighty effort the fetters of a bit, the leaden weight of Routine, the cloak of many Cares, and the slavery of Home, man feels once more happy.

—Sir Richard Francis Burton

Deborah Harris strolls up the picturesque Parisian street carrying a long French baguette and a bottle of red wine, and you just know that she is an African-American woman. It's not just because she is black; there are plenty of black folks walking the streets of Paris, but Harris is different. She has that African-American sister-girl stroll that only African-American women have. Head erect, stride long and confident, her stroll says, "Forget 'Still I Rise;' hell, you'll never get a chance to knock me down."

She's about ten minutes late, and there's the immediate inclination to attribute her lateness to "colored folks time," but as Harris makes her way to her door, she reminds me that in France, everyone is late.

"You're lucky that I showed up anywhere near our agreed time," Harris laughs. "The French will show up to a three-o'clock brunch at six o'clock with no apologies."

Harris's old Parisian building, with its Old World features of wrought-iron balconies and whitewashed stucco sides, is beautiful. But the tiny two-and-a-half-person elevator gives you an early indication about the dimensions of the abodes in their building. And it is very accurate.

Harris's apartment is very tiny by any standard, and very expensive. Take five steps in either direction and you run into a wall. The kitchen is nothing but a Bunsen-burner-sized oven and a bar-style refrigerator. The bedroom? You're in it the minute you walk over the threshold. The bathroom? There are American closets larger than the one in this unit. But ah, walk out to the balcony, you soon find the payoff. Views of the Eiffel Tower and the Parisian skyline dominate. Yes, the apartment is no larger than your average prison cell, no make that smaller than a prison cell. But instead of feeling imprisoned, Deborah Harris is probably feeling more freedom than the ordinary person gets to experience in a lifetime. She is doing just as she wants, where she wants, for whom she wants. And that "whom" is Deborah Harris, living happily in Paris.

"I had been to Paris a few times before and liked it. I had met a tour guide at the Castle of Versailles, and he told me how he got started, and it sounded interesting—like something I could do when I retire. The woman I was going to work with was already in Paris and had been for about two or three years.

"I arrived in Paris on Wednesday, September 20, 2000," says Harris. "Originally, I'd planned to work with another sister and her company doing tours in Paris, but we could not see eye to eye on the arrangement. I thought that, hey, I could do this on my own. My sorority, Delta Sigma Theta, ran a story about my company in its national publication. French and American friends told their friends, and the business was begun."

So Harris moved to the 9th arr. of Paris, sort of a Parisian financial district dotted with major department stores, for the beginning of a one-year sabbatical.

"I am a telecom professional and have been in the industry for more than fifteen years. Just prior to moving to Paris, I was working for U.S. Sprint as a branch manager for transport services (ATM, frame relay, network services, etc.), handling global business customers, with headquarters based in San Jose, California. I wasn't tired of my job, because I love the telecom industry. However, both my mom and dad had died within the last five years at the time, and I started to look at life differently. I decided that I would actually do things I had always imagined. Visiting Paris was my mom's dream, but she never got there. By the time I was able to afford to take her, she was too sick to go. It was a major disappointment. [It made me realize that] I don't want any more major disappointments in this life."

Perhaps no other European city evokes comparable images of cosmopolitanism, glamour, and romance as does Paris. What many don't realize is that African Americans have contributed significantly to the qualities that have helped create these images. Paris has both a large romantic heart and an African-influenced soul.

Ever since the turn of the twentieth century, African Americans have traveled to Paris, often deciding to make the City of Light their home. Escaping the ravages of racism in their native land, they left an unforgettable impression on the entire country and culture, creating both a hunger and an admiration for any and everything African-American.

Paris, unlike any other city in the world, has been a place of refuge for many of our African-American historical greats: James Baldwin, Josephine Baker, Langston Hughes, Sidney Bechet, Duke Ellington, Toni Morrison—the list goes on. According to some expatriates, visiting or living in Paris afforded them a sense of freedom and equality that eluded them in their native country. It was in Paris that they found the peace that they had dreamed of: the dignity of simply existing as human beings. Jessie Faucet, a visiting writer, described the Paris of 1924 as a place where it was lovely just to be by oneself and not bothering with color prejudice.

Today, in a city of nine million, there are 375,000 French-speaking West Africans, 425,000 French West Indians, and about 6,000 to 10,000 African Americans living in Paris. As you drive the streets of Paris, you see and hear their presence via the red fez of the West African Senegalese, and the patois of those from former French colonies such as Martinique.

So there is indeed a reason for the black community to continue to make pilgrimages to Paris: it is a missing link in our history as Americans. Under the dust of this city, along the grand boulevards and avenues, in forgotten alleyways and small, winding streets are pieces of a broken mirror glimmering with the images of our legacy.

That legacy includes poet Countee Cullen writing his sonnet "At the Etoile" under L'Arc de Triomphe, and World War I African-American troops marching under the same Arc in triumph. In the present day, that African-American legacy means the presence of African-American establishments such as Haynes Restaurant, the oldest soul food restaurant in Paris, opened by a former Morehouse College football star in 1949.

Harris was able to tap into a clientele, African Americans, who have been traveling internationally for a time now and are looking to discover something in Paris beyond the typical tourist areas.

"African-American visitors to Paris, generally business professionals, are generally my customers. Many have been to Paris several times, and some are making their first steps through Europe. I also had African Americans who live in Brussels and Germany take my tour.

"Typically, via phone or E-mail in advance of their travel, arrangements are made for our meeting in Paris upon their arrival. Sometimes I provide assistance with transportation to and from the airport, and bookings for tours outside of Paris. I have the ability to personalize and customize my tours.

"I meet with the client at their hotel; we review their itinerary, determine a walking tour time, and meet at the time arranged to conduct the tour. I also provide shopping and restaurant information based on the needs of the client."

"Tours run approx. four and a half hours, and I am busy at least four days a week. My largest group was fifty people, but most of the time the groups are small, normally about three to six people. There isn't a lot of competition, because Paris is a pretty big place—and there's enough business for everybody."

One of the places on Harris's itinerary was 15 Avenue Montaigne, Theatre des Champs Elysees. The Theatre des Champs-

Elysees is significant because on October 2, 1925, Josephine Baker made her Paris debut with Louis Douglas and black clarinetist Sidney Bechet, called the founding father of jazz, in the musical *La Revue Negre*. Other African Americans who appeared on this stage were Florence Mills, Louis Armstrong, Katherine Dunham's dance troupe, Art Blakey and the Jazz Messengers, Alvin Ailey, Langston Hughes, and Ray Charles.

The site of the old Hotel Langeac has recently become a hot tourist haunt, as it is the place where, in 1787, future President Thomas Jefferson began his thirty-eight-year relationship with his slave Sally Hemmings.

"If an African American could visit just one place in Paris, then my vote goes to the American Cathedral in Paris. Recently renovated and reopened during my stay, the grounds are simply calming and beautiful. Plaques are maintained in the hallway commemorating troops and battalions from World Wars I and II. Many clients were moved to see the recognition given to these African-American war heroes. Given more time, a trip to Normandy and viewing its surrounding areas is extremely moving. Hard to imagine that such a beautiful, tranquil countryside area was the scene of one of the worst wars of our time.

"The American Cathedral is also where huge crowds of Americans attended commemorative services in April 1968, after the assassination of Dr. Martin Luther King Jr. Also, memorial services were held for James Baldwin there in 1987."

One of the obstacles that Harris had to overcome was her lack of fluency in the French language. And in a country that protects its language and culture, it was imperative for her to gain some level of proficiency.

"Yes, I learned French, but it was not great. I took intensive classes four hours a day, Monday through Friday, for much of the time I've been here. I learned enough to have a very basic conversation and how to deal in an emergency.

"Although racism exists, it is different than in the United States in that it is often more of a nationality divide than a color divide. Algerians and Africans were oftentimes not treated well in my view.

"As an African American with a noticeable American accent, in my whole time here I experienced only one incident [of racism], and that was with a friend in a department store. We laughed about it. An old woman was annoyed that we weren't moving fast enough and shouted at us an obscenity in French. Thanks to the French classes, we were able to respond in kind," she laughs.

There was an African-American support system in Paris. Various African Americans living in Paris regularly have soirees and meetings, even getting to the point where African-American artists and authors would present their works and hold book-signings.

"I joined a group called 'Sisters,' which is comprised of primarily African-American women living in Paris," says Harris.

"The Sisters group provided me an opportunity to fellowship, network, etc. Some of the women I met through the organization were like me, planning to stay in Paris for a short time, say about two years or less. They were doing specific work, traveling or researching. Many others had been here a long time, more than fifteen years, and had become more accepting of the French system and way of life. Many had married French nationals and had children, so their lives and expectations were very different from us short-timers. Probably the most interesting phenomenon of the African-American women who had been in France for a long time and had no plans of returning to the States to live was their perception of rampant crime in the United States. Providing a safe environment for their children was of major importance. In many conversations, I found that crime throughout the United States was thought to be a major problem and hindrance for their returning."

Harris has some simple advice for anyone looking to move to Paris.

"Do the homework," she advises. "Read up on the regulations for living in France for an extended period; there are a few great books on the market that will help your research. I planned for approximately nine months before going to Paris. But living in Paris is substantially less expensive than living in the United

States. The exchange rate is seven-point-five francs to the dollar. That's a lot of buying power, and many goods in France are simply less expensive. A great bottle of wine could be had for three dollars. A hundred and fifty francs bought a gourmet meal. But still, make sure to bring money, and a fair amount of it.

"If you could change one thing about Paris it would be the weather. It rains a great deal, or at least for the year I've been here. Although I didn't let the rain stop me, slogging through got on my nerves. The winter wasn't much fun either. I'm Californian and I love sunshine!"

Harris's sabbatical ends in one year, but she intends to keep the business going. She has built relationships with travel agents and has a steady stream of clients requesting her services.

"I have another friend who is interested in doing the same thing. We have worked together before, so I'm confident this will work out. She will come to Paris in October 2001 for four months, in order to get a lay of the land, and then she'll make plans to return permanently by summer of 2002. We have a tour group already booked for the summer of 2002," Harris says with a smile.

But if Paris is so wonderful, how come Harris doesn't move there permanently like the other African Americans in the city?

"I had never planned to live here permanently. I'm from Oakland, California, and I love that city and the whole San Francisco Bay area. I have a greater appreciation for living in the United States since my experience in Paris. I enjoy Paris; I will always continue to spend time here. I love the relaxed lifestyle, and the way of life for women in Paris is wonderful. One gets a feeling of safety, so I travel the city at all hours using mass transit and I feel comfortable. I love the friendships I've established here. But I'm clearly an American that firmly believes the United States is the best place to live on earth. If you're lucky enough to live in California, then aces!"

"This Parisian experience has taught me to believe that I can do anything and anything is possible. I think the biggest obstacle in the beginning was with me. I was disappointed that the original partnership didn't work out and that a friendship had been lost. But as one door closes, another opens. I was able to make a friend here who had a steady stream of visitors coming to Paris, enabling me to get off on my own with a great start. I'm not in as big a hurry as I used to be to get on to the next thing. Still, it could be my age, it's hard to tell!" she laughs.

"I can tell you this: that when do I leave Paris, I'll miss the bread, pastries, and my friends."

And after her year there, it seems as though Paris will also miss Harris.

13

The Friday Night Gathering

Chicago, Illinois

There is a vast world of work out there in this country, where at least 111 million people are employed in this country alone—many of whom are bored out of their minds all day long. Not for nothing is their motto TGIF—"Thank God it's Friday." They live for the weekends, when they can go do what they really want to do.

—Richard Nelson Bolles

The First Friday party was supposed to start at 6 P.M., but if you're African American, you pretty much know that people will not show up on time. In other circles, it may be called being fashionably late, but in the African-American community it is called by another term, "colored people time." Rather than attributing a negative connotation to colored people time, it should be looked at charitably as a sort of cultural style that we African Americans enjoy. As an original First Friday organizer, Danielle Carr is used to folks showing up in their own good time.

"And if you really look, you'll also notice that the women show up about two hours later than the men," says Carr as she awaits her guests. "They have to get off work and then get ready for the party. But the men reap the benefits in the end."

Eventually the fashionably late begin to make their way to Chicago's Club Allure, the location of this month's First Friday. Soon the music filters into the room, the bartenders are filling martini glasses, and the party has officially started. Smiling black faces and amorphous chatter are the background for this warm evening in July.

First Fridays was a concept developed over a decade ago, when in various cities organizers brought middle-class, professional African Americans together in a casual social setting on the first Friday of each month. In theory, the parties are designed to help these professionals network, but in practice, the parties are more of an occasion to feel reaffirmed by others in similar circumstances. The pressures of being an African-American professional are what unite them.

"I stole the idea for First Fridays from another First Fridays in San Diego," Carr said. "There were originally four people that sponsored [Chicago] First Fridays, and we had already thrown informal parties in the past. We had a couple of hundred people at our first event, and it kind of grew from there."

Ten years later, Carr is the lone organizer, and she continues to sponsor First Friday events at Chicago area nightclubs. The events normally draw between 200 and 400 attendees each month.

"We don't do public advertising; we only let people know about our parties by word of mouth," says Carr. "We like to keep a certain standard and clientele for our parties. The average person who attends our parties could be between twenty-five and fifty-five years old, and both blue-collar and white-collar. One thing that I like about these parties is that there is a mix and we all get along."

A quick survey of the black folks assembled here gives rise to some quick and convenient stereotypes. There are the white-silk-suited players, who are portraying a cool that often ensnares those who dare to wander too close. There are the superbusinessmen, the ones who need to use their cell phones every thirty seconds and try to make it obvious to everyone nearby that they are considered a VIP somewhere in this world. Then there are the women, who travel to the club with at least three of their girlfriends—a group large enough to keep the conversation going, but small enough to ditch if the right man comes by.

But in the midst of the stereotypes are real people. Some are just glad to be somewhere other than at home or at work. Others are trying to pursue their dreams through networking. Maybe this stranger they are talking to has the key to furthering their career.

"I'm trying to make it as an actor and a film producer, but to kept the bills paid, I work as a building administrator for a trucking company," said Joey Thornton as he sipped his drink.

"I'm just happy to be out," said Tim Johnson.

Local Chicago celebrities such as Jesse Jackson Sr. and Jr. have stopped by in the past, but Carr says that many don't come by because they won't get their egos massaged by the patrons of First Fridays.

"Honestly, we don't get a lot of celebrities in here because our guests don't really care about them," laughs Carr. "And if they don't get sweated, they won't come back."

Club Allure has two floors, with two distinct moods. The bottom floor is more a mingling area, with people standing in small groups, while the second floor is more sedate, with groups sitting at round tables, sipping on cocktails.

Sitting in the corner of the second floor are three friends: Nedra Jackson, Chinika McMillan, and Dawn Murphy. Young and fashionably dressed, the three friends survey the First Friday scene.

"This is my second First Fridays event," said Nedra Jackson, a social worker in Chicago. "I decided to come with my friends because I wanted to try something new. This is a chance to meet people and see who's out here. Since I've been here, I found a lot of common things between people, and it is a great mixer."

"It's just great to be around people, especially men, that have jobs!" Dawn laughs. "These are brothers with educations, and jobs with benefits. Not that this is really important, but it is nice to be around people that are at your level."

Chicago has long been an end point for African Americans looking for employment, especially throughout the Great Migration of Southern black families to Northern cities in the early twentieth century. Mostly poor, these rural Southern blacks provided the backbone of an urban Chicago renaissance. And even today, Southern blacks are still making their way to Chicago in search of a better life.

"I think that it is more diverse here in Chicago than in Alabama," says McMillan, an Alabama native who moved to Chicago five years ago. McMillan is a human resources recruiter.

"But I think that it is more segregated here in Chicago than in Alabama," she continues. "You find black people who have lived on the South Side of Chicago that have never been to the North Side. And I think that some of that is prejudice because being from south Alabama, you know where the racism is, but here it is more implied and subtle."

It's about three hours into the party now, and the players are beginning to hold sway over the crowd. The networking party is beginning to morph into a regular dance-and-have-fun party that could happen at any club. For the people who sought out First Fridays to network, this transformation seems to be a missed opportunity.

Norman Fleming, an information technology specialist, feels that these business networking parties tend to perpetuate an immaturity within the African-American business community.

"It's very important for us as a people to understand the business game and the discipline of networking," Fleming says, with a serious tone. "I'm not sure that we have that level of education and understanding. Normally, we have subsets of groups at these functions that don't leverage the opportunity to meet other African Americans that could have a professional connection that could build your career. I think it's time for education, communication, and information. As far as First Fridays, I would love to know how First Fridays as an organization educates African Americans to understand what networking is all about and what the purpose of this event is, as opposed to meeting ladies and men.

"I think that this party is an extension of what potentially our culture represents," he continues, "as it relates to having fun, partying, but not necessarily understanding the purpose of why we are here."

While First Fridays may not reach the expectations of Fleming, the aspirations of most party-goers seem to combine both professional and career success, as espoused by Nancy Harris.

"I would like to be happy in my career and job," she said. "I don't want my career to be like a job, but something that I get up every day to do because I love it. And of course, I would love to find the man of my dreams, wherever he is!"

All of Nancy's friends laughed at her remark, but none too hard. It seems that the dreams of Nancy were reflected through the actions of everyone at First Fridays. They are networking not just for business, but also, hopefully, for life.

14

The Fiddler on the Stage

Chicago, Illinois

Music is the universal language of mankind—poetry their universal pastime and delight.

—Henry Wadsworth Longfellow

"It's funny, but some black and Latino garbage men recognized me when I was in New York," Boyd Tinsley said. "They were like, 'Hey, man, you're in the Dave Matthews Band!' It blew me away.

"I see a few African Americans in the audience, but not a lot," he continues. "That may have something to do with the fact that we are not played on BET, and I would love to see our videos on BET."

Odds are that if you are African American, you don't know who the hell Boyd Tinsley is. You don't know that he plays the violin in a rock band. You don't know that this band has one of the largest fan bases in the world and has been selling multi-platinum albums for nearly a decade. You don't know that this band is also technically a "black band," meaning that the majority of the members are African American. So who the hell is Boyd Tinsley? Tinsley is a member of the Dave Matthews Band, one of the most popular bands in the world.

Formed in 1991, The Dave Matthews Band consists of Dave Matthews as lead vocalist, Carter Beauford on the drums, Leroi Moore on the saxophone, Stefan Lessard on bass, and Boyd

Tinsley on violin. Tinsley, Beauford, and Moore are the African-American members of the band, although the white South African-born Dave Matthews technically is African American also.

"And if you ask him, he'll tell you so," laughs Tinsley.

Soldier Field, in Chicago, is the latest concert tour stop for the Dave Matthews Band. Their new album, titled *Everyday,* has shot up the charts, and in the parking lot, thousands of devoted and some would say fanatical, Dave Matthews fans have been camping for a week. Like Grateful Dead fans generations before them, they have a certain kinship and bond that transcends just being individual fans. They come in recreational vehicles and follow the band from tour stop to tour stop. These are not casual fans. This is a devoted citizenry.

While wafts of marijuana smoke and a general good vibe percolate among the faithful in the parking lot, Tinsley sits in his tour bus checking his E-mail. It's about three hours before the start of the concert, and this time is the calm before the storm. Fragrant incense has been burning in this home away from home, and this muscular brother with dreadlocks seems pretty relaxed. But the question remains, how did Tinsley get here, and what is a brother doing playing a violin in a rock band?

"It was a complete accident [that I play the violin], man. It all started in middle school when I signed up for music class and realized that I had signed up for the string orchestra instead," he recalls. "I decided to give the violin a try, and it was an instrument that I fell in love with from the beginning, and it was the first thing that I had an immediate connection with."

The Charlottesville, Virginia, native got off to a late start on the instrument but rapidly progressed to the point where he was asked by the concertmaster of the Baltimore Symphony, Isador Zaslov, to attend the Performing Arts School in Baltimore, Maryland.

"I loved the instrument and I was catching up to people who had begun playing before me," said Tinsley. "Zaslov was my mentor and he had me up to his house for a couple of summers. He basically taught me intensively for a couple of weeks in the summer for two years. He really had these detailed plans for me moving to Baltimore. He had enough faith in my talent to have me move to Baltimore and go to the performing arts school there. His wife was a concert pianist, and I was going to live with them and then he was going to be my mentor so that he could lead me to a music conservatory. He had all these big plans, and I mulled it over, but it was a commitment that I could not make. It would have meant basically an eight-hour day and forty hours a week of serious, serious, serious study. I would have had to eat, live, and breathe that, and I really didn't want that."

But even though Tinsley enjoyed playing classical music, he knew that he wanted to do more with the instrument.

"But I got to the point where I loved the instrument, but I didn't love that [classical music] aspect of it," said Tinsley. "I found that I didn't want to study classical music, that it wasn't a drive of mine. "I got to know about Stephane Grappelli, the jazz violinist, and Jean-Luc Ponte and a lot of the other musicians like Papa John Creach. Some of these violin players were doing stuff that was not traditional classical music or what you'd usually label as violin music, so I knew that there was another avenue out there for me."

After arriving as a student at the University of Virginia, Tinsley gave the violin about a year's rest. But when his guitar-playing friends began to ask him to jam with them, he began exploring the rock elements within the violin.

"It was very strange at the time because up to that time, all I had done was read music," Tinsley recalls. "Before, it was like, 'Okay, if we have sheet music, we can play this,' but I didn't really know the concept of just playing. But a lot of friends encouraged me to just do that, and just play. I didn't play a lot at first because I had to get to the point where I said to myself, 'Okay, I know where all of these notes are; now the only thing I have to do is have confidence and let my fingers do the walking.' That was sort of the beginnings that led me to here. Just being around lot of guitar players."

Honing his chops by playing University of Virginia fraternity houses and local clubs, Tinsley began covering Bob Dylan, the Grateful Dead, and Neil Young.

"The fraternity that I wound up joining at UVA, Sigma Nu, was mostly at that time a music fraternity," said Tinsley. "About seventy-five percent of the guys there played guitar. On the weekend, we'd turn our fraternity house into a coffeehouse, where community musicians would come down and play from seven o'clock at night to seven in the morning. We would have acoustic music from midnight until the sun came out. It was a great mixture of townspeople and college students, and that to me was where I got the buzz and I knew that that was what I wanted to do. It was just a cool experience."

Fast-forward to 1991, and a local Charlottesville musician named Dave Matthews is forming a band. He has already recruited fellow Charlottesville musicians Moore, Lessard, and Beauford, and Tinsley is the last piece of the puzzle. But even though the band is currently one of the best-selling bands year-round, Boyd talks about the fact that the success of the band was no way guaranteed.

"It was definitely a fucked-up band, but fucked up in a good way," laughs Tinsley. "You had a violin, an acoustic guitar, a sax, a drummer, a bass, and an occasional keyboardist. And with that, we are supposed to go out and rock a crowd? But somehow we did it, and even we didn't understand it. We just sort of just played."

The newly formed Dave Matthews Band began to cut their teeth by continuing to play small clubs, small concerts, and generally honing their sound. Gradually, their audience began to build, first regionally, then through college radio, and then nationally. Suddenly, eight albums later, the Dave Matthews Band was year after year selling out concerts. It had arrived.

The band has been called a jam band in the past because of their tendency to improvise songs on a whim, but they are much more than that. A more correct assertion would be that instead of being a jam band, a term that is used disparagingly by music critics, they are an ensemble that spotlights each musician. And this freedom gives Tinsley chances to explore with each performance.

"My playing comes from everywhere," said Tinsley. "It

comes from wherever I'm coming from on that particular day. Some days, even within a set, there are some things that I play that are only for accompanying with almost classical lines. And then there are times where I just dig at it and play hard-jamming solo that's influenced by a Neil Young or Jimi Hendrix. That's what I would call untamed music. It's coming from the heart and the passion. But violin depends on the player because I really think that it is as versatile as the human voice. It's very expressive instrument. In rock music, I think that we've only begun to tap into it."

Like a jazz ensemble, this rock band takes its music and allows it to metamorphose into something new each time they play. But in order to do this, they had to trust each other.

"That [trust and teamwork] has always been a common denominator," said Tinsley. "Everybody working together, and everybody listening to each other. There's really nothing else beyond that with this band.

"We basically work it out every night. There are nights where Leroi would have a solo, but the next night he will look at me and basically say, 'You take it tonight.' We feed off each other. Sometimes there are more appropriate places for a sax or a violin and we recognize that. We are always changing as a band, and I hope that we never get to a place where we just say, 'okay, here we are; this is what we sound like and this is what we do.' Because I think that if we do feel like that then we are pretty much done as a band. There are not many bands like us, and what each musician brings to this band is very special. We're always striving to take the music further."

One of the things that make the Dave Matthews Band appealing to their fans is that they are unpretentious. Tinsley believes that the small-town values they learned in Virginia have continued even through all of their success. Even after ten years of touring, it is not unusual for them to go out and meet their fans before a concert. And they are one of the few bands that allow their fans to record their shows. Even their stage appearance is downplayed.

"I'm probably the flashiest one of the group in terms of how

I dress," said Tinsley, who is renowned for his concert gear. "But I'm pretty much alone in doing that. Everybody else will probably wear the same thing on stage that they show up to the gig in. They might put on a clean shirt, but then again, maybe not!" he laughs.

"[Glamour] has never been the focus of this band," he continues. "Once we got to the level that we are at now, meaning the rock-star thing, it's still not the focus. In this band, everybody would much rather go back home to Virginia in the country than go up to New York and party with so-and-so. The only reason we're here is for the music. And if we're not first and foremost concentrated on the music, then this thing isn't going to last much longer."

Tinsley is an avid bodybuilder (there's a mobile gym and trainer that accompanies them on tour) and often wears Jim Morrison-style rock-star leather pants on stage, but ironically, as outgoing as his wardrobe appears on stage, it is in direct contrast to the fact that Tinsley is a shy man. He hides somewhat behind sunglasses.

The music is the thing. The music is the thing. This is the constant message of Tinsley, because to him, the quality of the Dave Matthews Band comes from not only knowing their music, but also recognizing the musical influences of rock, blues, and world artists from various genres. He feels that the band is able to bring these influences to their fans. These are musical influences that their fans may not have been exposed to without their efforts.

"There are really cool things that happen," he says, recalling an earlier incident today. "I went to the mall to get a cup of coffee, and immediately swarms of kids came by, asking for my autograph. I accept that. These kids see us on MTV or hear us on the radio and see us live on shows, and we're their heroes.

"Like to me when I was growing up, I liked the Grateful Dead. They were like my heroes. These were the people that defined a generation for me. And these people look at us as special, and I know what I do and what this band does is special, but I know that there are some bad muthafuckas out there [that can really play music]. Maceo Parker has played with us, and Al Green has played with us. Buddy Guy's here tonight. We've had the guys that made funk music play with us. And this opens up their music to a wider audience.

"I don't think that kids are getting the same kind of historical [music] knowledge that we got when we were coming up," he continues. "I think that we did have a little bit of understanding about music that happened in the early fifties and the sixties, and even some knowledge of the thirties and forties in regards to jazz. At least we had a limited knowledge of who Miles Davis was, or John Coltrane, or even people like Little Richard. But I don't think a lot of these kids know about these people. I think that their lives are so inundated in the present by who's on top now, and which pop star is on top now, and who MTV is going to put in their face constantly, constantly, constantly, that they somehow have not been exposed to [the older music].

"I guess it's because we didn't have MTV or videos. We just had radio," he laughs. "I mean between the AM and FM, we got all of that oldies music from the sixties and seventies. I don't think that the kids are getting that same type of exposure. Now, some of the kids are. Sometimes during an interview we might mention our influences. Especially Carter. And when he does that, the drummers out there that are influenced by Carter will go and investigate those musicians."

Tinsley says that sometimes when the band plays covers of other musicians, the audience sometimes has to be told that what they had just played was a classic, and not their own composition.

"We'll get a comment like, 'Al Green, who's that?' " he says, frowning. "Hopefully, I'm wrong and I've just met the ones that don't know much, but I do check out the Internet newsgroups and listen to what the fans are saying, and I do see a lot of 'Who was that?' "

Back to his place in the Dave Matthews Band, and his uses of the violin, Tinsley wields the violin in a way never heard before in rock music. Where the strings were often used as an accompaniment, Tinsley and the band put the violin out front in most of the songs. Combined with Tinsley's energetic stage presence, where the violin seems to almost smoke from the intensity of his play, he has changed the instrument's role in rock forever.

"People are not afraid of the violin anymore," he says. "In the seventies, there were a lot of strings in a lot of the discos and R and B music, but it stayed in the background and never came up front. One of the things that this band has done is put the violin out in front more, and also in more solo positions. Now I listen to some music and say, 'Wait, that's distinctly a violin playing,' and it's not way in the back, but in front with all of the other instruments. I think people understand now that this is an instrument that has not been fully tapped into yet. Rock and roll has been mostly about the electric guitar, electric bass, and drums; but that has been played, played, and played, so more and more people are saying that this is an instrument that can also hang in this music."

And as a result of his rock revolution, a violin company has named a special model after him.

"I play a Zeta, an electric violin. It's probably the industry standard of violin players. A lot of the major country players like Charlie Daniels play it, and Mark O'Connor, a big jazz-folk violinist, plays a Zeta.

"Zeta just named a violin after me called the Boyd Tinsley Signature model. We've nicknamed it the 'fiddlelin' because it's kind of like a violin, but it's set up so that it can be strummed pizzicato. And sometimes I even strum the violin like a mandolin.

"It's a great honor to have an instrument named after you. I'm blown away by it. One of the cool things about what I do is that a lot of kids are getting into the violin because of the exposure of this band. Kids that see me on the violin will see what I'm doing and will end up taking it further.

"I think that we have great fans. They're very dedicated and very devoted and they really love this band. They're nice kids, also. When I see them on the street, say like last month in Philly, they are really chilled and they are really respectful. And a lot of times, their parents are just as into the band as the kids. So when they come to the concerts with their kids, they are not there to chaperone. They may even be bigger fans than their kids."

But how come an African-American-dominated band hasn't been able to capture the African-American audience? It seems to have all of the elements—funk, jazz, lyrics, and an R & B vocal style that plays well in the African-American community—but they have yet to, for lack of a better term, reverse-crossover to the African-American community.

"I think that black people who have been exposed to us really love our music. I mean they really love our music," says Tinsley. "So I think that if there was more exposure in the Black community that more people would find us. We don't have a video on BET, and it would be nice if we did. We are not on Black radio, so it makes it hard."

But even though the African-American audience has not found the Dave Matthews Band, the band members still give back to their Charlottesville African-American neighborhood through their charities. It is important to them that other African Americans have the opportunity to thrive via community support in the same manner that the community helped them.

"Carter, Leroi, and I all grew up in the same neighborhood in Charlottesville," he said. "And we all wanted to do something to give back, because we had been given a lot. Our band started with grassroots fans and people supporting us, and we just wanted to give back. All of a sudden we were making all of this money, and that was never the prime motivation on anyone's part. Yeah, we wanted to buy a house and we wanted a car, but we weren't just out here to make money. But we all still live in the Charlottesville community, and we wanted to give something back. I mean, this community gave me a lot, and the school system gave me the violin lessons, and the support that we all grew up with. I mean, Carter's drum teacher, and Leroi's horn instruction—these were people that took care of us.

"There's a park that all three of us used to go to as kids called Washington Park," said Tinsley. "It's in the black neighborhood and it [historically] didn't receive the same amount of funds as some of the affluent parks in Charlottesville. A couple of years ago, they were having a big renovation, and we were approached. So we gave them a big chunk of change so that they could get that finished, because that was where we played. That was the park that baby-sat us."

With that, it's time to get ready for tonight's concert. Overnight there was a typical Midwestern summer storm rolling through the Chicago area, and that had threatened tonight's outdoor concert. But all of that is the past now. The skies are crystal clear, and the stands are full of fans. The only thing left to do is to go on stage and play the set. For Tinsley, there will be the usual high that comes from being a rock star in front of 50,000 fans, but at this moment, there is only one thing on his mind before he goes out to play his set.

"I've got to make sure to call my wife and kids before I go out," he says, walking to the phone.

15

An American In Brazil

São Paulo, Brazil

The emotional, sexual, and psychological stereotyping of females begins when the doctor says: "It's a girl."

—Shirley Chisholm

Zakiya Carr's heart is torn in two. In the past two years, she has become a true Paulista, or citizen of São Paulo. She speaks fluent Portuguese, has a Brazilian boyfriend, and can tell you about the best clubs in the city. Yet even though she cherishes her experiences in Brazil, she remains a sister from East Palo Alto, California.

Howard and Syracuse University educated, Carr came to Brazil to do work for others, and that has been accomplished. She has advocated for those Brazilians who have traditionally been without a voice; Afro-Brazilian women. And in the process she has seen learned more about herself than she could have known at the beginning of her residency in Brazil. But her heart is still torn because she is set to come back to the United States in three weeks, and she surprised herself by being glad. Even though she knows life in her own country is also rife with racism, she yearns for some of the simple advantages of home.

"Every time I come back to the United States, it's a culture shock. My sister lives in Atlanta, and she had a baby last year," Zakiya reminisces. "So I went back when the baby was born. While I was there, we went to a restaurant outside of Marietta that served Creole food. I was just excited because everyone in the restaurant was black, and I was wishing that Brazil were like this."

We are sitting at a São Paulo restaurant with her Brazilian boyfriend, Vinicius Roche, eating a nice, hardy lunch. In some Brazilian restaurants, you pay by the kilo; so the more that you eat, the more you pay. This is one of those restaurants. The food is delicious, and Zakiya is reminiscing about her time in Brazil. She got here through a circuitous route.

"I went to Howard in 1992 and graduated in 1996 with a degree in film production," she says through bites of salad. "After graduating, I got an internship at *National Geographic,* but I didn't like it. I really thought that I wanted to do documentary films, but I didn't see any career opportunities in the field.

"So I got a job at the Children's Defense Fund, working with Marian Wright Edelman. That was a good experience. After leaving CDF, I worked for a quick minute at another NGO [nongovernmental organization] as I prepared to go to graduate school. It was then that I went to Cuba for an International Women's Rights Conference that was my first conference that I attended, and I knew that I wanted to go into international relations."

Zakiya's first trip to Brazil occurred when she spent a semester abroad in 1995. She studied at the University of São Paulo and eventually became fluent in Portuguese. She thought about returning to Brazil as she embarked on her graduate school career.

"I got into Syracuse [graduate school], and they had a really good study abroad program," says Zakiya. "I really wanted to get as much international experience as possible. I stayed at Syracuse for about a year before I went abroad. I traveled to Geneva for a couple of months and then went to Ireland. I left there and came to Uruguay for a conference where we studied economic trends and how it affected politics.

"I also studied in Uruguay for a while, doing a traveling workshop. We traveled to Chile, Argentina, and then we came to Brazil. We were supposed to go back to Chile, but I made the decision that I was going to stay here."

What made Zakiya interested in staying in Brazil was an offer to work at GELEDES, one of the first Afro-Brazilian Women's institutes in Brazil. Founded by Afro-Brazilian activist Aparecida Suely Carneiro, GELEDES is a response to the marginalization of Afro-Brazilian women in both the Black and women's rights movements. The late 1970s found both of these movements strengthening within Brazil, as the black movement attempted to empower the Afro-Brazilian community, while the women's movement worked in the areas of fairer divorce laws and better health for women. But each movement failed to address the specific concerns of Afro-Brazilian women, who are burdened by the triple whammy of being poor, black, and women.

"Because in its popular form, [the women's movement] is very white and middle-class, and it doesn't really address the needs of poor, black, and marginalized women," Zakiya explains.

"Basically, the Afro-Brazilian women were part of the general social movement, and they felt that their issues weren't being met by their white sisters. One of the issues that white women were fighting for was the right to work. Well, that concept is not germane to black women because black women have always worked. It has never been a luxury for us. Black women had always worked, but where had they worked? In the homes of these same white women! They were always helping and providing a service for someone else, but they had never had an opportunity to help themselves and their families. They took care of someone else's kids, but they never had a chance to take care of their own." A lot of the white women wanted to be treated as equals to men, where black women wanted to figure out how to survive.

GELEDES works in three different areas: health, human rights, and communication. Zakiya's specialty is international relations.

"When I was hired, I was asked to create links with other black organizations and like organizations in Canada, in the United States. I had to find out about other issues that concern Afro-Brazilians, like the argument for reparations for slavery," she said.

Through GELEDES health workshops, black women from

poor communities are able to explore reproductive health issues (sexuality, contraception, sexually transmitted diseases, breast feeding, etc.). GELEDES is also interested in exploring alternative health care practices that derive from the African-based religions that are still thriving in Brazil's black community. In addition, the health program sponsors discussion and support groups and publishes educational pamphlets on black women's health.

GELEDES's second strategy is to implement a legal aid program that will bring discrimination cases to court in an effort to apply the newly won constitutional guarantee against discrimination. Through GELEDES's Human Rights/SOS Racism program, Carneiro's program, GELEDES filed twenty-one suits on behalf of racial discrimination victims.

The third feature of GELEDES's three-pronged strategy is to disseminate this work as widely as possible through a communication program that uses pamphlets, publications, media, and seminars.

As part of that lobbying and communication effort, Zakiya will be traveling to South Africa as part of the United Nations Conference on World Racism. But as for the movement against racism in Brazil, Zakiya feels that Brazil is behind the United States.

"Afro-Brazilians are in a pre-[American] Civil Rights era," said Zakiya. "However, before the Civil Rights era, Blacks were still united in their churches and their community organizations, and we had a sense of being collectively oppressed. We had a feeling that we were in the same place. There isn't the same level of solidarity here in Brazil. This sounds very sad to say, but if you talk to other people who have read a lot and have studied the dynamics, you would understand."

The dynamics of race in Brazil is very complicated. Officially, Brazil considers itself a nonracial society; however, the question of race permeates everything within Brazil. Race in Brazil is not only black and white, but also many shades of brown. Frequent past and present miscegenation between the races means that there is a large mixed-race or mulatto population in Brazil. Today, even though most Brazilians have some African heritage, what remains is the legacy of white superiority.

"Racism exists every day. Those people who feel it, know it. But unfortunately, the majority of the people who feel it refuse to deal with it. Because it makes it easier to cope if you just don't react. You don't have to feel the pressure," she notes.

Being black in Brazil is in many respects a symbol of being the lowest of the low. Hence, everyone tries to be anything but black. Pride in being Afro-Brazilian is overwhelmingly eclipsed by Brazilian society's need to attain the white Brazilian aesthetic.

"How many people classify themselves as Afro-Brazilian? Probably one percent [of the population thinks itself] black," Zakiya laughs. "I mean, 'Why would you choose to be black in Brazil?' is the thinking of most people. Here, I think that people know that they are black when [bad] things happen. But on a daily basis, I don't know. We have a saying, 'Black Brazilians look down too much.' They don't make eye contact because they don't have pride in themselves. There are tons of women wearing blond hair, many of them black, and you have sisters walking around thinking, 'I wish I looked like that.' "

Zakiya believes that it is difficult for the Afro-Brazilian community to feel a sense of collective pride because Brazil tends to co-opt African traditions as its own. Any efforts to recognize the Africanness of Brazil are routinely submerged within a general Brazilian culture that assimilates all cultural differences.

"I won't say that there isn't any [black] consciousness, but it manifests itself in different ways. It is very difficult to articulate, but sometimes it manifests itself in culture. Except that Brazil tends to take the culture and makes it its own," Zakiya explains.

"Take, for example, a dish like feijodada, which is like chitterlings to African Americans [in terms of tradition]," she continues. "Brazil calls it the national dish. It would be like the United States saying that jazz is the national music. Afro-Brazilians try to say that this is mine, but the country always co-opts the culture. [Afro-Brazilian] culture becomes the national culture. The

Brazilian government, when they promote tourism in Bahia [northeast Brazil], for example, which is eighty-seven-percent black, never says come and see our Afro-Brazilian culture."

Even as an African American, Zakiya feels the pressure to be close to the white Brazilian ideal. Her dreadlocks and African features do not match what the typical Brazilian, both black and white, sees as beautiful. If you are black, you are encouraged to look as mulatto as possible. And if you are a mulatto, you try to be as white as possible. And even if you are white, you are encouraged to look like the white, blue-eyed, blond Brazilian ideal.

"Generally, I think that I have high self-esteem. I feel good about myself," she says. "But I think living in Brazil as an African woman is very difficult. It doesn't matter if you come here or if you've always lived here. The ideal beauty is a completely different creature. It encourages you to be more mulatto; it encourages you to be lighter. I think that this is one of the biggest issues. You know, not to harp on it, but you never know how much you can count on that affirmation that you receive in America [that being black is beautiful]. Here in Brazil, there is a feeling that if you are a black woman, then you are not beautiful."

The Afro-Brazilian culture is also suppressed through the suffocating poverty that hinders the population, most notably the Afro-Brazilian population. At the beginning of year 2000, white men earned the most. White women make 60 percent of what white men make, and black men earn only 40 percent of this. At the bottom, black women make only 45 percent of what black men make. And this is if things are all equal, with the same level of education.

In her two years in Brazil, Zakiya misses some things that she took for granted in the United States. Although she doesn't consider the situation of African Americans to be a utopia by any means, she misses the collective sense of community.

"One thing I noticed is that here in Brazil, there are no looks of conspiracy between black people," she says.

Zakiya is referring to the often silent acknowledgment African Americans give each other in public. It's often demonstrated by a simple word, a look, or a head nod in the other's direction. And more than likely, it is designed to be signaled under the radar of others, particularly white people.

"There's no getting on the bus and going . . ." [she nods her head]. "I think that African Americans realize that no matter how distant you may get to others in the black community, you still acknowledge black people."

Zakiya's dream is to try to create that sense of community by training young leaders of African descent in how to lead their communities. Once she gets back to the United States, she is going to try to fulfill this vision.

"What I really want to do is create some sort of leadership institute, internationally, that works with people of African descent in order to help put young black leaders in positions of power," she explains. "The power could be national or it could be local, but we have to have voices. We've got to be able to speak about our own issues. We've got to write about, create, and manifest our own culture. They've got to be active parts of their own community and take them wherever they want to take them. It would be a shame not to do this."

But for now, it is time to go back home. But she doesn't close the door on returning to Brazil or another country other than the U.S.

"Before I came here, I thought to myself that I could see myself living here. That was in 1995, but now I think I'm at a crossroads. It's not that life is so horrible here, and that there aren't a lot of things that I could do, but someway, somehow, São Paulo is the wrong city for me. It would be great if I could find a reason to live in another country. I don't like living in America that much. But I do like the way being black in the United States makes me feel. I feel proud to be black in the U.S.A."

But while in Zakiya's eyes the Afro-Brazilian community may have a ways to go before they feel a sense of pride in their culture, she does see changes happening. The changes are happening slowly, but they are coming nonetheless.

"This [black Brazilian civil rights] movement is the next revolution in the world in terms of black people," says Zakiya, leaning forward. "If I could look at Brazil from a satellite, I can see hot spots in Brazil. People are sick and tired of being on the bottom rung [of society] all of the time. And they take the majority of the slights.

"There are some conscientious people in Brazil, and those people are not at their wits' end, but they're making themselves crazy," she continues. "But I think that in the last ten years, black people have become more popular than any other time. They want to hear their own voice, and their own experiences, and not some white anthropologist that has their own subjective agenda. I don't know how many people have been able to actually see the inside of what's happening [in Afro-Brazil]. I think that I've had the blessing to be here during this time of change, and I hope that I continue to have contact with people here."

What is her greatest hope for the people she will leave?

"I think that for the rest of my life I'll be helping Afro-Brazilians and Afro-Latinos discover themselves," Zakiya concludes. "Not that they don't know who they are, but I want to be here when they finally figure it all out. They will demand respect, and tell people how they want society to treat them."

16

São Paulo by Day and Night

São Paulo, Brazil

Do what you can, with what you have, where you are.

—Theodore Roosevelt

Marcio Macedo, or Kibe, as his buddies call him, is a typical college student. He's a senior, studying social sciences and anthropology. He likes women, beer, and having a great time. He laughs easily, listens to hip-hop, and has a parent-shocking earring through his lower lip. In other words, he could be any American college student. But Kibe is not like every American student; he's an Afro-Brazilian student at the Universidad de São Paulo. And that makes him a rare person indeed, as he is one of only one hundred Afro-Brazilian students at this 60,000-student campus.

The bus to the Universidad de São Paulo takes you right through the heart of this city. Nearly twenty million people make this city their home, and at midday it looks like each one is trying to drive on its crowded streets. It is no wonder that Brazilians make great race car drivers.

"Here the pedestrian is not king!" laughs Kibe as pedestrians scurry through the traffic, narrowly avoiding the cars.

Alex and Batista, two of Kibe's friends and fellow students at the university, have joined us on our tour of the campus and, later, the city of São Paulo. Alex is a white Brazilian, and Batista is an Afro-Brazilian with long dreadlocks. Among this group of students, the plight of Afro-Brazilians in Brazil is a burning topic.

Batista is the older sage, having participated in earlier black pride movements, and is somewhat cynical about the future of Afro-Brazilian people.

Alex provides an understanding ear and appears to truly understand what Afro-Brazilians are trying to accomplish.

Kibe is the cautious optimist who wants to believe that he can make a difference.

Our bus driver, ignoring pedestrians crossing the streets, traffic accidents on the side of the road, and the general, constant honking of horns, creeps his way toward our destination. Soon, after all of the disorder, we finally arrive at the campus.

We get off the bus and begin our walk through the campus. Nothing about the University of São Paulo looks particularly extraordinary. The buildings are mundane and somewhat drab. As one would expect, you see students all around the campus, and you hear a constant patter of Portuguese. But one thing is missing. Where are the black people? They are here, but you have to look for them very hard.

"When I first arrived on campus, I was shocked because I didn't see any black people," said Kibe over lunch. "Then I decided to get to know the people who work at the university."

This is where you actually find black people at the University of São Paulo. They are the janitors, the cooks, and the people who make sure that the numerous free-coffee tables have hot coffee available for the students. In other words, they serve the university but don't attend.

Even more ironic is the fact that the University of São Paulo is surrounded, like most prosperous areas in Brazil, by favelas, of which most of the residents are Afro-Brazilians. The city has tried to hide the favelas by building a Berlin Wall-style barrier between the favelas and the university, but it doesn't work. The favelas overwhelm the presence of the wall, yet there is an unmistakable unconscious message being sent to the favela residents and the mainly white university students: the university is not a place for black people. And that message reverberates throughout the country.

"Although most racism is covert, it is now becoming more overt. For example, traditionally, the university is not the place for black people [in the minds of Brazilians]. The people think like this," says Kibe.

"Now, I admit that black people shouldn't think like this, but when a black person arrives at a Brazilian university, she's walking around saying 'Where am I?' There is no support for them on campus. You have white people here. You have rich people there. You have middle class over there. And she thinks, 'Oh, my God, this is horrible! Here is a place where people listen to rock music!' And then she begins to doubt herself. She walks around and thinks that she is ugly and that she doesn't belong at the university."

Kibe looks off into the distance and sees a lone Afro-Brazilian student walking across campus.

"I think I have a mission on this campus," he continues. "I have many responsibilities. There are one hundred students in the suburb [satellite] schools and only one at the main university.

"In American universities, black students have a place to go to make a link together. You have black student unions and things like that. In Brazilian universities, we don't have those places. You see one big thing about our experiences that is different from the African-American experience, is that you had segregation. Black people in America stuck together. In Brazil, we don't have [a history of] segregation, so we didn't stick together. We don't have things such as black neighborhoods.

"So now, what we have done is start a pilot project where we provide support for black students at the university. We try to be mentors to the students. But we only have money for one session. Still we have programs where we talk about the situation of black people. This Friday, we will talk about affirmative action, and in the coming weeks, we will talk about other things dealing with black people. It's a good thing because we get to meet all of the black students in the university during our programs and let them know that they are not alone."

We take a walk through the campus and enter one of the colleges, the College of Philosophy and Social Science. The building looks as though it hasn't been updated in years, and this is a sore spot among the three students.

"On this campus, the College of Economics is very resented because they receive all of the money," says Alex. "You will see a big difference in the condition of our college and the condition of their building."

He is right. The College of Economics building looks like it has been pulled out of a downtown business district and placed on the campus. It has gleaming glass doors, a new library, and new wall-to-wall carpet. However, students at the College of Philosophy and Social Science rebel and show their resentment by scribbling graffiti on the new, shiny business palace. It is one way for the students to protest the inequity.

"Afro-Brazilian students go to schools where the education is bad, so we are not good in subjects like engineering and economics," says Batista. "So most of us are in the social sciences and philosophy. And the resources are not put in our college."

In the College of Economics we walk past an employment advertisement for the Americas' largest multinational company, General Electric. It pictures the face of an African-American student, happy about having chosen to work for the company. All three laugh at the advertisement.

"Ah, the African-American middle class!" laughs Kibe. He finds it quite ironic that an African-American model is used to illustrate the Afro-Brazilian middle class. It is obvious that GE couldn't find someone to represent the Afro-Brazilian middle class because it is so small.

The stark differences between the rich and poor in Brazil have Kibe and other Afro-Brazilians aching for an African-American-style middle class. It is the Holy Grail for change among their community, but to them it seems to be an elusive objective.

"Our black middle class is very small and it seems to me that they don't have a sense of responsibility to the black community," he explains.

"This is a racial democracy and there isn't a black middle class or a black bourgeoisie. And this is where we have to get to first," adds Batista.

"Black people have to be able to live in clean places. Other blacks have to see a black middle class or bourgeoisie in order to know what they are missing, and that they have to go fight for that."

"Our future is so sad," laments Kibe. "The black middle class is very small. And what is even more distressing is that when you find these black people, they are marrying whites. They know that they are black, but they are marrying white people to be whiter than they are black."

Miscegenation between Afro-Brazilians and white Brazilians has resulted in a large biracial population. Termed mulattos by Brazilian society, their lack of identification with white Brazilians rather than Afro-Brazilians is a sore point for both Kibe and Batista.

The obsession with color is so strong here that when you see a mulatto whose skin is darker, an African-American would see the person as being black. However, Kibe says, "But here, they don't identify as being black, as they would in America. It is quite the opposite in Brazil. They would think that because a person is not chocolate-colored but is instead light-skinned, that person is closer to being white. And a lot of mulattos try to be white, but they just are not quite white enough to be fully accepted by white Brazilian society.

"Being a black man in Brazil is difficult because you don't know who identifies themselves as black," Kibe continues. "A lot of people that look black have decided to identify themselves as being mulatto. Why? If you are black, people in Brazil think that you will harm them. It is very difficult to walk around in this society as a black man, because you don't know what preconceptions people may have about you. It is a very fluid situation in our society."

With that, we move from the campus and get back on the bus toward the old downtown of São Paulo. Our destination? The Bronx, a galleria named after the New York borough.

As we ride past the graffiti-scarred buildings of São Paulo, it seems as though no building in the city has escaped the wrath of the graffiti artist. All have been tagged in some way or form.

São Paulo is the second city of Brazil; forever compared, often negatively, to the allure and glamour of Brazil's first city, Rio de Janeiro. They write songs about girls from Ipanema, while in São Paulo there is more interest in whether the stock market went up or down. São Paulo is the Chicago to Rio's New York. But São Paulo does have a gritty charm, and the old downtown is reflective of it.

We get out of the bus, which is in the middle of the street, of course, and from there weave our way through the kamikaze traffic. Remember, Kibe said that the pedestrian is not king in Brazil. He's right.

Safely on the sidewalk, Kibe reflects on how the lack of cohesiveness in the Afro-Brazilian community has resulted in a lack of pride. But with the influence of African-American culture, Afro-Brazilians are finally beginning to find themselves. And they like what they see.

"In the last ten years, I think that we have more pride," he says. "In the last few years, we have been influenced by things such as the hip-hop movement. We heard things such as Public Enemy's "Fight the Power," and "Burn, Hollywood, Burn," and we began to listen to the message, and how it applied to us here in Brazil.

"The hip-hop movement changed my life because it brought me another perception of life. I began to think more clearly about my own situation here in Brazil. I began to think that maybe white people are the devil. I read the autobiography of Malcolm X and began to make a transition. We began to think about our situation here, and this provided the momentum for everything dealing with Black Pride in Brazil."

We arrive at the Bronx, and if you don't blink, you really do believe that you have actually been transported to the Boogie Down Bronx. About a hundred shops, none occupying more than thirty feet of frontage, bring African-American flavor to this part of São Paulo. The only thing different is that the patois is Portuguese instead of English.

Hip-hop shops, each with its own window tribute to slain African-American legends Tupac and Notorious B. I. G., compete with barbershops and beauty salons, each with "Black Power" in their name. Black Power Dana's Hair Salon competes with Black Power Mario's Barbershop. Each store, hip-hop and hair shop seems to come equipped with either a Malcolm X poster, a posturing b-boy in front of the store, or a constant rap beat flowing into the common area of the mall.

Kibe seems to know everyone here. From the deejay who is passing out flyers to a party, to the Japanese reggae hat-shop owner, each one seems to have a word or two for him. To the inhabitants of The Bronx, he's like the Cuba Gooding character, Trey, in *Boyz N the Hood.* Those in The Bronx who are up to no good recognize that Kibe is a university student and he's doing well, so they give him his respect. But they also know that he's still one of them.

It's eight o'clock and that means it's time to visit a chopp, which is a Portuguese-style beer and steakhouse. Kibe, Alex, and Batista are joined by two of São Paulo's leading deejays, as the chopp shop owner places a table outside for us. He's moved us out into the mall walkway because he's got to mop his floors, but that doesn't stop the sale of beer.

"Only in Brazil," laughs Kibe.

In a place that replicates African America, the talk turns back to what are the differences in the experiences of Afro-Brazilians and African Americans. Kibe goes back to talking about one of the historical negatives for African Americans that Afro-Brazilians think turned out to be a positive experience.

"You see, one big thing that is different about our experiences is that you had segregation," notes Kibe as he sips a beer. "Black people in America stuck together. In Brazil, we don't have [a history of] segregation, so we didn't stick together. We don't have things such as black neighborhoods. In America, you have black people that live in the suburbs, but the majority live in black neighborhoods. In Brazil, the poor people live in the suburbs."

But Afro-Brazilians do have something that correlates to the African-American experience, and that is the community's connection to religion.

"In America you have the Christian church, and in Brazil we have Candombles. In Bahia, at the turn of the century, Candombles was the core of the black people. The leaders of Candombles are normally always women, and they are called "mothers." It served as the social function for black people, and it was the place to meet other people, and possibly to meet your future mate. But today, things have changed. Here in São Paulo, the black people are now either Catholic or they are Baptists. Sometimes I think that we don't have allies in those religions [that keep the Black community together]."

Candombles, an African religion from the Yoruba tradition, competes with Brazil's official state religion of Catholism. Strong in northern Brazil, where the population is 87 percent Afro-Brazilian, you can find Candombles trying to reassert itself in the urban areas of Rio de Janeiro and São Paulo.

"We are just now asserting ourselves, and we are doing this through recognizing how proud we are to be Afro-Brazilian and to have the traditions that we have as a community," Kibe says.

With the cervejas, or beers as they are called in English, now consumed, the next destination is Tango and Cash, a peculiarly named samba club a few blocks away.

Named after an obscure and quickly forgotten Sylvester Stallone movie, Tango and Cash is what would lovingly be referred to in America as a hole in the wall. Packed wall to wall with young Afro-Brazilians waiting in anticipation for the arrival of a local roots samba band, the brothers and sisters begin dancing to a deejay playing local samba hits. Eyes closed, one woman who's dressed in jeans and a tank top dances to a rhythm beyond the amplifiers and speakers. Her hips sway in a rapid samba movement, conjuring up Brazil, Africa, and the long journey in between.

"This is where you will feel the spirit of Brazil," says Kibe with a smile.

Soon, the samba band appears. Six young Afro-Brazilians carrying various instruments begin playing, and Tango and Cash becomes one large, orgasmic rhythm. The strumming of the guitar, the playing of the drums, the rhyming in Portuguese becomes intoxicating, and time stands still. The only thing that matters is the samba, and the worries of Afro-Brazil seem far away indeed.

"This is our music, the music that we created, and is something that we can look to with pride," says Kibe as the night ends and we leave the club. "I hope that we find more things like it in the future."

With more Afro-Brazilians like Kibe carrying the torch, that future does look bright.

17

The Angel of the Favelas

Rio de Janeiro, Brazil

The harder the conflict, the more glorious the triumph. What we obtain too cheap, we esteem too lightly; it is dearness only that gives everything its value. I love the man that can smile in trouble, that can gather strength from distress and grow brave by reflection. 'Tis the business of little minds to shrink; but he whose heart is firm, and whose conscience approves his conduct, will pursue his principles unto death.

—Thomas Paine

The residents all stand in the filthy entryway of a giant housing project. At first there are only a few, but as the minutes go by, the numbers begin to build. When you look for an architectural description of this building, think Cabrini Greens in Chicago. Think of the worst Soviet-style architecture. Think of a hulking, gray, nondescript mass of concrete sitting in a middle-class neighborhood, warehousing the Brazilian poor, thousands of residents at a time. Think of a building built with an inhumane indifference as the main cornerstone of its philosophy.

But nevertheless, the hundreds of anonymous faces wait for the elevator to arrive so that they can get to their individual tiny apartments. Intermittently, their eyes frantically search the overhead elevator floor meter for movement, even though their minds already know that the time of arrival is predetermined. The elevator will arrive on the bottom floor at 10 A.M. Why 10 A.M. and not within minutes or even seconds, like normal elevators? Well, that is the schedule. If you miss that elevator, there is an automatic thirty-minute wait for the next one. Imagine that! A housing project that contains thousands, and you have an elevator that only works every thirty minutes.

Suddenly it's 10 A.M. and the red doors of the elevator part. People pile out of it as though they were part of a Keystone Kops comedy. They offer no greetings to those anonymous faces that have been waiting to replace them. And vice versa. Such is life at an urban favela.

Jose Marmo, an Afro-Brazilian dentist who has been patiently waiting for twenty minutes, joins this group of old men, young women, and everything in between, who crowd their way onto the elevator to make their way to the sixteenth floor. Even though he doesn't live here, he is one with all of those who call this favela home.

When you finally arrive on the sixteenth floor, you realize that one of the great ironies of the favela is that it is located in a section of Rio de Janeiro that provides breathtakingly panoramic views of all Rio. The windows, large and expansive, bring a world of wealth almost within rock-throwing distance. But it is a painful illusion. You are not able to touch this wealth, because you are immersed in poverty.

The poverty that encompasses this structure makes one think of the famous island prison of Alcatraz. Just as the prisoners were tortured with their spectacular views of San Francisco, the residents of these favelas are tantalized with the spectacular sights of Rio de Janeiro. For both the prisoners and the residents of the favelas, the views could just as well be mirages in the desert.

Marmo is in the favela to teach youth about the dangers of sexually transmitted diseases. He began his work nearly three years ago and is now the health coordinator for the non-governmental organization Afro-Reggae Cultural Group.

"I am many things to many people," Marmo laughs as he walks through the favela's hallways.

Marmo began his work in the favelas determined to speak about some of the myriad health issues associated with the slums. But he found that his first approach didn't make an impact.

"When I first began work in the favelas five years ago," he

recalled, "I would come in and talk about AIDS and HIV prevention, and the residents would just hear 'blah, blah, blah.'

"Then I realized that I had to mix the Afro-Brazilian culture with the message," he said. "When I did that, the residents would rush up to me, saying 'Marmo, we get it now!' So I knew that I had something that worked."

Marmo's merging of Afro-Brazilian history and religion with the health message immediately reached his favela audience. And as an added benefit, he was able to get the youth of the favela to participate in educating their fellow residents so that he could make an even greater impact.

Besides AIDS and HIV prevention, Marmo also deals with the problem of mental health.

"Pregnancy in the favelas is a big problem," he says. "You see, when someone becomes pregnant, the person doesn't go to school; the father may leave, and they may not have work. They become poor, and it becomes a strain on their mental health."

Over the years, Marmo has worked through a number of organizations, but for the past few years he has been working with the Rio-based Grupo Cultural Afro Reggae.

Founded in 1993, the Grupo Cultural Afro Reggae, or Afro-Reggae Cultural Group, is located in a dingy office building interconnected by dark, labyrinthine hallways. Inside the spartan office, a few posters of Bob Marley and an old Lyricists Lounge hip-hop poster share wall space with a government bulletin explaining the official dress code for organizations receiving government money. Apparently there has been a problem with nongovernmental organization staff members wearing Bermuda shorts to work, and the Brazilian government wants to stamp that out.

The Afro-Reggae Cultural Group uses the arts; with reggae and hip-hop music in particular, to accentuate issues within the Afro-Brazilian community in Rio de Janeiro. The purpose is to illuminate subjects that get ignored in Brazilian society, while also effecting change through a number of programs.

Through Afro-Reggae, organizations produce workshops that teach ethnic and modern dancing, percussion, capoeira, singing, and ballroom dancing. In music, the workshops include courses for guitar, bass, saxophone, drums, and keyboard, with the objective of training professional musicians and instructors.

Projects run by the Afro-Reggae Cultural Group include Nice Child, which deals with initial pedagogy and culture for children between two and seven years old. In this project the children also participate in percussion lessons, dance, capoeira, and music.

Urban Connections is a new project of GCAR. The main subjects are workshops for deejay and graffiti directed to youngsters from fourteen to twenty-one years old.

Also, the Afro-Reggae Cultural Group is the home of the Afro-Reggae Band, a musical group consisting of Afro-Brazilian musicians and dancers using capoeira to interpret the music. They have performed around the world, most recently at the 2000 International Stop Racism Concert and Awards Show in Canada.

Finally, Afro-Reggae runs a health program. This program was developed to improve the current situations in the favelas: unstable and poor nutrition, lack of knowledge of sanitary basics, and prevention of diseases. This program works on three levels.

The Health Tent: This project is developed in a partnership with the Brazilian Interdisciplinary Association for AIDS. There are tents equipped in the Lapa section of Rio, and a traveling tent (that is used in various events, seminaries, etc.). This project has as its main objective the distribution of informational material, brochures, educational materials, and condoms. You will see these tents in front of Copacabana nightclubs, protecting the prostitutes and their johns.

Louis Lopez, a Rio disc jockey known as DJ Rastafari, stands in front of these nightclubs and tries to make an impact.

"We try to target teens and adolescents," says Lopez, who

has been distributing condoms for six years. "I stand as a barrier between the people and the disease. If I give them the information, I feel that I can make a difference, even as a disc jockey."

Lopez also goes into the schools and passes out material. He says that he has seen behavior change from 1995, when he first began, to the present.

"Now people are more open to information," he says. "Before, they would think that AIDS was only a gay disease, but now they all know someone that has been affected with the disease. Now they won't have sex without a condom."

The Health Team: The team uses frank language to talk about the problems that HIV can cause to human organs. The target groups are the youngsters who study and live in favelas, and they get their message across by having youth from the favelas produce song-and-dance skits with information about HIV as the underlying message. This is Marmo's area of expertise.

With phones constantly ringing, a small staff of young Afro-Brazilians move swiftly about the office, answering phones, meeting with community members, and satisfying the requests that flow into the office. The staff is responding to requests for performances from the community, the various organizations that use their umbrella organization, and others interested in working with the youth. But always, money is an important factor in whether programs get done.

"I am the manager of the foundation," says Romario Santos, an administrator with Afro Reggae. "It is difficult when you are working with young people, but we get financial support. It is very important because without that financial support, these young people will be out on the streets. But our financial support allows us to bring programs to the schools. You see, most of the poor people in the community don't have jobs, or if they do, they are at the lowest levels in society, maybe as a low-level office worker. So without our programs, it is possible that they will stay on the streets and fall into criminality. So we create programs to support them a little bit.

"We work in the slums," he continues. "We don't like to pretty it up by calling them something else. They are not low-income areas, or housing projects. They are slums. In Brazil, we like to deal with the reality of the situation. And as long as we know what the reality is, we can deal with the problem effectively and help the residents. It doesn't help if we call slums something that they are not."

Back to the favela, where you can see that the Afro-Reggae Cultural Group is providing help to these particular slums. The help it provides is reflected in one special room on the sixteenth floor of the favela.

In this oppressive concrete structure sits an old amphitheater. Now, although this amphitheater has seen better days, all around the paint is peeling and the concrete is broken in so many places, it is still a beehive of activity. With the help of a single instructor, dozens of children are tumbling on mats, while others are performing circus tricks worthy of the Cirque du Soleil. Long sheets of multicolored cloth, some hanging nearly fifty feet in the air, are climbed and manipulated by these youngsters. They twist their bodies in various gymnastic shapes, spinning themselves upside down or defying gravity by holding on with only one hand, all the while performing with a flourish and confidence that this impersonal structure doesn't deserve.

When Marmo enters, the teenagers all run to him, vying for a second of his attention.

"Jose, look at this!" says one tumbling little girl, her brown body flying through the air.

"Jose! Jose! Jose!" says another as she slides upside down on the ropes. She does this with absolutely no fear, even though she's about forty feet high.

"This is the reason that I'm only a dentist two days a week," he smiles. Marmo literally touches and speaks to each child.

This gymnastics class is part of a concerted effort by community groups to create some beauty within this depressing edifice. At various times you'll find dance classes, capoeira instruction, and art classes for the children.

Soon it is time to gather a group of the children and take them into an anteroom. About ten children, the youngest eight and the oldest sixteen, all sit down at the table. They are about to work on a sex-education project for the favela.

Marmo acts as a facilitator for the students, and instead of coming with a plan of action already plotted for the students, he gives them the freedom to express themselves, and also develop themselves, as they see fit, around an outline of action. Today, Marmo begins the discussion by telling the students that in about a month, there will be a celebration of Zumbi's death.

Zumbi is a historical hero for Afro-Brazilians that has been emphasized in recent years. This is where Marmo's formula of mixing culture with message comes to fruition. What Marmo proposes is a mixture of dances and songs that talks about AIDS and HIV within the context of celebrating the legend of Zumbi.

November 20, 1995, marked the three hundredth anniversary of the death of Zumbi, the last leader of the maroons of Palmares, and Brazilians have been celebrating his death ever since. Palmares was a state founded by maroons, or runaway slaves, which flourished in Northeastern Brazil throughout most of the seventeenth century. This date looms large in the popular imagination, since Zumbi embodies for many Brazilians, especially those of African descent, the strongest resistance to the slave-based colonial regime, and, consequently, the struggle for economic and political justice.

"They are beginning to learn the importance of Zumbi, and he is turning into a hero for blacks in this country," Marmo says.

The teenagers' task is to come up with effective skits that not only get across the information but also entertain and engage the sometimes fickle favela audience.

"And not only must you talk about AIDS and HIV, but you need to talk about sexually transmitted diseases," Marmo tells them.

This elicits a cacophony of laughter as their bright faces begin naming the various diseases that they know. But even though this is a youthful, bashful laughter, it is not an immature laughter. These children know the impact and seriousness of these diseases in their community.

One teenager comments that if you get a sexually transmitted disease, you are prone to get pregnant also.

"There is a girl at school that is only about twelve years old that is pregnant right now. I don't want to be like her because I don't want to have a baby right now. Besides, I'm a little person and you have to get big to have a baby," she says and laughs. "And I don't want to get big!"

All of the other students laugh and agree that they don't like to take care of babies. Marmo then decides to have them talk about their first sexual experience. Through his casual manner, he is able to find out if any of these teens and preteens are at risk for the very diseases they are going to be talking about before their friends and relatives.

Except for a very embarrassed little boy of eight years old, all of the students have had some sort of sexual relations. He then speaks about how important it is for them to use protection when having sex, and to be able to understand the responsibility that goes along with having sex. One gangly sixteen-year-old pipes up.

"Hey, Marmo, I just don't want to be like those others in my school that have children."

That's the type of attitude that Marmo wants to cultivate through his work. It's a sentiment that says the cycle is being broken one child at a time.

Marmo and the children work on the project for a good part of the day. It will provide just a bit more information for the children and residents, and bring Marmo a little more of a sense that he is making a difference in a community so often ignored by the Brazilian government.

"It is very important that we effect change in Brazilian public policy, because the black people don't have health programs. The black people don't have good schools. The blacks don't have money. Black people don't have work so that they can get money. It's a depressing situation. It has been very important to go back to the community, because the people in the favelas don't have anything. So you must go back to show them that you can get out. But it is very difficult for them to see themselves out of the favelas."

As dusk falls on Rio, it is quite obvious that Jose Marmo and the Afro-Reggae Cultural Group are trying to light the way out of the darkness of the favelas.

18

A Teacher's View of Life

Rio de Janeiro, Brazil

Better keep yourself clean and bright; you are the window through which you see the world.

—George Bernard Shaw

As the evening sun settles over the Atlantic Ocean, the beach restaurants, or chopps in Brazilian parlance, begin to fill with a mixture of locals, tourists, and prostitutes. The locals know the waiters, and their dishes come hot and ready without their having to order. Meanwhile, the tourists fumble along with their pidgin Portuguese, trying to explain which type of steak they'd like to order. The prostitutes, sitting alone at tables they've purchased for the evening from the restaurant management, usually don't have long to wait for customers, as European tourists supply plenty of johns.

At an indoor table, Rosangela surveys the scene.

"It's pitiful, but I guess they have to do what they have to do," sighs Rosangela, commenting on the prostitutes. We nibble on appetizers. They all fade into the background as Rosangela orders us dinner. It's time to hear about Brazil from the perspective of an Afro-Brazilian woman. It's a casual conversation, a riff on anything and everything that's Brazilian.

In her forty-five years, Rosangela Valle has seen a lot, and as an Afro-Brazilian woman, she sees things even more acutely than the average Brazilian.

As an Afro-Brazilian teacher in Rio, and for more years than she can count, she has been a tranquil oasis for African-American students visiting Brazil. She eases their transition by being their friend, mother, and confidante as they make their lives in Rio.

An English teacher at two language schools in Rio, Rosangela has had the unique opportunity among Afro Brazilians to view the problems of her country through the prism of other Africans from throughout the Diaspora. She's lucky. Her middle-class status has lifted her out of the favelas, and her education has made it possible to travel throughout the world. And her journey began peculiarly with the man who sang the "Twist."

"I became interested in languages in the first place by an influence from America," she recalls. "I had an uncle who liked Chubby Checker, and he had all of these [English-speaking] records, and he was the first to talk to me about learning English.

"Why don't you learn English? Why don't you learn English? He asked. But I really didn't think anything about it. But then I decided to become a teacher, against my father's will, I must say, because teachers everywhere in the world, especially in Brazil, make low pay. He wanted me to be a secretary or something to do with business. But when I decided to be a teacher, I thought about what my uncle had said, and decided to concentrate on my English courses. So I began learning English at the age of fifteen."

So from that beginning, Rosangela went to college.

"I went to the Federal University, where I studied English, American literature, British literature, and learned about the structure of both languages, Portuguese and English. I have been a teacher for twenty-three years, and at public and private schools where I teach the English language," she said. "I teach near my house, which is in a private area of Rio de Janeiro. In public schools, I teach Portuguese, because in these schools, they have a bit of segregation. [When I started there] they only had English there, and I don't think that it is fair, because there are students there that wouldn't like to learn English, so I teach them Portuguese. Because I think that they should learn their own language correctly. Now, the school has a French and Spanish teacher there, but I continue to teach Portuguese to the students. However, at the language school, I teach English."

The educational system in Brazil is notoriously poor, and especially so for Afro-Brazilians. Some have said that for Afro-Brazilians the educational system is reminiscent of pre-Civil Rights America, with the African-American community under the segregation system receiving inferior materials. In Brazil, poor education leads to badly paid jobs. As of 1991, only 6 percent of black children in Brazil make it to secondary school. And almost half of Brazilian blacks take home less than the minimum wage of eighty dollars a month. A larger proportion of black women take home less.

With knowledge of English being a passport to a better life, today there is a better opportunity for Afro-Brazilians to learn it now, compared to when Rosangela first learned it.

"It is a bit easier for people to learn English today. Because you have many language schools in Brazil, and they compete among themselves so they can offer low prices and better quality to potential students. I'm forty-five years old, and it wasn't like this when I was in school. In those times, it was pretty difficult because learning languages was something for the middle and upper class of Brazil. English courses were very expensive, and therefore it was very difficult for me to pay for it. So only those that could really afford it had been designated as being candidates for language school.

"Nowadays, I think that knowing English is necessary, but it remains a luxury. We usually define the learning of a foreign language in two aspects, the mental one and the cultural one. The mental part, meaning what are you going to do about this language? The cultural part goes over whether you are going to travel and live in the country of the language you have learned. Do you want to become a member of the target community? In my case, I think that I was already looking for reasons to become a teacher in Brazil. And I knew that if I had learned some foreign languages, I would be able to have a career apart from teaching."

It was at university that Rosangela began to become aware of

Brazil and its historical mistreatment of Afro-Brazilians. It was also through school that she became aware of Africans throughout the Diaspora.

"It was in the 1970s, when I was finishing university, that I became more aware of the politics of Brazil. I realized that the poor community of Brazil mainly consisted of black people. The universities and religious institutions brought people into Brazil that would talk about black people from throughout the Diaspora, and from that I began to make contacts with black people outside of Brazil. So I began going to congresses, and I would see other black people. We began discussing the problems of black people within the African Diaspora.

"One of the benefits that I received from learning English is that as I began understanding our condition as blacks in Brazil, I could also communicate with other brothers and sisters from around the world. I think that was the main thing that could open doors for me. Communication, apart from earning money, fueled me. But being able to communicate is one of the best things."

One of the curious aspects of Rosangela's black consciousness is the fact that it came during Brazil's time under military rule. One would think that military rule would clamp down on any type of enlightenment, particularly any knowledge that would question society and the state, but as Rosangela reflects, military rule for Afro-Brazilians was complicated.

"I have mixed feelings about military rule. The military regime was trying to create equality by guaranteeing the basic social needs, health, education, etc., to the Brazilian population. Black people, who didn't have access to these services because we couldn't pay due to our lack of financial power in Brazil, thought that the military regime was good. They gave us quality public schools. There was a guarantee of being able to enter university. It happened to me. However, it is impossible nowadays because the government has destroyed the philosophy of quality public schools. So in this case, I would say that yes, the military was good for black people because it gave a guarantee of basic needs; inflation was under control, so we could have some

The bleak winter accurately reflects the mood within Oklahoma on the day of the execution.

Determined to have Gloria Leathers remembered, LaToya Leathers and Robert Ferguson, Jr., hold a cherished photo of their slain mother and sister.

Unrepentant in his desire to see Wanda Jean Allen executed, Robert Ferguson traveled from Johnson City, Missouri, to see Allen die in person.

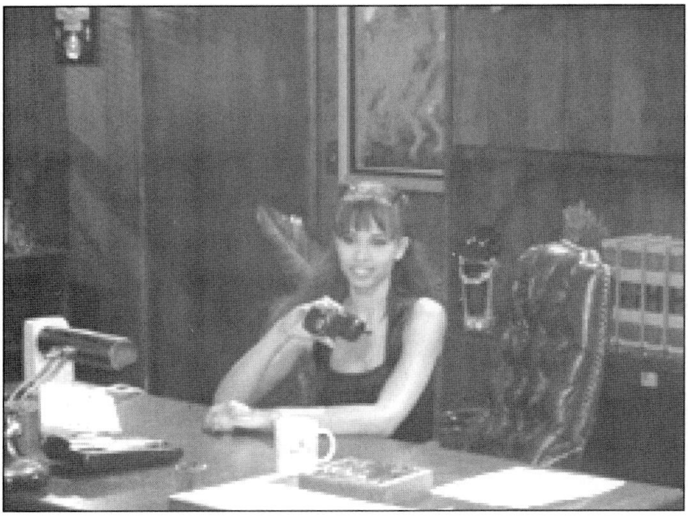

Playing the part of a real estate agent in the adult movie *Open House*, actress Nikki Fairchild rehearses her lines. In the next scene, she will have sex on the desk with actress Obsession.

Maria Manning, owner of Manning Hair Designs, awaits the morning rush. She has steadily built her clientele, yet hopes to expand her services in the near future.

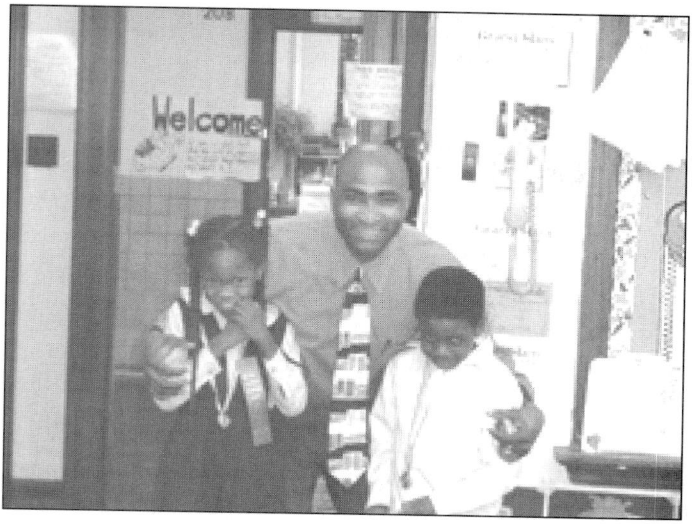

These young students may be camera shy, but they aren't shy about reading books.

Since Salome Thomas-El arrived at John Reynolds Elementary, students have made reading books a priority and a source of personal pride. These students have been rewarded with medals for having read the most books in their class.

Awaiting her nightly customers, the bartender at the Real Jerk takes a break from prepping her station.

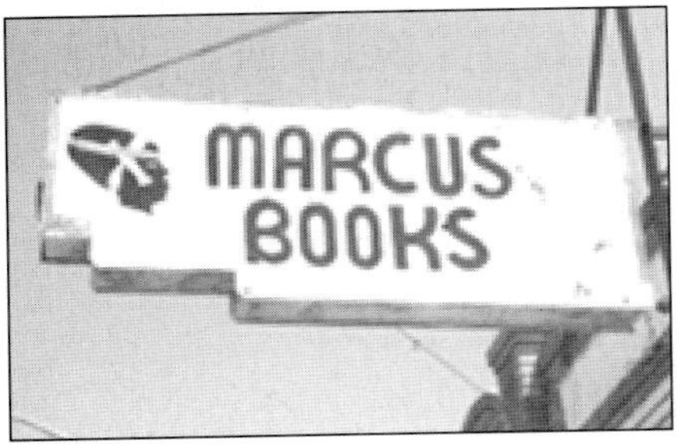

Beginning in 1960, Marcus Bookstore has been serving the African-American community in both San Francisco and Oakland.

Able to hold large audiences, the Oakland Marcus Bookstore branch is packed for a booksigning by *The Wind Done Gone* bestselling author Alice Randall.

American poet Osagyefo performs his poetry at the Kensington Library. The New York based poets, performing on their Babylon By Foot tour, were a big hit with audiences throughout England.

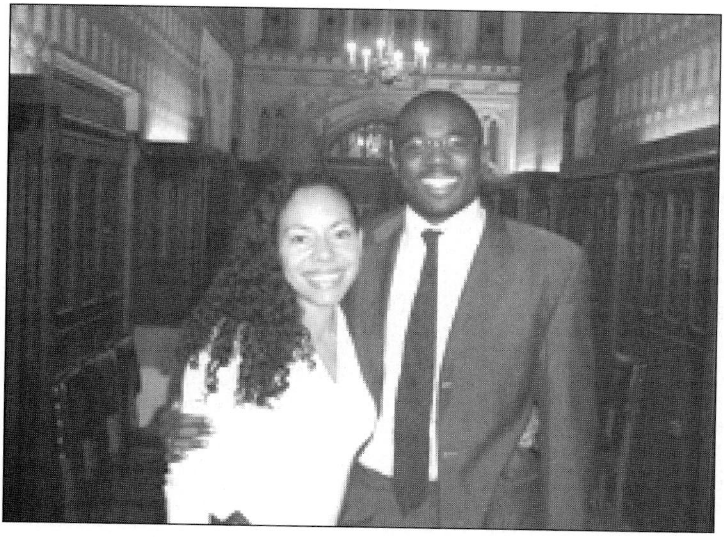

Meeting in the halls of the British House of Commons, British MPs Oona King and David Lammy know they not only represent their own districts, but also black Britains nationwide.

A temporary expatriate, Deborah Harris stands in the vestibule of her Paris apartment. In less than a year, Harris was able to create a successful tour agency in Paris.

Normally the violin was played as an accompaniment. Boyd Tinsley was one of the first musicians to bring this instrument to the forefront. Here, he plays in front of a sold-out Soldier Field in Chicago.

For the past decade, The Dave Matthews Band has consistently been one of music's most popular bands, selling millions of albums. Touring almost nonstop, it sells out arenas worldwide.

As an African-American woman, Zakiya Carr found working with Afro-Brazilian women rewarding, but she feels the struggle will continue for a long time after she leaves the country.

Club Tango & Cash begins to fill up as the samba band warms up. When the band started up, bodies began swaying to the music nonstop.

A little slice of the Bronx, Brazilian style! African-American culture influences urban Afro-Brazilian life to the point where you will often see portraits of Martin Luther King, Jr. and Malcolm X in many shops. Another common characteristic is the Afro-Brazilian embrace of the 1960s' American Civil Rights chant, "Black Power."

In the favelas of Rio de Janeiro, the hand built brick and tin roof homes crowd the hills surrounding the city. Ironically, some of the best city and ocean views are contained in some of Rio's poorest neighborhoods.

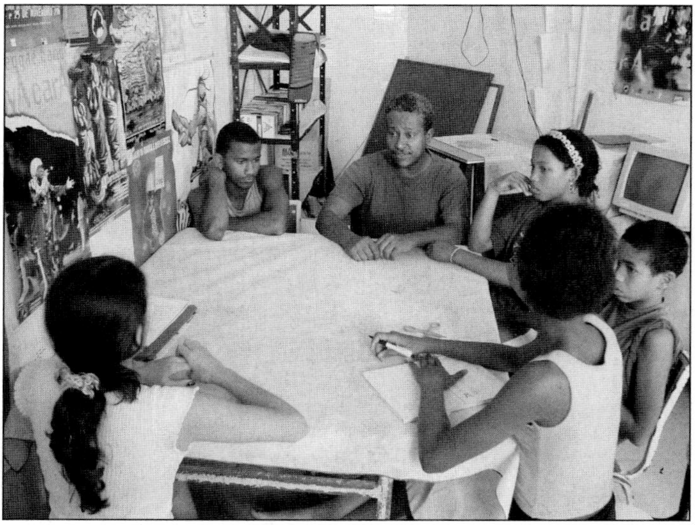

Afro-Brazilian dentist Jose Marmo, center, teaches children of the favelas about sexual education. During his visits to Brazilian favelas, Marmo attempts to connect Afro-Brazilian culture with modern Brazilian health issues through workshops run by the favelas residents.

Homes within Miguel Cunto ranged from unfinished to complete. This home across from Mother Beatrice's compound is a finished home.

Looking casual and feeling relaxed, former Atlanta mayor Bill Campbell prepares to deliver his weekly radio commentary.

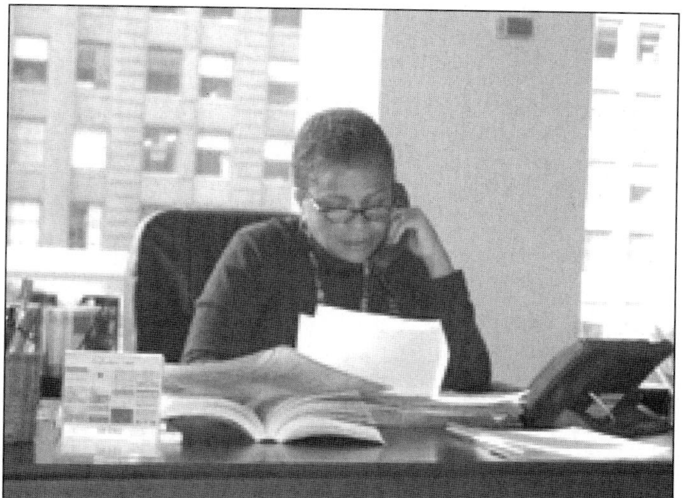

For *Essence* editor-in-chief, Diane Weathers, each day is a juggling act of meeting deadlines, creating new ideas, and managing staff.

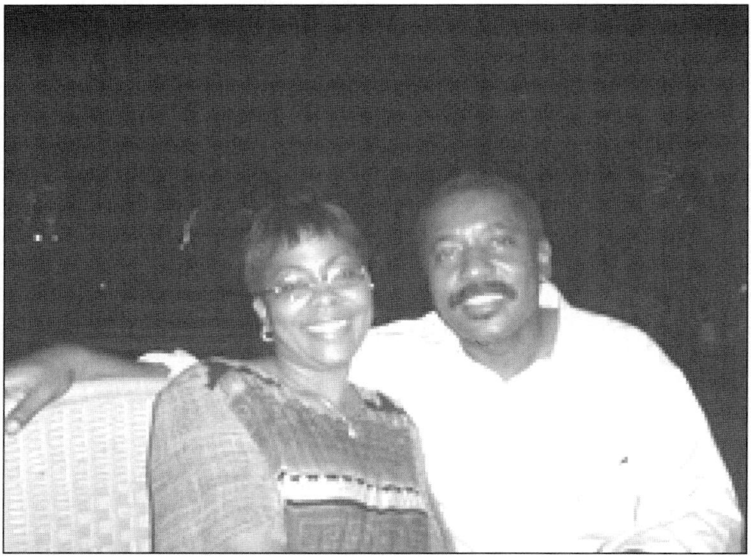

Sitting with her fiancé, Victoria Cooper, left, has made West Africa her home for the past twenty years.

As the wife of a U.S. diplomat, Tamice Parnell has gotten used to the idiosyncrasies of life outside the United States. The water had just gone off at her house this afternoon.

Throughout Ghana, there are forty-two European castles and fortifications that were used as dungeons for the millions who lost their lives or whose descendants comprise the African diaspora of today. Cape Coast Castle, one of the best preserved and the second largest slave castle in Ghana, is becoming an official museum of the slave trade.

Thousands of slaves captured from the Ghanian interior would be held in this Cape Coast Castle courtyard temporarily. After being recorded and classified, they would be led to crowded underground dungeons, where they would stay for months until their ultimate transportation to the New World as slaves.

The slave castles of Ghana have become an emotional symbol of the legacy of slavery for African Americans returning to Ghana. In recent years, African Americans have made a point to mark their presence at these castles.

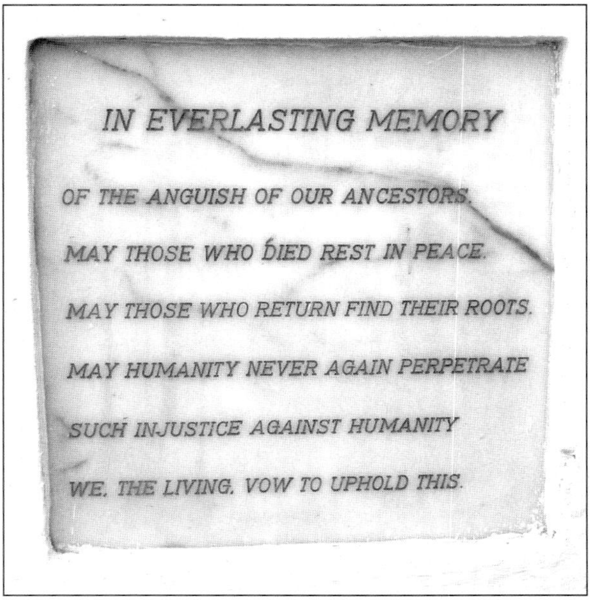

IN EVERLASTING MEMORY
OF THE ANGUISH OF OUR ANCESTORS.
MAY THOSE WHO DIED REST IN PEACE.
MAY THOSE WHO RETURN FIND THEIR ROOTS.
MAY HUMANITY NEVER AGAIN PERPETRATE
SUCH INJUSTICE AGAINST HUMANITY
WE, THE LIVING, VOW TO UPHOLD THIS.

Ronald and Anne Gordon moved to Ghana after looking at other places, including Morocco. Now they live in a jasmine-scented home on the outskirts of Accra.

African-American Michael Williams has thoroughly integrated himself in Ghanian society, however he finds most of his African-American students have problems adjusting.

Escaping for a little quiet time before his speech, E. Lynn Harris relaxes with a glass of wine.

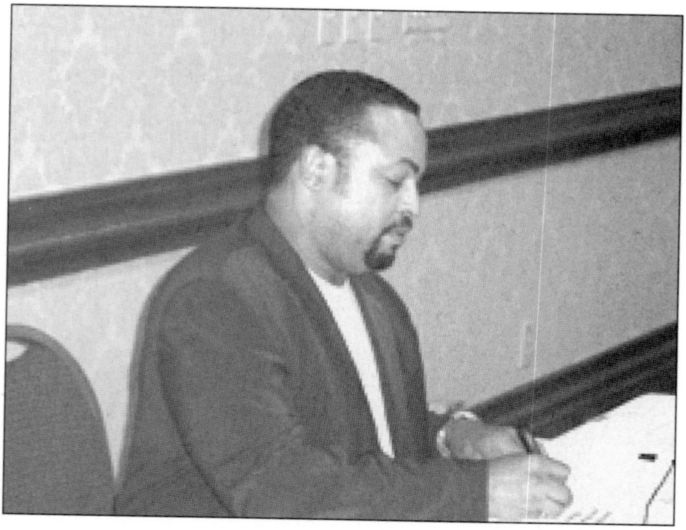

Since beginning his writing career by selling his books in beauty salons, Harris has become one of the bestselling African-American authors of the past decade.

Guru, a Morehouse College grad, has combined street smarts and business acumen to remain a player in hip-hop. Stretching the bounds of the genre, he was a pioneer in linking hip-hop with jazz.

Both old school and new school hip-hop artists from throughout New York visit the Manhattan studio to watch GangStarr record their new album.

Coach Rob Evans guides his charges through a pre-game practice. Arizona State would put up a valiant effort, but lose in the end to UCLA.

Facing the media after the game immediately after the loss to UCLA, Evans has the unenviable task of recounting what went wrong.

Ringmaster of the morning circus, deejay Frank Ski has made his V-103 show number one in Atlanta.

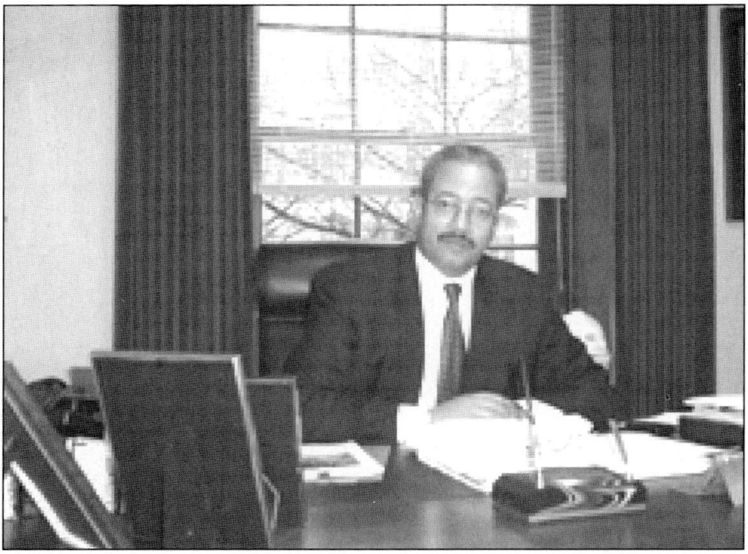

Looking to forge new alliances from unlikely partners, Democratic Congressman Chaka Fattah has worked with conservative Republicans to move his education agenda forward.

change. We could use our money; we could see our people going to school.

"Now, it was bad for the sake of democracy. You constantly had to think about, what could I say? What can I write to the paper? Or will what I say or write to the paper get me persecuted? That was bad, especially if you were at the university. You really had to watch what you said. Otherwise people disappeared. In the 1970s, mind you, I used to see some people attending classes, then disappearing. These were spies looking for people who dissented against the government. Then all of the sudden, a friend of ours would disappear as well. Those would be the people who had been targeted by the spies. We all became very conscious of what we said. And many, many people died. There are some people who we never knew where their bodies ended up. So it was a deal with the devil."

Historically, Brazil has tried to marginalize the Afro-Brazilian politically as well as psychologically. One of the more destructive policies to the Afro-Brazilian community in Brazil has been the ideology of branqueamento or "whitening." This theory was dreamed up in the 1920s to stop Brazil from becoming a predominantly black country.

In 1945, the country's immigration policy declared the need to "develop within the country's ethnic composition the most convenient characteristics of its European descent." And a 1966 Foreign Ministry leaflet guaranteed that the Brazilian population was white, with a minute proportion of the population being of mixed blood. As recently as 1988, an advisor to then governor of São Paulo, Paulo Maluf, proposed a national birth control campaign aimed at blacks, mixed-bloods, and Indians, to prevent them from becoming a majority. From these types of policies, Brazil has created a society that rewards closeness to whiteness, rather than a uniting of all blacks as one race.

"There is a big difference between African Americans and Afro-Brazilians, a *big* difference," says Rosangela. "Here, our government puts Afro-Brazilians into different categories in order to determine who is really black. The government talks about the blacks and then they talk about the mulattos. In Brazilian society, the mulattos are considered beautiful, so they get the better jobs. And the Brazilian government segregates [the Afro-Brazilian] community from the rest of society. If you are mulatto, then you can work at the hotels, or you can be a waiter. But if you are pitch black, the people will say, 'Sorry, but you aren't getting the job.' And it is difficult to get our black people together under these circumstances."

Essentially, black people in Brazil begin to become invisible nonfactors in society, and that black invisibility begins early, particularly in schools where virtually all books are written by white authors. The only mention that black children hear of their ancestors is as anonymous slaves; Princess Isabel freed them in 1888. As of 1991, only 6 percent of black children in Brazil make it to secondary school.

Logically, this poor education leads to badly paid jobs. Even when they do have the training and experience for better-paid work, the dice are loaded against black people. Many advertisements demand a "good appearance," subtle shorthand for "Black women need not apply." And certain jobs are no-go areas. In Rio, for example, there are said to be only five black waiters; white diners do not want to be served by black hands.

This whiter-than-white ideology is all-pervasive. For example, the 1980 census required blacks to fit themselves into one of the 136 color categories, including "burnt white," "toasted," and "cinnamon." There has been progress in the past decade. The 1991 census reduced the options to five: white, black, pardo (mixed race), Asian, or Indian. Brazil's black movement (which has been growing since the independence of African countries in the 1960s and 1970s) played a vanguard role in suggesting that all those with black genes should identify themselves as black. *Mulatto voce e' Negro* ("If you are mulatto, you are black") was their slogan.

"Unfortunately, those mulattos that are closer to being white are the most rewarded. They are the most valued. Black men, for example, tend to marry white women because they think that they will have some added status. Their society ranking will be better if they mix with white women; then their children will be mulatto. But of course, we have a few mulattos that are very proud of being black. They integrate themselves and fight for the rights of black people, but unfortunately it is not the majority. And as you look around Brazil, it is easy to see that the great majority of people are mixed."

Although Brazilian President Fernando Enrique Cardoso is fond of saying that he has a "foot in the kitchen," meaning that he has black ancestors, with "the kitchen" being the place where most Afro-Brazilians worked, the most dominant and powerful people in Brazil are white Brazilians. Only a handful of the 503 members of Congress are black; two out of twenty-three state governors are black, and there are no black ambassadors. And the only Afro-Brazilians you see in Brasilia's government buildings are serving coffee, mopping floors, or chauffeuring around white Brazilian bureaucrats.

The actual number of Afro-Brazilians in this country depends on what the issues are. According to official census figures, Brazil has a large population of people of mixed race: of about 159 million people, about 38 percent are classified as "mixed," about 6 percent are black, and about 55 percent are white. Still, there is no larger community of people whose roots are mostly African in the world except Nigeria.

But when, for example, the local *Globe* newspaper recently published the demographics of students finishing college, they reported that 2 percent of blacks finished college, but 16 percent of mulattos finished college. This is an example of the "divide and conquer" mentality that resides within Brazil, according to Rosangela.

"The way I look at it, I consider mulattos to be black. But things like this divide us and are some of the reasons that we haven't developed our political power or created movements in regard to education. No one will give us our rights; we have to fight for them. But the way it is today, it is through education and through health, which are our poorest services, that the government is able to keep control [over the black community]."

In the most recent census, one of the key black advocacy groups who were trying to get more representation for Afro-

Brazilians adopted a more ambiguous stance, with posters showing three people of different shades of blackness under the slogan, "Don't let your color go unregistered." Although the census numbers show that more and more Afro-Brazilians are recognizing themselves as black, there is still a reluctance to be a member of this downtrodden community.

With this inequity within Brazilian society, the outsider might be tempted to ask how the government is able to keep a massive population of Afro-Brazilians from revolting. Rosangela offers a simple opinion.

"The Brazilian government tries to keep black people down through music, religion, and sports," she says disdainfully. "In sports it's football. In music it is the samba. And in religion, it happens that we are officially a Catholic country, but we have the freedom to practice whatever religion you want. And our black religion, which comes originally from Africa, is the Candombles. So whenever there is a bone of contention [within the black community] that has the possibility of turning into a riot, they [the Brazilian government] have a carnival or a festival to take our minds off of the problem. I think that that's how they keep control. But with those things, they are still having problems [keeping order]."

As was so often stated by Afro-Brazilians familiar with the African-American experience, Brazil is like the United States before the Civil Rights Movement when it comes to the power of the Afro-Brazilian community. The power is underneath the surface, and there has been a lack of national leadership in the Afro-Brazilian community.

"In terms of national leaders, we don't have many. Benedita da Silva is the only one, and she's paid a hell of a price," said Rosangela. "But for the great majority of blacks that attain a position, they lose the language of the favelas when they get into power. And we feel so bad about it."

Fifty-four-year-old Benedita da Silva worked her way from the dire poverty of the favelas surrounding Rio de Janeiro to become the first Afro-Brazilian woman elected to Brazil's senate.

She was born on the wrong side of Brazil's rigid class line as one of thirteen children. Working various jobs as a teenager, and rarely making enough money to live off of, she tells of her days eating out of garbage cans, of the deaths of two of her four children from curable diseases, and her work as a live-in maid—"humiliating" work where she was "treated like a slave," according to her autobiography, *Benedita da Silva: An Afro-Brazilian Woman's Story of Politics and Love.*

Da Silva said that it was the poverty she saw every day that compelled her to enter politics, an arena that she prefers to believe in despite the corruption that plagues the Brazilian version of democracy. "We must change things," she said in a recent interview. "And in order to make these changes, the only way is through politics."

Da Silva rejected the commonly held notion that the racial situation is, if not better in Brazil, at least different. "The situation is very similar in Brazil, the U.S., and South Africa," she said. "We [all] have to deal with drugs, gender issues, and problems with education. Brazil, the U.S., and South Africa must unite together in order to solve these problems.

"We are trying to reach the level of identity and representation that Afro-Americans have in the U.S.," da Silva said. "In the U.S., people with African origins have reached a better standing in society. In Brazil, race is not a physical question; it's an identity. We are from Africa, but we are not Africans. We have to separate what is black from what is white."

It is that separation from the white aesthetic, and, more important, a revolution of the mindset that devalues their worth as Afro-Brazilians, that Rosangela Valle and Benedita da Silva are striving to change. As Rosangela picks up the check and we get up to leave, I ask her if she has hope for the future.

"Oh, yes, even though things sometimes don't look bright, I do have hope for the future," she says. "And I make sure to teach my own children that they are black and they should be proud to be black."

19

Echoes of an African God

Miguel Cunto, Brazil

The most beautiful thing we can experience is the mysterious. It is the source of all true art and all science. He to whom this emotion is a stranger, who can no longer pause to wonder and stand rapt in awe, is as good as dead: his eyes are closed.

—Albert Einstein

It's a hot and muggy Saturday, and thirty kilometers south of Rio de Janeiro, just past the stagnant river waters that crisscross Brazil, and around the corner from the polluted and congested highway, sits a little section of a favela called Miguel Cunto.

Miguel Cunto is about as nondescript as a dot on the map can be. Miguel Cunto is a collection of red brick buildings piled upon each other like millions of broken and dirty Lego blocks. Old Volkswagens speed their way through alternating paved and dirt roads, their destinations known only to their drivers. The neighborhood is a maze of humanity and inhumanity living side by side. The only constant is the poverty that suffuses every square foot of this little community. But like most places in the favelas of Brazil, this is a poverty of material goods, not spirituality.

In spirituality, Miguel Cunto is rich because it is the home of Ile Omio Juaro. And within the walls of Ile Omio Juaro reside the worshipers of the African religion of Candombles.

Candombles centers of worship are called *terreiros,* and they encompass a sacred indoor and outdoor space with sanctuaries for the orixas, saints, and Indianlike spirits called Caboclos. The head of the terreiro is either a priest, sometimes referred to as a *babalorixa* or a *pai de santo* (father of the orixas), or a priestess, called an *ialorixa* or a *mae de santo* (mother of the orixa). This religious leader is traditionally a black woman who, in addition to being responsible for the spiritual well-being of the Candombles members and the terreiro's material needs, uses divination to communicate with the orixas. To ascertain an individual's personal orixas or to help find a solution to a devotee's personal problem, the mae de santo will toss sixteen cowrie shells whose resulting patterns reveal the will of the orixas.

Mother Beatrice is the mae de santo, while her son, Adailton Moreira Costa is the pai de santo. Together they lead the worshipers through the Candombles ceremony. Today people are coming from throughout the Rio area to participate in the ceremony.

"Our community, for example, is a mixed community," Costa says. "We have professors, lawyers, cooks, maids, and each can give one or two real to the community. Whatever they have, they will be equal in the community. Our community is open to all people."

The origins of Candombles began in the hinterlands of Africa. Portuguese colonists brought the first African slaves to Brazil in 1549, about sixty years after Columbus landed in the West Indies. Yorubas, Adjas, Fons, and other Africans from the "Gold Coast," present day Ghana, Benin, and Nigeria, were brought to cut cane, pan for gold, build churches, and construct roads. Before the trade ended, in 1888, nearly eight million slaves had been shipped to Brazil. One of the religions that the Africans brought to the New World was Candombles.

"We have a saying that we are black, but our traditional religion is for the orixas, and we don't have a place in our religion for prejudices," notes Costa. "But the white people [in Candombles] must learn to respect the black historical aspect of our religion. It is a slow process, but it begins with a dialogue."

There are three different types of Candombles in Brazil, each one associated with different *nacoes,* Portuguese for *nation.* The nations refer to the different African regions of Candombles. The first is the Gege-Nago Candombles, and it is based on Yoruba religious traditions and language. Angola-Congo Candombles and Candombles de Caboclo are based on Brazilian and other African traditions, but are still influenced by Yoruba beliefs. Another variation of Candombles in the New World is Santería.

"When you talk about Santería and Candombles, the essence is the same, but there is a cultural difference," says Mother Beatrice.

"It is a question of adaptation to the place and the history. Like in Nigeria, Candombles is not the same as here in Brazil. We have a tradition that is different from another part of Nigeria. Santería in the Caribbean is just another name and another adaptation of our religion. But when some people who practice Candombles in Brazil go to Cuba and see Santería, they may proclaim, "That is not Candombles." But it is. But it is very difficult for people because we have our own sense of tradition and how we worship."

In Candombles, the worshipers believe in one Supreme Being, known as Olodumare, and numerous intermediary spiritual beings, known as orixas. These orixas were similar to the Christian God and Catholic saints of the Portuguese colonizers.

Quickly, the Africans recognized the similarities in characteristics between the Christian saints and their orixas and began to identify some of their orixas with the saints. For example, they identified Obaluaiye, the orixa of smallpox and epidemic diseases, with Saint Lazarus the leper. African and Catholic religious traditions in some Candombles blended the two religions, while it was only superficial in others. In either case, it allowed them to secretly worship their African deities behind the facade of the saints, and contributed to the formation of a religion known as Candombles.

In Brazil the predominantly black state of Bahia continues to be the cradle of Candombles. Although the religion is openly practiced today, historically its practice has been covert because of repression by church and state officials. Beginning in the nineteenth century, police raided Candombles houses of worship, confiscating their possessions and arresting their members. The repression of some Candombles lessened in the 1930s, when participants in two Afro-Brazilian congresses advocated the preservation of Candombles as part of Brazil's African heritage. But it was not until Brazil officially declared its commitment to fostering religious freedom, in the 1970s, that Candombles devotees began to practice their religion openly.

"There is a lot of religious intolerance in Brazil, and especially when it comes to Candombles," says Mother Beatrice. A lot of people think that we worship the devil, but our duty is to worry about the people *in* Candombles, and not what people think *about* Candombles. The fanatical people, like the Protestants, have religious preconceived notions, but not really the other people. But with other people that are not so fanatical, we really don't have problems with them."

Following a 1983 conference on the orixas tradition and culture in Salvador, Bahia, some Candombles priests and priestesses proposed doing away with the Catholic elements in Candombles, principally the imagery of the saints, which they regarded as no longer necessary for the worship of their African deities. Today, whether or not to desyncretize Candombles continues to be a hotly debated issue.

Today is the celebration of a Candombles orixa, Obaluaiye, an orixa linked with the healing of disease and good health. In the backyard, women dressed in calico chant songs to the gods while lanky teenage boys with braces on their teeth drum a continuous rhythm. The music, the chanting, and the periodic firing of firecrackers make for an almost hypnotic atmosphere.

Costa leads a group of worshipers into a small building where ritual slaughter of animals will take place. In Candombles, a devotee "belongs to" multiple orixas, who control the devotee's destiny and act as his or her protectors. The orixas are intermediaries between humans and Olodumare, the creator of the universe. As the children and servants of Olodumare, the orixas are all related by a common mythology, which is used to explain the social relations between people who worship different orixas. People's actions are understood individually in terms of their personal orixas. What a devotee does, eats, and wears on a daily basis is often influenced by his or her orixas, which are associated with specific days of the week, foods, animals, and colors.

"There are some orixas that we can speak about and then there are some that we can't speak about," Costa says. "We can't even say their names."

In addition to respecting the preferences of their orixas, devotees usually exhibit personal qualities akin to those of their orixas. For example, a devotee of Xango, the orixa of thunder and lightning, will tend to be proud, aggressive, and stubborn, all of which are characteristic traits of this orixa. In this way, orixas often determine their devotees' behavior and daily decisions.

From out of view, a squealing pig is being led to the terreiro. As the worshipers and devotees continue to chant, drum, and sing, the pig seems to sense that death is only a few feet away. Now inside the terreiro, the pig squeals incessantly as the final prayers are made to the orixa Obaluaiye. Suddenly, a deep guttural noise emanates from the pig as its throat is being cut. The chanting and drumming reaches a fever pitch as the worshipers rejoice that they have pleased the orixas.

Costa leads the other devotees out of the terreiro, their hands and shirts red from the pig's blood. Another firecracker goes off as the worshipers announce to the community that a sacrifice has been made.

"The people inside of the building, they have a special relationship with this particular orixa," says Costa. "And the ones on the outside don't have the same relationship. The inside of the house contains a special family, and we were initiated for this particular orixa. And this orixa has particular priests."

Over the next hour, various ducks, geese, chickens, and other animals will be sacrificed to Obaluaiye. Some will be killed outside, others inside the terreiro. All will be collected for the great meal and celebration later tonight.

"Basically, all of the animals are equal," says Costa. "A big animal will provide us with more food, or it will produce more blood, but it is the same as a small animal. When an animal is sacrificed, it means that we will have the qualities of that animal."

Besides providing a religious base for Miguel Cunto, one of the main missions of Ile Omio Juaro is to work within their community. So they try to integrate their Candombles ceremony with the needs of the community as they make their terreiro the center of the community by tackling social issues outside their religion.

"Here we have more room for our social movement. Mother Beatrice for example, she's a very important person within the AIDS community and within the homeless problem. She's a very conscious person. Our purpose is not just to sacrifice animals. That's just the religious part. Our role is serving other people. That can be the problems of the streets, our neighbors, or our community," says Costa.

"Most people in the community are poor people, and most poor people are black people. There are other Candombles communities in Rio, but they don't have that same sense of responsibility. When we sacrifice our animals, we use all parts of the animals, from the skin to the blood and the bones. And we are able to give this back to the community, because the community is a poor community. So we share our bounty as a feast. We hope that other communities of Candombles will have the same type of projects as us."

After the animals have been sacrificed, the worshipers and devotees make their way into the main hall of the terreiro. Mother Beatrice sits in a chair of honor, and the worshipers all make their way to her. She radiates presence, and when she walks around the room, the worshipers immediately lie prostrate before her.

The drums have been brought inside, and now devotees are moving to a new rhythm. A spiritual force referred to as *axe* sustains Candombles, and devotees increase their *axe* by carrying out daily devotional rites and through possession ceremonies. During these ceremonies, drummers play a sequence of rhythms, each corresponding to the orixa being summoned, while devotees sing songs and execute dance steps associated with their personal orixas. The songs and dances collectively reenact the mythology of the orixas and individually reflect the human activity and aspect of nature that an orixa oversees. For example, the choreography of Oxossi, who presides over hunting and the forest, involves the hunting and capturing of game. During these ceremonies the orixas often descend into the bodies of their devotees, inducing an animated state of possession in which the devotees dance.

"Inside, the orixas come as a manifestation. It is a very special visit for us. We think that it is wonderful," Costa says.

For African Americans, this feeling would be akin to a Christian "catching the spirit." As the orixa comes to more and more people, the dancing becomes more and more frenetic. The devotees' sweaty bodies glisten as Mother Beatrice rocks in her chair, overlooking the spectacle. Every so often, she gets up and dances along with devotees. Then suddenly, it's over.

The women go into the kitchen as they begin preparing the banquet for this evening. Mother Beatrice and Costa take a seat just outside of the terreiro, as the children begin playing.

Tired, as she sips a drink of water, Mother Beatrice reflects on how Candombles is perceived in Brazil.

"In Brazilian society, there are preconceived notions about Candombles. But it is not a problem for us. We try not to hide our sense of religious traditions and culture. We try to live like what we think is right for us.

"One of the missions for our community is to announce the condition of the poor in the newspapers, television, and on the radio. The rich people from Rio don't care about the poor, and it is up to us to let the poor people know that they have rights, and that we need to work together.

"We help people in the community with a bunch of problems. It could be problems of love, where people come to us and say, 'Ah, my love has left me,' and we try to resolve problems. Also, we get financial problems, marriage problems, pretty much anything. Sometimes people just come so that they can just talk to someone."

How does one qualify to become a member of the Candombles?

"To become a member, all you have to be is human," laughs Costa.

New initiates to Candombles go through an elaborate initiation process that lasts several months and eventually allows them to be possessed by an orixa. During this induction period, initiates are kept in a secluded room where they learn the songs, dances, and mythology of their orixas. In addition, their bodies are ritually prepared with herbal baths and drinks to receive the orixas. Initiation culminates in a ceremony marking the spiritual rebirth of the initiate, who becomes what is sometimes referred to in Portuguese as a *filho* or *filha de santo* (son or daughter of the orixa). In Yoruba, initiates are called *iaos.* The initiation process creates a family of devotees related by spiritual rather than genetic ties.

As Mother Beatrice reclines in her chair, non-Candombles members from the Miguel Cunto community begin entering Ile Omio Juaro. Some ask about the coming banquet, while others ask to speak with her privately. She gently talks to each one as Costa helps with the cleanup.

"We've been up since five this morning and we probably won't be done until five in the morning tomorrow," Costa says wearily. "But it is well worth it."

20

The Essence of Womanhood

Times Square, New York

It is not enough to show people how to live better: there is a mandate for any group with enormous powers of communication to show people how to be better.

—Marya Mannes

Diane Weathers silently walks into her office, a corner office in the heart of New York's Times Square. Her office is saturated with the giant, bright multicolored lights of omnipresent scrolling billboards right outside her office window.

"US High Court dismisses Affirmative Action . . . Taliban leader thought killed . . . CIA Agent murdered in Taliban Prison Firefight . . ." the constant scroll reads. America is fighting the Taliban in Afghanistan, and after the tragedy of the terrorist attack of September 11, the public is hungry for information, any information about the war.

Before she sits down at her desk, Weathers is immediately given a stack of papers by her assistant, Hyacinth, a young college graduate who seems to have mastered the delicate balance of being ever-present yet unobtrusive.

"Make the copies for the COB meeting. Make about, say ten copies?" she says to her assistant. Hyacinth rushes off.

"[A typical day] consists of a lot of meetings," says Weathers as she settles in behind her desk. "Meetings take up a lot of the day. Some go on too long, and I'm trying to cut back. The COB meeting shouldn't go on longer than two hours, but it always seems to keep going on and on—much too long."

She takes time to look over her desk, and picks up the magazine *Men's Health.* It is not unusual for magazine editors to take a look at the competition, but what does a men's magazine have to do with a women's magazine?

"One of my favorite things about *Men's Health* is that they really know how to package stories," she says, riffling through the pages. "They know how to deliver information in a way that is smart and witty. It's well edited. I just like the way they deliver information. It's really solid. A lot of times I mention *Men's Health* to the editors and just say 'take a look at it. See how they do things and get some ideas from it.' "

Hyacinth returns to give Diane a rundown of things left to do and things needed for the future. As though the staff instinctively knows that Diane has arrived, the phones begin to ring. Employees pass by the office, poking their heads in, getting instructions for the day. And, of course, there are more papers needing to be signed.

"My husband says that I am the only person who can do three things at once," laughs Diane as she signs the papers, talks on the phone, and flips through a magazine.

A wife and mother of two, Weathers began her writing and editorial career in 1975 with *Black Enterprise.* Throughout the years, she has worked as either an editor or writer at *Newsweek, Consumer Reports, Family Circle,* the *New York Times,* and several other publications. This is her second stint at *Essence;* she previously served as a senior editor from 1993 to 1997, and earlier this year she was appointed editor in chief.

Mikki Taylor, Essence's stylish beauty editor, enters the office, and the two editors immediately begin a discussion about a possible trip to Cuba. Finding new and exotic locales is part of shooting any fashion or beauty piece, but there is one small problem with a photo shoot in Cuba; it is off limits to most Americans. But journalists are exempt from this restriction, and Weathers wants to feel out Taylor on the possibilities of traveling there.

"Are we going to Cuba?" asks Weathers.

"I don't think so," says Taylor.

"Jan told Barbara that we were. She even gave her a date."

"We haven't been getting great information about what's going on there."

"I was talking to a friend of mine," says Weathers, "a relative who has gone back and forth to Cuba, and she thinks that Castro would love us. She thinks that he would hook it up so much. She feels, and she's going to make some calls, to be sure that he would love to pave the way. I told her that there would be the fashion and the beauty, but there would also be the connection with the Afro-Cuban community. So I want to make some calls and talk to some people to see."

"One thing [that concerns me] is the cost, because we really have to hire a production crew to work with you and shadow you there. And then there's the whole security thing, so there's that concern," says Taylor.

"They don't have any crime there, sweetheart."

"But when Americans go there . . ."

"But what I'm saying is that she gave me a sense that, and I'm sure that she's right, that he would set it all up," Weathers insists. "I mean, a black women's magazine [in Cuba]? And I think that [the Cuban government] would procure everything. We would probably get such incredible treatment. I mean, we're not just going down there spending money, and I think we need to pursue it along those lines."

"I would like to pursue it along those lines, but I would like to look at everything," reiterates a hesitant Taylor.

"We need to have all of the players come together and discuss it," says Weathers.

"I guess that we would be going around the tenth of January?" asks Taylor.

"That's what the date would be."

"So this shoot would be for the June or July issue?"

"You know why it would be good? July is our adventure issue. Could we do it for July?"

"We could; we could make a July cover out of it."

"Wouldn't that be wonderful? We could make a June or July cover out of it."

"Yes, it would be."

"And also, I think that there is a vibrant art community [in Cuba]," Weathers continues. "They have been going on, thank you, without us. Europeans are going there and it is a big tourist destination. And for black women, I'm saying that it could be such an experience. And I've spoken to Tanya, Tanya Banks. She's my husband's cousin, and she's going down there in March. Tanya said that she would make some phone calls to some of the folks here in New York that have the really strong Cuban connection."

"When do you think she'll get back to you?"

"She said that she could get back to me in a week."

"So yeah, maybe we could all come together. I'll talk [to New York Cubans] and see what they say. I just would like to get some feedback that I can share with you."

"There's so much going on there [in Cuba], and we know our African-American readers are interested."

"Let's try to come together and say, 'Here it is, guys; it sounds favorable and let's work toward it.' "

"And I can get away from editing copy," says an exasperated Weathers. "I need to go out and talk to people, but instead I'm line editing copy. I'm taking stuff home and line editing."

Tamara Jeffries silently sits in her office, just adjacent to Diane's, prepping for the meeting that is to come later today. She has made her daily two-hour commute from Philadelphia, and she knows that what lies ahead this afternoon will require her to juggle, inspire, and reach interoffice political compromises with a staff of strong-willed women. Maybe that is why her bookshelves are lined with books on yoga and meditation? Tamara just laughs.

"Just the life of an editor," she says with a smile.

These two women are part of a team at *Essence* magazine, regarded arguably as the most powerful African-American magazine currently on the market. Weathers, who is the editor in chief, has been charged with the task of improving the quality of

Essence, while also continuing to make it relevant in the twenty-first century.

Jeffries, the managing editor, is responsible for corralling the ideas of her young senior editors and meddling with it all so that it corresponds with the visions of not only Weathers, but also *Essence* matriarch and longtime executive editor Susan Taylor.

All of this is a balancing act. *Essence* magazine has for most of its history had the market of African-American women all to itself. Covering issues of health, career, and relationships, *Essence* for years has been all things to all African-American women as it filled an essential void left by the general-market women's magazines such as *Vogue* and *In Style,* which tend to focus on white women while ignoring the specific needs of African-American women in their pages.

But lately, *Essence* has been challenged on the newsstand. New African-American women's magazines, such as *Honey,* are trying to cull some of *Essence*'s readership by appealing to younger African-American women. Also, African-American faces are beginning to appear in mainstream publications. *Essence* is finding that it has to balance its traditionally older demographic with its need to attract and retain the young readership that advertisers covet. Hence you have the input of the young *Essence* senior editorial staff, and today's COB meeting.

COB, magazine parlance for "center of book," is one part editorial meeting, one part bull session, and one part combat. At every magazine—and *Essence* is no different—there is a passionate fight for ideas. Editors will decide such things as which articles will be chosen to set the tone for the magazine, and what headlines will draw a potential reader's interest. Nothing is too small to fight for, and people are honest and up-front about their opinions. This is a cooperative effort that requires people to leave their egos at the door.

It's ten o'clock, and Tamara enters Diane's office and asks about the start of COB.

"Why don't you all start, and then I'll come in at noon?" Diane says.

As Tamara leaves, Pamela Edwards and Stephanie Scott enter

the office. Pamela is a fashion and beauty writer, and Stephanie is the assistant beauty editor. And while they go over future ideas such as what to do with toes, rings, toe rings, and a new section called "Looks We Love."

"'Looks we love' is that great eye, that wonderful shoe, that outfit that so-and-so wore; it's a hodgepodge. It's just great things that we've seen. And that's in every single issue," Weathers notes to Pamela and Stephanie, trying to define the section.

Meanwhile, as Weathers talks about that hodgepodge, there's a discussion going on in the conference room. The topic is "Drama Queens" and whether it is a viable subject for the magazine. The conversation among the senior editors goes something like this:

"Drama queens have relationship things going on—they spent the rent on a seven-hundred-dollar Gucci and all of the areas are going simultaneously, and when that friend calls you, you know who she is . . ."

"My thing is whether or not drama queens know that they have a choice, and I don't think so . . ."

"The drama queen is the person who can't visualize why her life is like it is—she has a fight with her boss, or just got fired, or is dating someone who is married and—"

"I would think that for a drama queen, this life is very scary, because it really isn't a choice . . ."

"And I don't think it is about control, because drama queens don't have lives that are in control . . ."

"No, I think there are drama queens who are professionals and they have it together. They go to work and win awards, so that's not the issue. It's the way they maneuver around everything else in their personal lives."

"I have two friends that are mistresses. One has been a mistress for about fifteen years, and she's fine. There's no drama in her life whatsoever. The other one has been a mistress for less time than that, but she always finds a way to get into confrontation with the man's wife, or his girlfriend, so her life is drama. So she does make the choice, because her life is not complete without drama . . ."

"But I'm also a fan [of being a drama queen], and I don't

think that there is anything wrong with a healthy dose of drama. The key factor is how you constructively—"

"But what's a healthy dose of drama?"

"I don't know."

"Well, somebody's got to have drama or we wouldn't have any good articles!"

Everyone laughs.

Finally, Tamara sums up the discussion.

"I think that [reader that identifies with the drama queen] is someone that looks at someone's life and sees that it is going smoothly, and then looks at her own life and wonders why nothing goes right. We could diagnose a person's drama issues.

"By the way, where is the food?"

They all laugh again, and another COB meeting is off and running. Sitting around a giant conference table, flanked by panel boards filled with the layout of the next magazine issue, the senior editors discuss and argue their points of view.

What this particular discussion was about is a potential article about so-called drama queens, and how women can change so that they have less drama in their lives. As with each story idea, the senior editors use free association in order to come up with a well-thought-out thesis for the article. However, one of the decision makers, Diane Weathers in particular, has not heard their ideas yet, and therefore anything they decide can ultimately be overruled.

At every magazine—and *Essence* is no exception—there are internal politics about what to print. Many considerations come into play, both spoken and unspoken. For example, in a period of rapidly declining magazine advertising revenue, no magazine wants to offend longtime advertisers, so that constrains some types of content, no matter how silently or how vehemently an editorial board may protest.

Also, when a magazine such as *Essence* decides whom to place on a cover, there are egos to consider. For example, the senior editors talk with Weathers about placing three men on the cover of its annual "men" issue, two of whom are icons within Hollywood. But there is a problem: The third is not considered strong enough to pull off a cover, and the two, despite their past collaboration, are not on good terms. Added to the mix is the fact that Susan Taylor has made it known that she definitely wants one of the icons on the cover.

So what to do? Well, they decide to ask one of the icons if he'll appear with the other. If he says no, then plan B goes into effect. They ditch the other rejected Hollywood icon and go with the one that Taylor wants and the lesser star. Got it? Good, now get on the phone with all of the parties, and try not to let them know your plan.

Senior editors are traditionally low on the editorial totem pole, and as progressive or daring their ideas may be, they still have to be filtered through the vision of Tamara, Diane, and Susan. It is that trio's task to maintain their overall vision of *Essence* while listening to new ideas and perspectives.

Diane has now entered the room, and the drama queen discussion is put off for later follow-up. A new-article discussion comes about when the senior editors discuss an upcoming issue featuring African American women in Hollywood. They are looking for fresh and new faces that they can introduce to the readership, but the paucity of African American actresses in consistent Hollywood roles inherently limits the discussion. Even when the list of potential subjects is expanded to not only movies but also television, the same old names pop up.

"Our Hollywood issue last year didn't do what we needed it to do," says Joan Morgan, a senior editor, "but it was very successful in Hollywood. Because the feeling was that none of the black publications ever have their finger on the pulse of who is emerging. And we did that last year. So Cicely Tyson is not going to do that for us. Angela Bassett is not going to give us that sort of cachet for that kind of Hollywood. If we are going to have a 'Women That We Love' [for Hollywood], then we need to make sure that the people we pick deliver."

"But you can have categories," Weathers explains. "They don't have to be all for the same reason. We can have Alfre Woodard because we don't see enough of her. We could have whatever hot upcoming person. [It could be] the most . . . whatever. I remember one anniversary issue. [Past editor] Pam Johnson did wonderful categories. It was the twenty-fifth anniversary and we had categories like 'Shoot from the Lip.' It was a whole hodgepodge. So let's think of it that way."

"Let's do the names," says Tamara.

They begin working on names, eliminating some while adding others. Once the names have been selected, the categories become apparent. Comedians go into the "Laughing Their Way to the Bank" category, while couples like Will Smith and Jada Pinkett-Smith are placed in the "Hollywood Couples" category.

And so it goes. As with most issues discussed in COB, there isn't a definitive moment when consensus is automatically met. Stories continue to evolve, even as the writer is writing.

What's last on the agenda for this COB meeting? A tragic story, as a former *Essence* employee recounts his life since losing his wife in the World Trade Center Towers on September 11. The main issue for the editors is, how do you approach this story? Will the story of September 11 be too old to tell by the time the story comes out, nearly six months after the event? Also, how will they word the cover-line tease so that it will entice readers to read this article?

A cover line is a small headline on the cover of the magazine that teases the prospective reader to pick up the magazine. Smaller than the main headline, it can be as small as six words long, and tell the reader on which page the article is located.

Susan Taylor enters the room and has specific ideas about what should and shouldn't be in the cover line. She doesn't want specific references to September 11, and wants to focus on the husband's tragedy.

"If we write a headline like 'I Lost My Love' and it's coming from a man, then I think that that is very impactful," says Taylor.

However, some of the editors balk at the vagueness of such a headline.

"To me that sounds like the breakup of a relationship. When I read the headline, I want to know that somebody died," says Weathers. "I mean, this is not just a breakup, and that is what pulls me [into reading the article].

"How about 'When A Wife Dies,' something that is very specific?"

"Now I'm wanting to read this," says Taylor enthusiastically.

"And it's a tragic story," Weathers continues. "It's the death of his wife, the death of a young mother. And it will be in the love issue."

The rest of the editors mouth their approval, but their faces don't seem convinced. They keep trying to find the right words for the headline.

"Burying a wife?"

"Death of a wife?"

"Loving a son, burying a wife?"

"What About 'Where's Mommy'?"

"When A Wife Dies: A Father Speaks."

"When A Wife Dies: A Husband Speaks."

"Mourning My Wife, Raising My Son."

"I think that is what he is doing," notes Susan McHenry another senior editor as they contemplate the latest cover line suggestion. "You have to do a few things at once. You have to suffer, miss the person and feel sad. And then you have to raise a child and keep your son propped up. It's heavy."

"What's holding me back [from the cover line] is that if we are not going with 9-11 World Trade Center, then we need to be really direct and say that this is a heavy-duty story you are going to read. This is a real tear-jerker."

After analyzing all of the possible cover lines, it is apparent that the September event will have to be mentioned in order for the average reader to initially care about the article.

"I think that if we mention 9/11 from our [African American] perspective, that we could be right there with the other women's magazines," says McHenry. "They have long lead times, too."

So what do the women finally agree upon?

"Remembering Felicia, Raising Sebastian" is the final cover line. How long did it take to come up with the final result? Nearly an hour, and one thinks that Weathers's earlier lament that COB meetings run too long was surely in vain. With each editor dedicated to providing just the right words, every minute of this meeting seemed necessary.

COB is now over, and the women disperse. Another issue has been fleshed out and it is on to the writing. It's just another day at *Essence*.

21

Public to Private Citizen

Atlanta, Georgia

He who controls the past commands the future. He who commands the future conquers the past.

—George Orwell

"Everyone wants to move to Atlanta because it has been viewed as an African-American mecca, and I would say justifiably so," said former Atlanta mayor Bill Campbell. "There are more black colleges here than any other place. You have the history of black politics, with Dr. King and the Civil Rights movement. I think that with Atlanta, you have a place where black people feel that they can achieve. And here, you can have a sense of solidarity with each other and feel a connection to the past. And that has made [Atlanta] a very special place.

"There's so much history of black achievement here. The black colleges really provide the axis around which so much achievement has been driven. Dr. King went to Morehouse. More black preachers are trained in Atlanta than anywhere else. DuBois taught here. Booker T. Washington gave his famous 'five fingers on the hand' speech in eighteen ninety-five. As a result of that, DuBois gathered his group and formed the Niagara Movement, and then NAACP. The SCLC was formed in Atlanta. I was the third black mayor, and now we have a fourth.

"In terms of entertainment, we are probably the hip-hop capital. I think that whether or not you are looking to start a business, or get into politics, Atlanta is an incubator that is unparalleled.

"I also think that Atlanta is a hot place for any young person. If you live in the South, and you are looking to 'move up and out,' Atlanta is the place that you would go. We have always been called the capital of the New South."

Bill Campbell has been out of office for less than a year, but he still sounds like the point man for the city. As Atlanta mayor, Campbell served two consecutive terms, and he is credited with improved public housing and increased affordable housing; business and economic development and downtown revitalization; new sports and family entertainment complexes; improved quality of life through increased youth facilities, programs, and services; infrastructure replacement and repair, including sewers, sidewalks, and bridges; privatization of the city's water system, the largest in the nation; operation of the busiest airport in the world; and host to the 1996 Olympic Games.

A reported $2 billion went toward building venues, infrastructure improvements and renovations. The Corporation for Olympic Development (CODA) spent an estimated $75 million on inner city redevelopment.

Hartsfield Atlanta International Airport gained a $300 million international air terminal, a $24 million atrium and overall improvements exceeding $250 million. All were part of the airport's master plan, but the Olympics created a catalyst to move the projects forward.

A 1997 Louis Harris survey to gauge the impact of the 1996 Centennial Olympic Games showed a big increase in favorable perceptions of the Atlanta area and the region among 620 corporate decision makers. Nearly one-third of the executives surveyed said Atlanta's handling of the Olympics caused them to be more favorable toward the city; 24 percent said they're more inclined to favor expansion or relocation to Atlanta as a result. Atlanta led in a similar survey in 1993, but the poll suggests the city broadened its lead because of the Games.

"The Olympics come once in a lifetime," said Campbell. "We've seen a post-Olympic boom. We are moving forward."

After eight sometimes controversial years as Atlanta mayor, Campbell is now beginning to settle into life after elected office. Currently, he's a bit of a jack-of-all-trades, dabbling in a little of everything as he tries to find his place in the private sector after twenty years of public service.

"I've been doing radio commentary, working with African-American companies trying to acquire media companies, and doing speaking engagements."

Today, Campbell is recording his syndicated radio commentary in Atlanta's Colony Square.

"I've been doing social commentary for the past few months. My topics range from AIDS/HIV crisis to the racial issues dealing with the death penalty. These are national issues."

In between takes, he decided to sit down and talk about his tenure as mayor, and what he thinks needs to be done.

He's relaxed, with the look of a man relieved not to have the day-to-day stress of being mayor, yet still looking for something to challenge him. But his time away from the mayoral office has given him time for reflection.

"Every African-American mayor faces a special challenge that white mayors don't have," remarks Campbell. "Both of us are expected to be mayor of the whole city, but there is a special responsibility that black people have as a necessity for you to deal with their unique issues. As difficult as it is just being mayor, being a black mayor is just an incredible challenge.

"I think that there were some issues where I took the position that I thought was the correct one, and it just seemed to dig me in with one section of the city or the other. But that's just the challenge of being mayor. And when you throw in the racial dynamic, then it makes it even more difficult. We had an issue in the wealthiest black commercial and residential area, the Buckhead area of Atlanta. Many young blacks started frequenting the bars, nightclubs, and restaurants. And it became such that the white merchants and many in the white community wanted, I thought, wanted the black kids to not frequent the area. That was incomprehensible to me in the year two thousand. And I said so. I [told] the merchants that there were racial dynamics at play and everyone was going to be able to enjoy the area. And we weren't going to do anything special as it related to police issues. And I felt that it was the right thing to do, but you can imagine [the fallout]. There's now, in many white circles, this reactionary [response] that [says] when you talk about racial issues, you are somehow playing the race. And that's preposterous and insulting."

Representing a quarter of the Atlanta population, the political power of African Americans in Atlanta has been well documented and established over the past thirty years, which means that African Americans don't have to rely on protest marches and boycotts. African Americans in Atlanta have direct access to City Hall, and therefore are able to get things done politically.

"I think that it is fairly clear that the black community [of Atlanta] has elected the past four mayors, all of whom have been black," said Campbell. "And each of us has had their own political machines, but in reality, it's just old wine in a new bottle. It's just the same machine that keeps getting recycled for candidates that the black community believes represents their interest.

"I don't believe that you would ever have [a candidate not representing the black community] because of the political history. Also, there is so much inquiry about who you are and what you stand for [as a candidate]. There is no walk-up leadership in Atlanta. And I think that you should pay your dues. I have my feet in both worlds, in that I'm a child of the Civil Rights movement, yet I know the dynamics of getting the nitty-gritty things done."

One of those nitty-gritty things Campbell had to get done was defending Atlanta's affirmative-action policy.

As Atlanta's first black mayor in 1970, Maynard Jackson deftly wielded his new political power into a visible measure of real black economic and social power. Jackson pushed for affirmative action in all public works projects and city hiring. During his tenure the city expanded the airport, skyline, convention center, and freeway system, and built Underground Atlanta and several other major public projects. Jackson arm-twisted large corporations to get more African Americans hired and promoted. Jackson joined with the former mayor and Atlanta Chamber of Commerce to convincingly brag that Atlanta is "The City Too Busy To Hate." This social environment made Atlanta a welcoming billboard as a top destination for even larger conventions, and the number one choice for corporate branch divisions in the South. By 1980, Atlanta attracted several hundred Fortune 500 companies to locate branches in the city, when they could have easily chosen Richmond, Charlotte, Memphis, or Nashville instead. Mayor Jackson's push for affirmative action on major pubic works contracts also enabled HJ Russell Company to become the largest black builder in the nation and acquire the experience to bid successfully for major private projects.

Atlanta has grown to a metro area of more than 4.7 million people, while its contemporaries of the 1950s are just breaking 1 million residents and have an order of magnitude fewer jobs. It can be said that African Americans in Atlanta owe part of their status to aggressive affirmative action policies.

In 1999, the Southeastern Legal Foundation, a conservative group, sued Atlanta. They charged that Atlanta was maintaining a system of preferences for minority contractors, and subsequently that those laws discriminated against white males. Even though many cities had decided to modify or eliminate their affirmative action programs, Campbell responded by passionately defending the programs. This passion also resulted in a feud with the main Atlanta newspaper and its leading African-American editor, Cynthia Tucker.

"Here in Atlanta, tragically, the local newspaper, the *Atlanta Journal-Constitution,* is so antiblack, and they have managed to have a perfect formula. They have a black woman as editor, Cynthia Tucker, who I think by all black accounts is what we call the Clarence Thomas of journalism," Campbell says angrily. "Her mission is to be an apologist for whites."

Cynthia Tucker, the *Atlanta Journal-Constitution*'s only African-American editor, argued that it was time for African-American politicians to prepare for a time without affirmative action and move toward a time where racial politics is less emphasized.

Campbell said that he would "fight to the death" to defend the policy, and believed that racial politics were a continuing reality. Subsequently, Campbell and Tucker staged a well-publicized feud as both exchanged charges and countercharges about who had the best interest of the African-American community. The feud turned personal and ugly, and even national publications such as *Time* magazine felt compelled to comment. Even though he was victorious in keeping the programs and policy, it is evident that the vitriol is still fresh and bitter to Campbell. Likewise, Tucker continues to wield the pen and attack Campbell nearly a year after he left office.

"[Tucker] gives those whites that are right wing, conservative, or reactionary [a person to point to]. And they are then able to say that if she feels that way, then my views aren't racist," he continued with disdain. "She validates that belief. Because she is one of the few black women editors, she is trotted out across the country. But the point that I am making simply is that the black community is strong, powerful, and independent here. Notwithstanding the newspaper and their peculiar point of view, race is still an issue.

"[De-emphasizing race in politics] is a fanciful wish by conservative politicians and many blacks who are just as conservative in their views, and is neutered racially. I have yet to come across any conversation among black people where the issue of race didn't come up. [We talk about] race in the workplace, race when shopping, race in human interaction. Race is still very much a factor in the America of today. So to think that you could have a mayor that would fail to appreciate that racial issues are very important, I think that this would be a disservice to the city that he or she runs."

Campbell says that opponents of African-American political power are trying to find candidates who are, in the words of Campbell, "race-neutered." These "new school" candidates don't have the same Civil Rights resumes as the first and second generations of African-American politicians.

"In Newark [New Jersey], you recently had an election that had these issues played out, with Sharpe James sort of representing the old school, and Cory Booker, I guess, who represents the new school of well-bred, well-educated suburbanite blacks, who I think don't have the same kind of appreciations for the issues of race. I just feel very strongly that race continues to be an issue."

James won that election, but the margin was close, as Booker drew 46 percent of the vote. So Campbell is right that race does continue to be an issue, but if the James-Booker race is any indication, the future may be different.

"I think that this is a continuing challenge to strike a balance, and that your leadership encompasses the entire city, but also understand that there are unique needs within your city that require special attention. An educator once told me that 'In order to treat people equally, you have to treat people differently.' And of course, we as parents, we know this when we talk to our children. We may love them all the same, but the children have different needs. We treat them differently to accommodate their particular issues, and so it is with governing."

With this political philosophy, Campbell advocated for children and seniors, diversity in the workplace, race relations, and neighborhood development. In an effort to close the digital divide, during the last two years of his tenure as mayor, twelve Cyber Centers were opened in neighborhoods and one mobile center, Cyberbus, was unveiled. More than 7,000 individuals, including seniors, have been trained in the use of computers as of December 2001.

"The problem of poverty in the black world is a shame even in the black mecca. In Atlanta, we have more public housing per capita than anywhere in America. So on one hand, you have all of this incredible black achievement, and contiguous black poverty. It is a dream deferred. It continues to be a major problem.

"I happen to believe that we need to bridge the digital divide. If we can do that, and we set up computer centers in Atlanta where people can come in and use a computer, then we can connect with people in the islands and other places. On the other hand, technology has never been kind to black people. Technology has eliminated a lot of factory jobs and farming jobs. But

I hope that it has a lot of positive factors that can help us. [Technology could] connect us not only from New York to Los Angeles, but also from New Orleans to Kingston [Jamaica].

With Atlanta's rich legacy of black political power, what does the future bode? According to Campbell, the future is mixed. The Civil Rights movement helped establish the political foundation in Atlanta, yet the beneficiaries of that political power have been apathetic at best.

"There's a disconnect in the African-American community that we haven't been able to solve. And that's a challenge for us in the future. I don't think that there are any tutorials when it comes to [being an activist]. I think that you've got to understand that politics is vitally important to the African-American community. On the one hand, I'm incredibly proud of African-American college students. On the other hand, I'm profoundly disappointed in their lack of involvement in the political process. In the last election, only about five hundred out of fifteen thousand students in the Atlanta University Center [the historically black Morehouse College, Spelman College, Morris Brown University, and Clark Atlanta University] voted. I think that's deplorable.

"I don't know where the next movement is going to come from, because in spite of our considerable efforts, we couldn't get the involvement on important issues. [It didn't matter] if it was the AIDS crisis or trying to reclaim our communities—we just couldn't get it done.

"I believe that some of the glorification of materialism, and the lifestyle that is identified with popular culture today, means that some of our young people have been distracted from the spiritual issues, but it is a temporary thing. But we'll be back on point—I just hope that it is sooner than later."

So how do the generations connect? According to Campbell, dialogue between generations is the key.

"I actually think that younger African Americans should think about how they can keep in touch with older African Americans. But we've lost touch with some parts of our history. We need to have respect for our elders."

Often, ex-politicians float in a netherworld. They experience a deflation because their responsibilities are lessening, and they experience a noticeable loss of power. Their egos are not fulfilled, and they drift. Campbell seems to be somewhat clear on what his future holds.

"I think that because I've had this incredibly exciting career, I would like to work on things that affect our community. Whatever means that I can use to make a difference, I will use," he concludes. "Five years from now, I hope to be able to help improve our community. At the end of your life, people ought to be able to say that you really helped improve the community where you lived."

22

Go to West Africa, Young Woman

Accra, Ghana

Two roads diverged in the woods and I—I took the one less traveled by, and that has made all the difference.

—Robert Frost

The year was 1980, and the newly married Victoria Jefferson Cooper had just settled in Liberia with her Liberian husband. Little did she know that three months after she arrived in this new land, she was going to be smack-dab in the middle of a military coup. Army personnel under the leadership of Master Sergeant Samuel K. Doe staged a bloody coup, and President William Tolbert and many of his aides were killed.

"It was very traumatic," she recounted, somewhat understatedly. "I had visited Liberia in 1976 in order to see if it could be a place to live. But the military coup turned upside down everything that had been considered normal. The country by that time had been independent for 133 years, and there had never been a military coup or takeover in the country. So it was all very new [to the country] and it was very bloody."

Liberia owes its establishment to the American Colonization Society, founded in 1816 to resettle freed American slaves in Africa. Six years later, native rulers granted a tract of land on Cape Mesurado, at the mouth of the Saint Paul River, to U.S. representatives, and the first Americo-Liberians, led by Jehudi Ashmun, began the settlement. In 1894 an American agent for the society, Ralph Randolph Gurley, named the new colony Liberia, and the Cape Mesurado settlement, Monrovia.

Other separate settlements were established along the coast during the next twenty years. Soon, however, conflicts arose between the settlers and the society in the United States. By the time Joseph Jenkins Roberts became the first black governor in 1841, the decision had been made to give the colonists almost full control of the government. A constitution modeled on that of the United States was drawn up, and Liberia became an independent republic in July 1847. Roberts was its first president, serving until 1856. Britain recognized Liberia in 1848; France, in 1852; and the United States, in 1862.

"The family that I happened to marry into was Americo-Liberian, and their family had [immigrated from America] in 1827. This coup was probably directed at them more than others. With me having been a part of that group, and with a name like Cooper, which was considered the epitome of that group, it was very, very traumatic, having been in Africa to live for only three months."

Cooper left Liberia, without her new husband, under the protection of an American embassy convoy, but soon returned to Liberia to live and work.

"Liberians weren't allowed to leave, but I left a week after the coup," she said. "My husband wasn't able to leave because the military government hadn't yet determined who they were looking for, so no Liberians could travel at the time. I stayed away for about two months, and then I went back.

"I went back after two months because I was a newlywed. You do all types of foolish things then. I don't think I would do that again!" she laughs.

The Liberian civil war had horrific consequences on the Liberian people. Over 10 percent of the population, mostly innocent civilians, was murdered; about three quarters of the population became either refugees or displaced people.

"I adjusted to a lifestyle where you were very careful about rubbing soldiers the wrong way or saying the wrong thing. It was very erratic and irrational for quite a while. But I was working for an international organization, which gave me some quasi status, protection, and free movement. That was useful for both my family and me.

"I loved the country, and I loved what I was doing [in Liberia]. The government wasn't directly involved in a lot of things that were going on in our world. It was just an unfortunate surroundings and environment. But I had gone to undergraduate school with a lot of Liberians, so a lot of my friends were there. We kind of hunkered down and enjoyed our little world and ourselves. After a year or so, Liberia stabilized, and we kind of got used to it. And soldiers did what soldiers do. But because Liberia has no history of coups and they were not a socialist country, Liberia's always been a capitalist country, there was no confiscating of property or anything like that. They were just looking for individuals and [settling] personal grudges. So it didn't take too long for them to settle down and become stable. I ended up staying there for ten years."

Victoria Jefferson Cooper was born and raised in St. Louis. A Boston University graduate with a degree in finance and development economics, she went on to Columbia and received an MBA in International Business and Finance. All of this was in preparation for an eventual life as an expatriate. This was no accident, as Cooper knew from an early age that she wasn't going to live in America.

"When I was a junior in high school, I went on a tour of Europe. It was during that junior year in high school that I had made up in my mind that I was not going to live in America; I was not going to work in America. My place was going to be London because I really liked London. At that point, I said that there is a whole world out there, and America is so insular and focusing on itself. I had set that in my mind, so the idea of leaving in 1980 [for Liberia] was not something that was far-fetched. I just didn't know what the vehicle for getting out was going to be."

Even though Cooper found her vehicle out of America, in 1990 she found her way back to the land of her birth. This time, however, she was back in America with two children who had never lived full-time in America. Although she tried to adjust to the American lifestyle, she felt like a fish out of water in America. In some ways she had become more a part of the African continent than the North American one.

"And after three years of living in America, I just realized that I can't stand America. I had started my own firm in America that was doing very well. [America] was too myopic. Maybe it was just St. Louis," she laughed.

"I had bought a house in suburbia and thought that I could do that. After two years, I decided to take the kids to London on vacation for a few weeks, and when I got back from London, I knew that I couldn't stay there [in St. Louis]. Because I knew that my world was larger than that. That's what had got me out of the U.S. for the first time."

So it was back to Africa for Cooper, but this time she chose Ghana.

"When I was in Liberia, I was working for Pricewaterhouse in consulting. The partner there at the time was from Ghana, and I started talking to him [about a job]. And when he made me the right offer, I said okay. That was in May of 1993. I came out to Ghana for three months to come and see how it was."

But even though she had lived through a devastating coup and civil war in Liberia, she was even more leery of living in Ghana. Her previous impression of the country was not a good one.

"The last time I was there was in 1987, and Ghana was a dirt-poor basket case at that point, and you had to bring everything with you when you traveled there," she recalled. "You had to bring your toilet paper, your food, your everything. And when he said come on out, I said what do I need to bring? He said, 'Nothing, Ghana's great!'

"I said to myself that I'll come out for three months and if it doesn't work out, I'll come back and just do fly-in consulting. But when I got here, it had changed considerably. The donor-funded consulting market was booming, and that was my sector. And I said okay, I can do this, and in August of 1993, I went back and got my kids and came on out.

"One thing you don't do when you are leaving America is go without a job, unless you know how you are going to manage [without one]," Cooper advised. "I've seen too many people do it. They have sold the car, the farm, the curtains, and everything, and they don't know that they need a work permit. They didn't know that you'll have to pay your house rent one year in advance. But they land [in Africa] sight unseen. Many come with glasses so rosy that that can't see past the glass. I have met more than my share of starry-eyed dreamers.

"I'm a realist, and I will put it on the line and say that if this experiment doesn't work, then [I need to] go home. Because at home you have a support system and here you don't have anything. What you need to do is plan how you need to come."

So just in case things didn't work out in Ghana, Cooper didn't sell her house. She left it with all of the furniture intact, and she left her "former husband in St. Louis" there also, as she laughingly says.

Ghana, and West Africa in general, have proved to be the true home for Cooper. She has since left Pricewaterhouse to form her own consulting company, and now advises the Ghanaian government on such items such as how best to make the Ghanaian bureaucracy more efficient. Her competition comes from Europe and America, but she feels that she has one particular advantage over them.

"Because I'm private sector, I'm involved in a lot of things. I do a lot of things that are highly visible. I'm the president of the African American Association and the American Chamber of Commerce. My work puts me at the minister level of government, and I consult at that level. I recognize that there is a different sense to what I do as an African American going into this advisory, than my competitors, who may be from Britain, or from France, or from wherever. For [those businesspeople], it's only business. There is no investment. I say [to the Ghanaian government], 'Look, I am working national reforms into government because I have a vested interest; I live here. I want my quality of life to improve, too. And so if I can give you quality advice, and help you can make quality decisions based on experience outside of Ghana and outside of Africa, then it will be better for all of us.' "

That includes Cooper's two daughters. Even though the two spent time in America, they both consider West Africa to be truly home.

"My daughters are much more Ghanaian than anything because they didn't spend much time in Liberia or America. This is home to them. My daughter is coming back to Ghana [from the University of Missouri] for Christmas. The idea of us going to America [for Christmas] is completely out because she says that 'All of my friends are here.' "

Cooper's challenge when her daughters were growing up was to get them to embrace their African-American heritage as well as their West African side. Growing up in Liberia and Ghana meant that they had close contact with their African relatives, but understanding their mother's African-American culture required a little more effort. The mingling of the two heritages means that they look at the world a little differently from the average African American or African.

"I think that what they add, as what they now call third-culture kids, is a new global thinking. This new global thinking comes from their separate-culture parents, and their own way of thinking and defining what they should look like. And they bring to wherever they go a fresh thought. It's clear when I see them with their [African-American] cousins that they bring something new into that dynamic, which opens the cousins up to new and different ideas that they may have never had access to or may never have considered."

That perspective was created through a conscious effort by Cooper to have her daughters experience life in America by visiting as often as possible.

"My oldest daughter was born in 1982, and the other one was born in 1985. It was always important for me to let them know, by living in America, about my African-American culture. Because I knew that they would be living outside of my culture for most of their lives, I made a very conscious decision when my oldest daughter was two years old, to send them away [to

America] for the summer. So she did what I did in the summers. When I was growing up, I left St. Louis and went to my grandmother's in Mississippi. And so my children did the same thing.

"Now they have a sense of what it is like to be an African American. It is not a theory thing [with them]. I made a conscious effort to give them as much of my African-American cultural experience as possible. At the same time, their exposure is very different, and they still require some adjustments when they go back to America. But they know what it's like to live in America as an African American. They know what an African-American family is like, and what the family structure is like. They know the importance of family as it relates to African Americans. And they know what it means within an African structure because their father is African. But they recognize the differences.

"What they've told me is that they realize how different the two families are. I'm from a close-knit Baptist family. Now, African families have large extended families and obviously we are familiar with that. The way the two families interact is different. They see my family in the U.S. as being very close-knit and tight, all over the place, but we have a connection. They see their Liberian and their Ghanaian families as different. The relationship between siblings is different. Now, I don't understand what they are seeing, because my experience is different than theirs, but they don't see the same type of closeness. One of the other differences is the relationship with children who are not a part of the marriage. In this environment, the children are accepted. In the African-American community, they better not show up! And these are life lessons that they have to reconcile in one's own mind, not as to being right or wrong, but what do I think is more appropriate for me in my life when I become an adult and make my own decisions? How do I handle these situations?"

Cooper's oldest daughter, Monique, is a broadcast journalism student at the University of Missouri and finds it ironic that African Americans who have never lived in Africa, think that she is not "African" enough. Somehow, she doesn't fit the vision of an African person that they have in their minds.

"African Americans will often tell my daughter Monique that she isn't Afrocentric enough," laughs Cooper. "And she says that 'I am me. I'm Afrocentric because my father is from Africa. Now I have lived there, so I know what it is like. So when you see me, you are seeing the epitome of Afrocentric. Now as for you, I don't know.'

"I think that in the evolution of her three years in college that she realizes that she is more African than American. And so she finds herself migrating to the African and International students instead of the African-American students, because they understand her. She says that she guesses that her paradigm is African, even though she has been immersed in the African-American community."

So how does an African American, even one who has lived on the continent for over twenty years, view herself within the context of being of African heritage?

"The difficulty is that many of the African Americans that come here are not coming prepared," reflected Cooper. "You see, many Ghanaians don't understand us as a people. They see us coming by the hundreds of thousands on a pilgrimage to the castles and forts. But they don't have an idea of what our experience in America was about. And [they don't know] why we really come. They see it as tourism and we see it as a pilgrimage. There is a significant difference in the two. They see television and they see poverty and deprivation and gang culture and rap as being African-American.

"And so when we try to share with them the breadth of our culture, the breadth of our experience, when we share with them our literary greats, our musical greats, politicians, civil rights, what happened as a people, as a very rich African-American culture with its own validity, they're surprised.

"My approach to my African experience, and my approach to all of my international experience is that when I arrive in this place, this is what I see, this is the hand that I've been dealt, and this is who I am. And it is as valid as anybody else's experience. So for me to come here and throw away the struggle of my people in America, I'm not going to do it. My people went through the passage and we survived. We are the survivors. I'm not going to fail their struggle, their blood, and their experience in order to build America, and then come to Ghana and say, 'You know, in America, that was my slave name.' I say exactly, Jefferson is my slave name because we grew out of slavery, and that is a valid experience. And we are who we are because of that. So when I come to the table in Ghana, I'm coming to the table with something that is valid. You are going to deal with me as an African American, and I respect the fact that my ancestral culture is from here. That's what makes me comfortable here."

23

Citizens of the World

Accra, Ghana

It is good to have an end to journey toward, but it is the journey that matters in the end.

—Ursula K. LeGuin

Technically, Tamice Parnell is not supposed to enter the Golden Tulip Hotel in Accra. For the wife of American Foreign Service officer Isaiah Parnell, the Golden Tulip is off limits to official American business because Libyan business interests own the Golden Tulip, and America has had an embargo against Libya for nearly twenty years.

"I can actually come to the hotel, but I can't buy anything," laughs Parnell as she sits down in the Golden Tulip's restaurant. "So I better not purchase a Coca-Cola!"

For the record, she doesn't purchase anything. Hostile hotels, different cultures, new residences: all are obstacles that Parnell is used to dealing with as a veteran Foreign Service member. Her husband initiated this unusual life soon after they got married.

"When we first met, I was working in Colorado Springs and he had been in ROTC in college and was fulfilling his three-year commitment to the army," she recalls. "He was a first lieutenant, and he took the Foreign Service exam three months into our marriage. He passed and went through a long process. Almost exactly one year after we got married, he was appointed a foreign service officer. He signed up, and I stayed in Colorado Springs because I was in contract with my job. He went to Washington and then I finally joined him for language training; we learned Spanish, and we moved to Mexico almost two years after being married.

"We've been out of the U.S. for about seventeen years. We've got four girls, none of whom have ever lived in the United States. We've spent most of our time in Latin America. Our first tour was in Mexico, and our second tour was in Paraguay. We spent a couple of years there. Our third tour was in West Africa, in Cote d'Ivoire. Our next tour was back in Mexico, and then Panama, and now Ghana."

The diplomatic lifestyle can be uprooting, to say the least, but they are a level above the average military family. Private schools and support from the American government comes in abundance, and when they are stationed in a country they can live a life sequestered from the harshness of Third World life. There is a community within a community, since members of the Foreign Service tend to work with each other.

"I love the service, and it was easy for us to adjust because both of us come from army families. So we're both accustomed to traveling—not quite the same way as we do in the Foreign Service, but I'd say that we live in a bit of an insular manner. Not as much so as the military do. We don't live on posts. We don't have a PX and commissary. We do actually live out in the community, although the embassy provides all of the support that we need. And so we probably get to meet and get to know the people of the countries better than if we were in the military. And it's great. We've seen all kinds of lifestyles, learned a couple of languages, and it's been invaluable for our kids. They speak languages as we go, and proceed to forget them as we leave, but it's in their brains somewhere," she laughs.

Ghana has been the second stint in West Africa for the Parnells, and their time in Cote d'Ivoire gave them a perspective of what to expect in West Africa. Unlike African Americans who are making their first visit to Africa, they didn't expect a "welcome home" mat from the Ghanaians when they landed.

"I think that all African Americans go through a period when they visit African countries or come to live in African countries—that whole sense of 'we've come home' and that sense of 'we're connected,' and Ghanaians, even though Ghanaians are nice, friendly, and welcoming people, don't have that same sense of connection for us that we have for them.

"Since this is our second time in this part of Africa, nothing surprised us when we arrived here," she continued. "But during our first tour of Africa, and going to Abidjan, we thought, now, this is the real foreign service, because we thought, this is the first place where we've arrived, and things really do look different from the way we are used to. All of the women wore the beautiful African fabric with the baskets on their heads. The men had the symbols of their villages burned into their cheeks. And we thought, 'Wow, this is neat.' "

On the second trip to Africa, Parnell and her family arrived with no expectations.

"So as far as preconceived notions [about Ghana], I don't think that we had any. The reason we are doing this is because we like meeting different cultures, and I don't think that we came with any expectations that it should be this way or that way. I think the thing that struck us the most was the weather. It is hot."

Parnell has been able to use the world travel to educate her four girls about the world and different peoples. In one way, they are exposed to different cultures, but in another way, the diplomatic life doesn't expose the children to their own culture, life in the United States, or particularly the life of African Americans. Like all international families, Parnell has the difficult task of describing the importance of race to her children, and this sometimes proves to be a difficult concept to explain. Sometimes they just don't get a concept that they have not experienced, and Parnell doesn't know if that is a good thing.

"They are kind of sheltered by the way we live, and that can be good and bad. [On one hand] they're not exposed to a lot of negative things that a lot of African-American kids grow up with in the United States. And so, there are not those kinds of distractions for them.

"They've been able to concentrate on school, so they are

more academic than may have been in the United States. The international schools have been very good, and the students that graduate from them have done well in terms of where they go to college. The schools that they attend are closed campuses, so they can't go on and off campus. And they are all small schools, from kindergarten through 12th grade. So people watch out for each other. If your kid is acting up, then you know that you'll get a call from the teacher. It's just kind of being in a smaller community within a larger community. It's kind of easier to keep an eye on them."

Parnell shifts a bit in her seat. Her face becomes a bit serious as she considers the negative side of that experience.

"On the other side, they're naive," she continues. "They're naive about race and issues dealing with African Americans in the United States. They are naive about our past, our history, or ancestors. I mean, they have an identity as an African American, but you know that the whole sense of racism, they have no idea.

"We have one child where this is an issue. We'll say something about an issue that, to us, clearly indicates a racial perspective, and then her response is always, 'How about if other people felt the way that you do?' or 'Why is it justified when you say something like that, and when a white person says something like that, they're racist?' Our answer is always that our history is different. Our perspective is different. I think that her perspective is more international than African-American.

"When we bring up an issue and we try to attribute it to race—and a lot of it is—they'll say, 'Oh, Mom, you're just being racist!' And frankly, these are some of the things, maybe not to this degree, that I said to my parents when I was growing up. But it's just the fact that I don't think that they have a real basis to know that prejudice and racism exist."

Educated to live in an idyllic, color-blind society, the girls find race to be a minor part of who they are, mainly because, as international citizens, apparently they have not had a reference point, so they can't recognize its significance in their everyday lives.

"We talk to them about things, and it is not a case of us trying to de-emphasize race. We tell them about it, but it's just not in their frame of reference. And what we expect will happen is that when they begin to go to school in the United States, they'll understand things a little better, and then they'll say, 'Oh, that's what Dad was talking about! Now I get it!' "

Frequent visits to the United States does what day-to-day experience cannot, but even with all of the advantages of seeing the world, Parnell admits that extended family ties are difficult to maintain while living around the world. These are sacrifices that come with the Foreign Service.

"It's really tough on the kids, knowing that they haven't established the types of bonds with their grandparents and the extended family that we as parents would like to see," she says. "So that's probably the most painful thing. But we do go back every summer, and we do spend a good amount of time with my husband's family and my family. And my kids are crazy about them, and they love going there, but nothing beats the proximity.

"[Their] cousins think that my children are interesting," Parnell laughs. "One of the things that a lot of Foreign Service kids run into is that they go back to the States and they talk about the experiences they've had and the things that they've seen, just because it's the way that they have lived. Just like American kids spending the weekend going to the mall, and the Foreign Service kids talk about going on safari. But it sounds like they're bragging. So a lot of times, you see people kind of turn them off. And we get to a point where we tell the girls to turn it down because I know that you're not bragging, but that's how it's perceived."

Either way, Parnell's life consists of maintaining roots in America, while helping her family adjust to new cultures and surroundings. When you've lived out of the United States for the past seventeen years, homesickness is relative to where you previously felt home was.

"Every time we get to a new post, my husband wants to go back to the previous one," Parnell laughs. "And when I arrive somewhere, I'm like, 'Wow,' and I want to see where we are and see what's new here. And so, I must say that the first time that I had culture shock was maybe here. [Ghana] didn't look quite like I thought it would. I expected things to look like things in Cote d'Ivoire, and they don't.

"Ten years ago, when we were in Abidjan, they were at the height of their economic growth. They were stable and they were kind of the "Pearl of West Africa." And now they are going through all kinds of civil strife. And so here, for an undeveloped country, [Ghana] seems to be pretty developed. Many of the streets, but not all of them, are paved, and many of the houses are relatively new. From the perspective of an American that has never been out of the States before, it wouldn't look like that, but if you've been to different countries, you notice it."

Still, even with all of their Third World experience, Ghana did provide some different living conditions. Whereas some previous stops were modern enough to compare to living conditions in the United States, some things about Ghana were a shock to Parnell.

"We were in Panama, which we thought was like living in the United States," says Parnell. "And then my parents came down and they said this is different, because they noticed all of the things that weren't like the United States."

But although Parnell was used to West Africa, Ghana did provide a little bit of a culture shock. And her initial impressions made her think that Ghana wouldn't be as developed as the other countries where she had been stationed. It had to do with a few more animals in the street than she was used to.

"When they took us to our house and they drove down our street, this was the first time that we had goats and chickens on our street," she laughs. "Now, we are used to seeing goats and chickens, but not on our street! And the water didn't work our first weekend; in fact, I just left the house without water. That's just one of the things that you get used to. So I just felt that it was going to be a lot more difficult to live here than it has actually been. We went to the grocery store for the first time, and again, even though we have lived in Third World countries, the grocery stores have been relatively good. They were big, and the stores here are not bad, but it's not like shopping at Giant. And so that takes a little getting used to."

But like most African Americans living in Africa, Parnell and her family have been able to see the good that Africa, and Ghana in particular, has to offer. It goes beyond the material, and it lies in the spirit of the culture and the people.

"There is a mentality here that is wonderful," she remarks. "I think that most people have their priorities in the right place, in terms of family and church. And that's probably because so much is not available here. Just kind of a basic niceness, for lack of a better word, is probably here more than anywhere we've been. I mean, people are so kind, nice, and polite. We talk about our daughter reaching dating age, and we talk about how glad we are to be here right now. I mean, the boys call and say, 'Hello, Mrs. Parnell, may I speak to Morgan, please?' and it is nice for our kids to see the type of manners here.

"Most of those who I know [African Americans] have lived here three or four years. I think that they have the same types of gripes that everyone else has, but because most of the people I know are married to Ghanaians, they live very much the Ghanaian lifestyle. They just learn to accept that this is the culture, a little more than people like us, who are here now, and we'll be gone in a couple of years. I perceive that many say that we've made this choice, and we feel that this is a better environment for our kids than living in New York City, so we're going to enjoy the good part of it."

As with all Foreign Service assignments, the Ghanaian post will soon come to an end. The girls are getting older, and a Foreign Service diplomat tends to have at least one tour within the United States every so often. The Parnells are overdue for this United States tour. So where does the Parnell family go from here?

"We're at a pivotal point right now," Parnell says. "We think that probably we won't tour again in Africa, and not because we don't like Africa. It is probably one of our best tours so far. But it's that parent thing. So we talk back and forth about going back to Washington, because our oldest will be going to college. If we can get a tour that is relatively close to the states, such as Canada or Mexico, then I think that's what we'll take."

But Africa and Ghana will always be remembered by the Parnells as the one Foreign Service tour that her family just had to take. Because with this tour of Africa, Parnell knew that her family, in particular her children, would benefit from living in Africa long after they left.

"We particularly came back to Africa for our kids," says Parnell. "We wanted them to see the same things that we have seen coming here. That [Africa] has a great culture. People ask us all of the time, why do you keep going to Africa, and why don't you go to Paris or London? Now, those are interesting parts of the world, and both my husband and I lived in Germany, but this is also an interesting culture, and I don't think that people know that. We wanted our kids to know that there is the Parthenon in Greece, and you've got the ruins in Rome, but you've got the ancient kingdoms in Ghana. And you've got great architecture in Cote d'Ivoire. And that this is also very interesting and this is where we come from, so we need to be proud of what this continent has to offer. Now, Africa has some things to work through, but it's still a wonderful place."

Taking a sip of her free glass of water, Parnell looks out the window and thinks about her experience in Africa and what others think of a land they may never have seen beyond television and the movies.

"I would like for people to spread the word that Africa is not huts out in the jungle or [people] swinging through trees," she says. "Now, there are huts and villages, but there are cities too. And we do have electricity and running water. It may not work all of the time, but it's there! And people are educated and sophisticated, and it's very different from what I think most people perceive."

24

Walking in the Spirit

Outside Accra, Ghana

The natural yearning to meet the Lord is innate in every human being, although most people seek Him outwardly, wherever His name is represented. If a man is disappointed in his search, again he turns to seek elsewhere, and so his life becomes a series of wasted efforts. As a child, man just plays. Then he goes on to indulge in all the sensual pleasures and the intellectual pursuits. Finally he begins to realize that there is no real happiness or lasting peace in all this and starts searching for something else. If his yearning is strong enough, and his search sincere, established within him, then the Lord Himself knows this and makes arrangements for the seeker to find someone to help him—someone who has already realized the Lord, someone who may be called by any name you wish, but is in fact a guru.

—Param Sant Kirpal Singh Ji Maharaj

The location could be rural Georgia, but instead it is about ten miles from the heart of Accra. The asphalt highway turns into a red dirt road, becoming as uneven and full of potholes as the highway had been level and smooth. Soon, the complex comes into view.

To the right is a silver Quonset building, and straight ahead is a home that, again, would look right at home in the American South. Surrounding the home is a meticulously maintained garden of vegetables and flowers. The light scent of jasmines wafts through the air.

It's hot and humid outside, but in the cool foyer, Ronald Gordon sits in a wheelchair, the result of an automobile crash in 1968. His breathing is somewhat labored, he tires easily, and therefore he sleeps a lot during the day. It is not an easy life. But in spite of this disability, or maybe because of it, it is very easy to see that he is a determined man. Gordon came to Ghana to find his own peace, his own sense of self, and you get a feeling that, damn it, no one is going to stop him, not even his family.

"My family has been here to Ghana, and I think their reaction to our moving here was, 'What has my insane brother done now?'" He laughs.

"[I know] some places where we grew up in the Deep South, and Ghana is a few steps up," he continues. "When we were kids, America was not nearly as cosmetic as it is today. You went to restaurants in those days because you wanted food. It didn't matter that all of the tables didn't match. But in America today, everything looks nice and smells nice. And that's not always the case here in Ghana."

A man of measured words, Gordon has lived an extraordinary life. He has been a physicist, worked in the aerospace industry, received a doctorate and taught at the University of Virginia, and been a part of United States military intelligence. He capped his professional career as a political appointee for the state of Virginia. Then, upon retirement, he began searching the world for a place to ultimately settle.

"We came out here first in 1994," he recalls. "It seemed like a pleasant place to come. I was surprised that the weather was as reasonable as it was, because Ghana was not on my short list of places to retire. Over the years, there were places that came and dropped off the list of places to retire. Ghana sort of evolved over time. In addition to Ghana, we thought about retiring in Morocco and Ecuador. But some of the advantages of coming to Ghana were that we knew some people in Ghana, and plus it was English-speaking. It seemed like a place where we could be comfortable. So we came."

The "we" includes his wife, Anne, who delightfully provides an animated yin to Gordon's subtler yang. She finishes his sentences, and her laughter echoes throughout the house.

"I was not uncomfortable moving to Ghana, because it seemed like a natural transition," says Gordon. "Since so many people we see on the streets look like people that we have known all of our lives. That, of course, has gotten me into some difficulty. When you live here a while, you can forget that there are some cultural differences. I always hope that I don't put my foot in my mouth. But what I say to my wife, very often we find ourselves in a situation where I have to apologize for not understanding Ghanaian culture. Then I told my wife that, heck, I'm an American, and I'm a guest here. People should understand my culture!" He laughs and sits up in his chair.

"Very often, I don't know the difference between our cultures; it's only after I've put my foot in my mouth I am made aware! And so sometimes it gets to that point, but now I don't bother [worrying about it]. I'm a very direct person, and I have difficulty working around to the point."

It could be argued that the clarity and directness that lead Gordon's life stem from his spirituality. He follows the Indian spiritual philosophy called "Ruhani Satsang."

Ruhani Satsang means literally "spiritual gathering" with no denominational or sectarian connotations of any kind. All persons, even though professing different faiths and religious beliefs, can be taught the principles of spirituality and encouraged to practice spiritual disciplines, in order to gain salvation and peace here and in the beyond.

"I am Episcopalian and I'm on a spiritual path that may be followed by those of any religion. If you look at the core teaching of the spiritual teachers on which most religions are based, they are the same. These spiritual teachers, whether Jesus, Buddha, Nanak, etc., all come from time to time to refresh these teachings. The world is never without one or more. Some are well known; some are not. Unfortunately, many of those who follow them after they leave the world establish these religions, and as the years go by, only the rituals seem important.

"Those who are hungry for more, search, often without knowing it, for the true teacher who can lead them to God and teach them the disciplines they should follow to get there. Our path is a worldwide congregation of these people, who are from many religions. Some are ministers and priests. Some are in jail. Some are high and others are low. I was initiated in 1964 by Sant Kirpal Singh, a well-known spiritual master.

Sant Kirpal Singh Ji, an Indian spiritual leader, is one of the more important religious figures of the twentieth century. Through his ability to make the spiritual teachings easily understood by people in the West, Sant Kirpal Singh Ji presented spirituality as a science; he showed that spirtuality could be practiced as an experiment within the laboratory of human body.

He undertook three world tours and toured India extensively, spreading the teachings of Science of Spirituality. He founded Sawan Ashram in Delhi, where aspirants from around the globe met to practice the teachings of Science of Spirituality.

Besides teaching individuals the art of meditation, Sant Kirpal Singh Ji also devoted himself to promoting human unity and world peace. In 1956 he gave the inaugural address to the Ninth General Session of UNESCO, held in New Delhi, India. His speech, "World Peace in the Atomic Age," is a road map for obtaining and maintaining world peace. That talk is a timeless vignette whose message is still relevant today. He taught that world peace could be attained when we recognize all creation as one family of God. During his life, religious leaders would even sit together on the same platform. His ability to unite people of different religions based on the commonality of all faiths resulted in his unanimous election as president of the World Fellowship of Religions Conferences held in 1957, 1960, 1965, and 1970. These conferences brought heads of different religions together on a common platform to understand each other in a spirit of love and respect.

As a scholar in comparative yoga as well, Sant Kirpal Singh Ji was one of the world's foremost authorities in the different yogic systems, and helped to guide people toward the one best suited to the goal they wished to reach. Heads of different religious and yoga groups visited him to obtain knowledge and guidance on spiritual subjects.

In 1969 he established Manav Kendra, a center to help people develop physically, mentally, and spiritually while practicing service to humanity and the environment.

In 1974, Sant Kirpal Singh Ji decided to hold a conference aimed at uniting people, not only at the level of religion, but at the level of their common humanity. Thus, in February 1974 he convened in Delhi the first Unity of Man Conference (now called the Human Unity Conference). Here, theists as well as atheists sat together as one family of God. He taught that God is one, though called by different names in different countries and religions. It was his lifelong work to help bring down the barriers that separate people and to unite them as one common family.

His books gained popularity and inspired people to develop spiritually. Among a score of books he has written are *Crown of Life: A study in Yoga; Prayer: Its Nature and Technique;* and *Naam or Word,* all of which bring out the underlying similarities in the different religions.

Numerous religious, civic, and social heads recognized his work. In 1964 Sant Kirpal Singh Ji was the first non-Christian to be honored with the Order of St. John of Jerusalem, Knights of Malta. On his tours he met with Pope Paul VI in Rome. In this meeting they exchanged views on world peace. He also received honorary welcomes from the grand duke of Oldenburg, the archbishop of the Roman Catholic Church, Prime Minister Lemass of Ireland, President de Valera of Ireland, and the governor of Massachusetts. In Colombia, he addressed the Council of Cali.

In India, many leaders came to Sant Kirpal Singh Ji to share ideas on bringing about peace and human unity. Sant Kirpal Singh Ji met with Jawaharlal Nehru and Lal Bahadur Shastri, who were the first and second Prime Ministers of India, and Dr. Rajendra Prasad, Dr. S. Radhakrishnan, and Dr. Zakir Hussain, the first, second, and third Presidents of India, respectively. He also met with Indira Gandhi on several occasions. In 1974, Sant Kirpal Singh Ji addressed the Indian Parliament, giving them his message of peace and hope for the future of humanity.

Today, Sant Kirpal Singh Ji is recognized all over the world as the father of the Human Unity Conferences, and people continue to honor him for laying the groundwork for peace and unity.

"When I met my master, he seemed to awaken something in me that made me feel that he truly represented something that I was hungry for."

In fact, their Ghanaian home is located right next to an ashram.

"We chose to live next to an ashram because it seemed the thing we should do. Like many things in our lives, if we look at the event that led to many life-changing experiences, it seemed that something else other than our reason and intellect led us here.

"An ashram is a spiritual center and sort of refuge for those people whose souls are hungry," Gordon explains. "This property over here was just the beginning of something that has evolved into an ashram. It is not communal in the fact that we live in the ashram; in fact, that is discouraged. But many people want to live around the ashram. We were told in 1994 that our home was going to be next to the ashram, and that was attractive. And since we are retired, it allows us to concentrate on our spiritual life.

"There was a group of those that followed this path who were already here, about 400 people. A spiritual master was here in 1980, 1989, and 1994. My wife, who was initiated in 1989, and I came here in 1994 to be with the master at that time, Sant Ajaib Singh, the successor of Kirpal Singh. The ashram had started being built before 1994, but it was going slowly."

Gordon looks at his hands and remarks pensively, "My spiritual life here in Ghana is probably the most important aspect of life here for me. Sometimes, from when you start your professional life until you get to the end of your life, there are many twists and turns. And often, you lose touch with who you really are. And when you are no longer required to earn a living or put bread on the table, you find that you want to go back to the beginning and examine who you are and where you are going, and how you can best spend your last days."

"Some of our children like a statement that I passed to them: 'If you knew that you were going to die tomorrow, how would you spend today?' So when you are not at that point where you have to be out earning a living, you like to reexamine what your real values are. And I think that we are at that stage."

Gordon is ambivalent about African Americans who are interested in coming to Africa, and one gets the idea that he is pretty ambivalent about being labeled African American, African, or anything but as a spiritual human being.

"I would probably say nothing to African Americans that are coming to Africa for the first time. It's difficult when this issue of race or culture came to mind. I think that we spend an overly great amount of time talking about these things. I'm too old for tutorials, especially for free tutorials. I'm at a stage in my life where I have my direction, and I don't have to explain or account to anyone. And the fact that we are here, whether it is of concern to you or not, is not a concern to me. It doesn't matter."

Before leaving to go to the garden, he adds one final statement: "The only thing that I miss about America is the stress," he laughs.

25

Never Felt So Loved

Accra, Ghana

Knowledge is of two kinds. We know a subect ourselves, or we know where we can find information upon it.

—Samuel Johnson

The sun is directly overhead as we enter the Art Centre. Located next to the beautiful Kwame Nkrumah memorial, the Art Centre is the place in Accra for Ghanaian arts and crafts. There you will find mud cloths, Ghanaian stools, Ashanti masks, and other crafts. Some are created in villages from throughout Ghana, while artisans make others on site. Since most vendors carry the same items, there is intense competition among shop owners for customers. And who are the most treasured customers? The African Americans looking to purchase items reflecting their African heritage are the most cherished. These tourists bring valuable dollars into the Ghanaian economy in general and the Art Centre in particular.

Natalie Gill, an exchange student from Wellesley College in Massachusetts, enters the Art Centre, and the hard sell from the vendors begins immediately. Even though she, like other African Americans, could pass for Ghanaian, Ghanaians recognize that she is an African American.

"Sister, sister, please come over here and take a look at my cloth," says one young Ghanaian man.

"Obruni!"

"Excuse me . . ."

"Hello . . ."

It seems as though hundreds of voices are directed at Natalie, but her eyes never stray from her path. She walks with a purpose. She is going to one particular shop in the Art Centre, and these invitations are not going to distract her. After navigating a quick left, right, and another left, she reaches her destination.

"How much for this chair?" she asks, pointing to an intricately carved chair. The dark mahogany furniture is an exquisite example of Ghanaian wood craftsmanship found throughout the Art Centre.

The shopkeeper, who has bargained with Natalie before, eyes the chair and her.

"Three hundred thousand cedi," he responds. At an exchange rate of 7,200 Ghanaian cedi to the dollar, that makes this piece forty-one dollars. While certainly a reasonable price, this price is the "American" price. Both the shopkeeper and Natalie know that this price is nowhere close to the final price.

"No!" Natalie instantly replies. And the haggling begins.

"What do you offer?"

"Fifty thousand cedi," says Natalie, stating an equally ridiculous low price for the piece.

"Oh no, I couldn't accept that," he replies.

They haggle back and forth, until they reach the agreed-upon price of 150,000 cedi. The shopkeeper meticulously wraps the chair, and Natalie walks off, satisfied.

"A lot of African Americans come here and pay whatever price is quoted first," Natalie explains as she moves through the marketplace.

"But the fun is to haggle. The shop owner wants to give you a fair price for the art, and I want to bargain shop," she continues.

"One conflict you have when you come to Ghana is that you don't want to exploit the people. For example, there are people who come on campus, sometimes young kids, but other times they are grown men, and they will do your [house] work for you.

They don't have money and this is their way of getting money. So you can't help but feel bad about them doing things for you, but you should feel worse if you don't use them, because sometimes they are begging you for work so that they can get some money. Even Ghanaians tell me to not feel bad.

Natalie has been in Ghana for four months, and in two months she'll be heading back to the United States. During her time in Ghana, she has fallen in love with this country, the region of West Africa, and African culture in general. She's traveled throughout Benin, Togo, and Nigeria and has stories about each one.

"The [national] borders in Africa were not created by Africans. European colonialists drew these borders, and it causes Africans to go through hell all of the time. The borders cut through tribe lines, so you'll see some Ghanaians that speak the same language as tribe members in Togo. It's really frustrating because people who are related can live in two or three different countries."

Her most eye-opening experience in Africa came when she visited Lagos, Nigeria. In a mixture of pathos and humor, she recalls her trip to the African city with the highest population.

"In Nigeria, I only stayed for three days, but Lagos is tough. It's crowded, like New York City times twenty-five thousand!" she laughs. "There are so many people in such a little space. Lagos is an island, and 14 million people are living right on top of one another. Every car ride in Lagos makes you think that you are at the point of self-destruction; there are so many close calls. And you add to the automobile traffic people riding on scooters. I've heard scooter stories of people having their arms and legs amputated because they are hit.

"There are so many people in Nigeria that a young man can go to a university and get a degree and then can't find a job. So he may have to drive these scooters to make a living. So he's doing this to only make some money.

"But Nigeria, of course, makes a great deal of money from oil because it has one of the largest reserves of oil in the world. But a Nigerian brother or sister can live ten meters away from an oil well and never see any profit. They are living in complete poverty. There are corrupt politicians, and the Americans and the Europeans that come in are getting all of this wealth.

"And then there are the police. If you ever want to know the worst extent to which bribery can occur, go to Nigeria. A Nigerian policeman will have no problem asking for your money. Between the Nigeria-Benin border and Lagos, a thirty-minute ride, we were stopped twenty-two times. At some of the stops, the police would ask us, 'Oh, what are you doing here? Okay, give me money and you can go.' They just want some naira, the Nigerian currency. At some stops, you could tell the police, 'Oh, we're just looking for water,' or 'We're just students who are traveling,' and they would tell you to go ahead."

There was one incident that left a big impression on Natalie's consciousness and signified how vulnerable young African children are when it comes to surviving poverty.

"I saw a little Nigerian boy fall into a gutter, and it was one of the most devastating parts of my trip. He was a small, small boy, and he almost went under. You know gutters. They are filled with dung, piss, and are completely unsanitary. But even with all of this, the Nigerians that I met in Lagos were really cool people."

These experiences fit right into the reasons that Natalie decided to come to Africa. She is trying to find the truth of Africa and how it fits her vision of herself as an African American in this world.

"I've wanted to come to Africa all of my life, especially when I realized how powerful African history is and how powerful it is to be a black person. I always wanted to discover my roots and come to where it all began, and I believe that this is where it all began," she said. "One of the biggest reasons for coming here was to find out the truth. Often in America, you get filtered media and filtered newspapers. And the only picture you see on television about Africa is the negative portrayal, the poverty and the crime. But you never see the beautiful things that I've seen while I've been here.

"I tried not to come [to Africa] with many assumptions and

preconceived notions. But I always thought of Africa as a place of tradition. It is a place of strong values and strong people. A lot of people would have you believe that everyone lives in poverty, but because I read outside of the box, I knew that it would be different. I knew that there would be difficulties because colonialism did to Africa what racism and the slave trade did to America. So I really didn't know what to expect.

"Basically, I came here to find a part of myself, to find my roots. In order to come to Africa, I had to find sponsors. I had to go back to my old high school, elementary school principal, and my old employers and ask them to donate money for this trip, because my family didn't have the money to bring me here.

"I know that my parents are from Barbados and Panama, and that people from the west coast of Africa were taken from here to Barbados and to countries that now have black people. So I had to come here, and it's just a beautiful place. The people are beautiful and they're kind."

Repeating what is a constant refrain from most African Americans who visit West Africa, she was disappointed by the initial reception once she landed in Ghana. She expected more of a welcome, because even though this is her first trip to Ghana, she considered herself to be a part of this land.

"One of the things that I expected was a little more of a welcoming reception," she says wistfully. "I know that they see foreigners a lot, and a lot of white people come here for different reasons. But when I see another person with brown skin in America, I give them love, or I say hello. Before they hear your accent, they don't always know [you're an American]. But once they hear your accent, [the response] is 'obruni,' which is the word for *foreigner* here.

"[Ghanaians think] that you're automatically rich because you're from America, because America is such a rich and wealthy country. And you know you have to break down this barrier between you and your brother or sister, because that's how I see all Africans, as brothers and sisters. You have to first say that I'm not here to take from you; I'm not here to exploit you, because so many people have come from outside to do that. I let them know that I just want to know about you, and I want to share myself with you so that you know more about me. If you have your prejudices and presumptions about me as a black American, because we're not called African Americans here. We're called black Americans because some [Ghanaians] think that there isn't anything African about us. So if you want to know more about black American culture, I can tell you, I can share that with you. And I want to know more about Ghanaian culture, and you can share that with me. And once people begin to realize your reasons for being here, and know that there's no undercover stuff, they begin to open up to you. But just the fact that I have to break this down is painful to me, because I always expected a reception like, 'Sister, I'm so glad that you've come home!' But I guess that was just a fantasy."

Natalie looks at her visit as an even exchange when it comes to truth. The media have colored her vision of Africa, while she has found Ghanaians with unrealistic views of America. To the Ghanaians she's met, America is the promised land. And the thousands of Ghanaians who apply for the few United States visas are a manifestation of the good life promised by the dream of America.

"In America, unlike in Ghana, all of the toilets flush. Food is always available, and you can get a job even if you are born on the street. The poverty in America is not as great as the poverty here. As an African, seeing the media that comes from America makes America look like a fantasyland. To them, everything in America is good; everything is wonderful because America is the land of milk and honey. So when you come here, and you come from America, the Ghanaians know that you are different from them."

Ironically, the African Americans are often not portrayed in a positive light. Some of this distortion is self-inflicted via the musical content produced by African-American artists; however, Natalie believes that there is a selectiveness of African-American images exported to the world.

"The view that Ghanaians get of African Americans is not always positive. For example, everything that they see, whether it is the television, the video shows, even the music, the hip-hop that they listen to is the negative hip-hop. They never hear KRS-One or the Mos Def, the positive. It's always the negative. So Ghanaians then say, 'Why are [black Americans] disgracing themselves over there? I wouldn't want to be associated with you because look at the women dancing naked in the videos.' They hear the cursing, and calling of women bitches, and hoes. They think Africans feel that at least they have their dignity. And you have to tell them that not everyone in America listens to that music, and not everybody is like that in America. Media is a very big player in our interaction [with each other].

"There are those chosen few Ghanaians that have had access and resources to educate themselves about [black Americans]. It's all about education and the lack of education on both sides. They know that not everything about America is good. They know that everything is not milk and honey. They know that the political system is warped. They know that the justice system is warped, and they wouldn't want to [live] in America; and if I did, I would only do it to check it out, but I would come back home to Ghana because that's where I want to be. And I'm going to welcome you as an African American coming home to Ghana. We've met people like that, but there are not enough.

"And African Americans have stereotypical ideas about Africa from the things that we see in the media. African Americans come to Africa and see villages and poverty. [We look at Africans] and say, 'Oh look at what [the African] is wearing, and look at his shoes!' And we won't accept Africans for who they are. But then there are the Afrocentric African Americans that want to get as close to Africa as they can, even if it is through other people.

"One of the things that Ghanaians ask, especially the ones that consider us to be brothers and sisters, is why don't African Americans invest in Africa? They know that we don't have a lot of money, but the little that we do have could be used to make a difference. African Americans in America could work together with Africans and make a powerful impact."

One way Natalie is going to try to make that impact is by

chronicling her own experience in Africa. Using a program that she participated in previously as a template, she hopes to give African-American students a new vision of Africa.

"For most African-American students in America, they are thinking of Africa as the continent they have read about in their books," she remarks. "They've read about strong empires and civilizations. But when you come here now, you're seeing Africa after it has been affected by the same white men that affected America. And it is disappointing because you know what it could have been like before these influences had tainted their civilizations. But then, if you dig deep enough when you get here, you can find the things that you are looking for. You can find the traditions and the power of the people.

"I'm taking pictures while in Africa. In America, I was in a program called Project Hip Hop, and we retraced the Civil Rights movement. We went all over the South and met veterans of the movement. We all took pictures, and from that we made a slide show. We went to different schools and community centers to show people what it was like in the South during that time. We were trying to inform the students about the people who walked with Rosa Parks and the Martin Luther Kings, and how they have passed along their torch to us. And I want to try to do the same type of thing with this trip. I want to document as much as possible. I'm not much one for writing, but I'm trying to journal often and I'm taking pictures in the hope that I can make a slide show.

"I'll have a dinner and invite people to come view the slide show. And if that works out well, then I'll develop my talk and tell people about what I learned in Ghana, Benin, and Nigeria, and how warped our view of Africa is in America."

Natalie wants to get close to Africa, and she has. It has allowed her to overlook the things that are different from her own native land, and see deeper into what is truly beautiful.

"The most beautiful thing about Ghana is the people, the children," she says. "To look into the eyes of these children and know that there is promise and potential for Africa and they are the key to changing every problem that Ghana has, now you realize how intelligent these children are. It's hard seeing children on the streets selling things, just trying to make money for their parents because they are providers for the family. Children come in from the villages, just so their parents will have a little money, and they are not able to get an education. But you see their intelligence and it is just so powerful.

"Another beautiful thing about Ghana is the land, the untouched land. The part that is not in the city, but the part that is just grassland, the plains, the beaches, the water, the oceans, it is here you just feel power of your ancestors in your spirit. It's just a beautiful feeling. There are so many beautiful things here in Ghana, just the friendliness of the people. You never walk into a Ghanaian family's house and are not offered water, or have people ask about your well-being. And you ask of them the same."

This feeling has translated to Natalie feeling better about herself than at any point in her life. More confident, more sure of herself, as an African-American woman she feels more beautiful herself as she lives in Ghana. But even that wasn't always a constant.

"As a woman of African descent coming to Africa, and feeling beautiful as an African woman, there are two different kinds of men [that you'll meet]. There's the man who is looking for the ideal white-featured beauty, and the men that love the black woman and would want nothing but that black woman. In Ghana, I found one special person, and I have never felt such high esteem. I've never felt so beautiful around a man."

She sees a difference between Ghanaian men and her experience with African-American men. In her eyes, Ghanaian men take more time to see her for herself, rather that just as an object.

"Often, a lot of African-American men are looking out for themselves and their own self-interest. Often in America, if you are walking down the street, a man is looking at your body before he really sees you. Now, you get that here in Ghana, but it is not to as great an extent as it is at home. They don't respect you as much back home. I'm not saying all men, but a good amount of African-American men. And you might find a man that you think is the right man, but then you found out that he is cheating on you. There's always that problem. And there is that problem here, too, but just the fact that I've met men that are different. And I think that that's a very beautiful thing.

"I leave in a couple of months. We're working on getting my Ghanaian boyfriend a visa so that he can visit in the summer. He wants to transfer to a school in the United States. If that is able to work out, then we'll work that out. If not, then I don't know. There's the Internet, E-mail, telephones, but some way, if it is meant to be, it'll work out."

But she still had an experience that reminded her of life in America.

"One of the first things that I experienced when I first came to Ghana, however, was that I was in a room with three white women, and a Ghanaian man walked into the room. He talked to the white women and ignored me as though I didn't exist. And it was very painful for me. And I was like, dang, is this what it is going to be like here in Ghana? I didn't come all the way to Africa for this! It was just painful, but a Muslim brother explained it to me. He said that even those men weren't finding white women more beautiful than you, but it was more that they see them as money and as a way out [of the country]. They think that they can more easily dazzle a white woman and give her good loving, in order to ultimately get to America. That is a major goal for a lot of men that are here."

According to Natalie, some Ghanaian men find African-American women different from Ghanaian women, and sometimes they have trouble dealing with them.

"One Ghanaian gentleman that we know says that the difference between African-American women and Ghanaian women is that African-American women have an attitude," she laughs.

"Every time we may get upset or express our opinions to him, he'll say, 'Oh, you black Americans!' I'm not saying that Ghanaian women are passive, but they are much more quiet and understanding. But especially since I go to Wellesley, I'm very proud to be a woman, and you know you can do anything that a man can do. But here, it's not like that. There are some Ghanaian women that do put their foot down too, but it is not that way for all women.

"In this society, Ghanaian women do everything. They are responsible for the care of the children. They cook. Sometimes they go out and run businesses. When I talk to my Ghanaian boyfriend, we talk about family and relationships of fathers and mothers [in African-American and Ghanaian families]. When I tell him about the ratio of African-American children with two parents, my boyfriend is like, 'Wow, men can just up and leave their children?' He can't understand how someone can do that. It's just not done in Ghana. Here, if you have a child, you better get married or you better take care of that child. It's just one of the things that is understood. And this is just one of the many things that have been saved by the African tradition, even after colonialism. They couldn't take away everything.

"[In America] it seems that there has been a mental breakdown, almost as though we were once slaves and now we are suffering from mental slavery. In America, they will never admit it, but some African-American men lose their self-esteem. Instead of dealing with things, they want to run away from problems, because they haven't been told how amazing they are. When it comes to the educational system in America, I know grown men that told me that teachers told them that they were stupid and that they couldn't do this and they couldn't do that. If someone is telling you that you can't, you can't, all of your life, then how do they think that you can raise a child?"

In a society where Africans run everything from top to bottom in civil society, Natalie believes that this provides a wellspring for positive reinforcement about what a person can accomplish.

"Here, all you see are black faces. Your teachers are black, your doctors are black; so there is a confirmation that yes, you can do things. In America, I've been educated by white people all of my life. And in order to learn about myself, I had to go outside of the school and find books written by black people. And I also had to find books about African civilization, in order to free myself from a little bit of my own mental slavery. Because even now, I think that I'm still oppressed."

The irony for Natalie is that although there is a long line of Ghanaians wishing to make their way to America, most African Americans she's met want to stay in Ghana. They've found themselves in this country, and they now realize that the riches of the world's richest country are not really needed.

"We tell Ghanaians that we don't want to go back to America. We tell them that everything that you'll ever need is right here in Ghana. One of the major things that I realized coming to Ghana was the amount of things that I don't need to survive. Like looking for laundry detergent, I mean, what do I need laundry detergent for when I have Key soap [a Ghanaian-brand bar soap]? What do I need a washing machine for when I have my hands?

"Africa has been a beautiful experience; it has definitely had its ups and downs. I've definitely had a climax of pure bliss and happiness, and then there have been downhill times where I don't want to be here, and I just want to go home. I'm sick of people staring at me and asking for money."

She laughs, but there is one inconvenience that has bugged her since she arrived in Ghana.

"If had one thing I could change about my experience, I would bless Ghana with toilets that flush. Some of the toilets here are almost like latrines. That's the only thing that is really a pet peeve with me.

"Seriously, one thing I would improve about my life here in Ghana is that I would spend a little bit more time on me here. A lot of the time I find myself giving more time to other people. I would like to spend more time reflecting on the things that I see, because I think that I've been taking certain things for granted, like the typical Ghanaian woman on the street, for example. These beautiful women, with the most amazing postures, hold huge amounts of things on their heads, and I just walk by that these days. You say to yourself, I've already seen that, so no big deal. But it is amazing.

And then when I go back home, I'll say wow, that just flew by! I want to make it so that I don't have anything I wish I had. But I feel that I could move here and live here though. It's definitely a place that I could see myself staying for a few years."

26

Meeting and Living in the Past and Present

The Cape Coast, Ghana

I may not have gone where I intended, but I think that I have ended up where I intended to be.

—Douglas Adams

When you ask someone in Ghana about the time it will take to travel from Accra to the Cape Coast, they will inevitably laugh.

"It could take from three hours to six hours," they'll say with a sly smile. "It depends on the time of day, the road conditions, and a lot of other things. This is Africa, you know."

Africa, indeed.

The history of the Gold Coast before the last quarter of the fifteenth century is derived primarily from oral tradition that refers to migrations from the ancient kingdoms of the western Sudan (the area of Mauritania and Mali). The Gold Coast was renamed Ghana upon independence, in 1957, because of indications that present-day inhabitants descended from migrants who moved south from the ancient kingdom of Ghana.

The first contact between Europe and the Gold Coast dates from 1470, when a party of Portuguese landed. In 1482, the Portuguese built Elmina Castle as a permanent trading base. During the next three centuries, the English, Danes, Dutch, Germans, and Portuguese controlled various parts of the coastal areas.

In 1821, the British Government took control of the British

trading forts on the Gold Coast. In December 1946, British Togoland became a UN Trust Territory, and the Convention People's Party (CPP), led by Kwame Nkrumah, won the majority of seats in the new Legislative Assembly. In May 1956, Prime Minister Nkrumah's Gold Coast government issued a white paper containing proposals for Gold Coast independence. The British Government stated it would agree to a firm date for independence if a reasonable majority for such a step were obtained in the Gold Coast Legislative Assembly after a general election. This election, held in 1956, returned the CPP to power with 71 of the 104 seats in the Legislative Assembly.

Ghana became an independent state on March 6, 1957, when the United Kingdom relinquished its control over the Colony of the Gold Coast and Ashanti, the Northern Territories Protectorate, and British Togoland.

My driver, Paul Sekyere, has arrived for his driving assignment early on this warm Saturday morning. It's about eighty degrees at 7 A.M., humid but, surprisingly, not very uncomfortable. Especially when you have the air conditioning pumped up on high.

"First we need to fill up the tank, and then we can go," says Paul as we get into the Toyota.

"Let's do it," I say.

The wide boulevards of Accra are teeming with people. The commuter buses, called tro-tros, are loaded with commuters, while taxis and private cars eternally jockey for position, move from lane to lane. Paul enters the fray and, like every other Ghanaian driver, is determined to reach his destination as fast as possible.

We pull into the Mobil station, and after a short interval we have gotten the car filled up. Paul turns on his CD player, African artist Daddy Lumba begins to sing, and we are on our way.

One thing strikes you as you drive through the streets of Accra. Almost everywhere you look, homes, large, Western-style multilevel homes, are being built everywhere. Construction trucks are everywhere, transporting concrete cinder block building materials to and fro. It is obvious that there is more money in the Ghanaian economy now, and these new homes are the result.

"There are a lot of Ghanaians that live in the U.K. or the U.S. that are now sending money back to Ghana and are building new homes," says Paul.

The crowded urban streets of Accra soon give way to a two-lane highway to the Cape Coast. Lush with green foliage, the scenic route hugs the West African coastline as you make your way north toward the Cote d'Ivoire border. Since this is a two-lane highway, the ways of the road dictate that drivers constantly overtake each other as they try to get to their various destinations. Slower, overburdened trucks, buses, and trolleys are never allowed to impede progress.

Paul's method of driving is the same as everyone else's on the road. He drives as fast as he can to the bumper of the slower vehicle, and when the coast is clear, he enters the opposing lane as fast as a formula-one driver, accelerates, and then passes with a gentle honk. After each pass, he gently adjusts his rear view mirror as though he really cares about what's in back of him. He doesn't. For him, everything ahead is important and things in back are not.

Paul is a Ghanaian student at an auto-mechanics school in Accra, who works as a house-sitter for retired African-American professor Michael Gordon. Gordon, who lives part of the year in Ghana, employs Paul as his driver and house caretaker.

Bright and engaging, Paul has transported plenty of African Americans throughout Ghana, and has a definite opinion of them.

"I am proud that African Americans come back to Ghana," he says. "For too many years, we saw white Europeans and Americans come to our country, and they were rich. Now we see African Americans come, and they have the same education and the same wealth, and that tells us that we can make it, because you have made it."

But even as Paul says this, he refers to me as *obruni,* which in the Twi language translates to *foreigner,* or more specifically, *white foreigner.* As an African American, am I not still an African brother? Paul smiles.

"Yes, you are," he says knowingly.

We continue rolling toward the Cape Coast. The highway winds with straightaways and cutbacks, and intermittently, about every quarter of a mile, there are people on the road selling various produce and game. Pineapples stacked pyramidally sit next to dark-green watermelons. As cars approach the stands, the sellers wave toward their produce. Bare-chested men hunt the lush, green bush, displaying their kills for the traveling customers. Cutting-grass, an herbivore that inhabits the region, is the most popular animal sold. The men either hold it by its hind legs as freshly killed meat, or they smoke it at roadside pits. Either way, it provides a quick meal for the hungry traveler.

Every fifty kilometers, we run into a village, and traffic creeps to a halt. Men and women crisscross the road with various foods and articles for sale. Most carry their wares on their heads, enticing travelers with ice-cold water, snacks, and even socks and toilet paper. A little deeper, just off the road, you can see the community from which these people have come. Often with unpaved dirt roads, these villages are also the legacy of British colonial rule.

We move on without stopping. After about two hours, we make a left, and soon we are on our way to the Cape Coast Castle, one of the many castles and forts built by the Portuguese and English to defend their territory and to export millions of human beings for slavery in the newly discovered Americas. For African Americans, the journey is akin to a Jewish person visiting a Nazi concentration camp. It is an extremely emotional event in one's life.

The castle itself is imposing and takes up a strategic position on the African coast. All white and ringed with cannon, the Cape Coast Castle intimidates both those approaching from the sea and those viewing it from land. One could only imagine the thoughts of men, women, and children who had to enter it.

"Thirty cedi for the American and five cedi for Ghanaian," says the man behind the Cape Coast Castle ticket booth. He fails to note the irony that a descendant of a slave who was brought here against his or her will is now forced to pay more to see this place than anyone else.

We pay and move on.

The main exhibition for Cape Coast Castle is titled "Crossroads of People, Crossroads of Trade" and tells the powerful and moving story in four distinct segments tied together by the underlying theme of trade.

The first segment talks about the history of Ghana from the earliest times through the ages of stone tools and terra cotta figures, to the Iron Age, the development of towns, the extraction and use of gold, and the eventual arrival of traders from the Middle East and Europe.

The second segment tells of the African Diaspora, and how Africans were rounded up and forced into slavery. With that in mind, there is one feature of specific interest for African Americans. These are the dungeons that housed our ancestors before they made their trip through the "Door of No Return." The tour guide brings a group of African students along for this part of the trip. He explains to the students that this door, with its sign that says "Male Slave Quarters," is where Africans from throughout the continent were brought to begin their journey.

"The Africans were sometimes brought here after having been captured in battle by other tribes and then sold to the Europeans," he says. "The Africans were housed either in the upstairs area," he says, pointing to a second floor of the castle, "or the men were brought here."

The stony mouth of the male slave quarters is like the venomous mouth of a snake. It opens wide and wends its way down to a dark and unknown hell. At the time of the slave trade, there were no lights to light the way, so this was like walking into a great stone beast. Packed with up to two thousand men at a time, for months at a time, the conditions were inhumane at best.

"The men would come into this room," says the guide as he leads us down the slippery stones to the bottom of the dungeon. "This is where they would stay until they were loaded onto ships."

There are three chambers at the bottom of the dungeon. Each is only about one hundred feet long and fifty feet wide and immediately claustrophobic. It is a place designed to crush the will and spirit, and it does so, impressively. If you look closely at the walls, you can still see the desperate fingernail scratchings on the wall.

About twelve feet high, near the top of stone walls, are three small inlets that let a little light into the dark, dank room. But letting in light was not their main purpose. The inlets were angled so that ocean water would come into the room to wash away the fecal matter that would accumulate. That was the theory.

"When this room was excavated, we found that fecal matter was this high off the ground," says the guide, pointing to a mark about four feet high. "These men walked, lived, and slept in this for centuries." The excavators left a square of the matter to serve as a reminder of what was left behind.

The second chamber has a single inlet built on the opposite side. In this room, a single opening provides light, but again, this light was not designed to alleviate the comfort of the captives. It was used to spy on the slaves.

Finally, we reach the third and last chamber. An altar has been set up where a man, sitting in the traditional dress, awaits. He chants a prayer for the Africans who passed through this chamber, and after he pours libations, our time in the chambers is suddenly over. The Door of No Return has been closed, so there isn't a way to reach the sea from this chamber, but there is a notice on the wall. It states that African Americans have returned and will continue to return.

The sun is now directly overhead and blazing. It is time to make our way to the next destination. Paul starts up the car and we head to nearby Elmina.

The drive to Elmina is only about ten minutes, but it includes some stunning visuals. On the right side of the road are brown thatch-and-mud huts, homes that fit the visual image most people have of life in Africa. On the left side is the Atlantic Ocean, lined with a coconut grove beach. You can't help but imagine that at some point, this stretch of beach will be filled with hotels and European tourists. But this is for the future.

When trying to find a destination in Africa, especially a commercial destination, it is best to look on the side of the road. In an Africanized version of the classic Burma Shave roadside ads, you see businesses advertising their services all along the Cape Coast Road. The business we are trying to find is called One Africa. Suddenly, a small road sign indicates that we have reached our destination. Make a small turnoff into a dirt alley, look to the left, and you have arrived at the gates of One Africa.

One Africa is a bed-and-breakfast complex set against the breathtakingly beautiful backdrop of the Atlantic Ocean. Opened by African-American expatriates Okofo and Imokus Robinson, the complex is designed to be a refuge for African Americans coming "home" to the African continent, and a place where any traveler can relax in comfort.

With land donated to the Robinsons as a reward for Okofo's being named a chief, the buildings are supposed to mimic the traditional mud-and-thatch African homes that dot the Ghanaian landscape, but in reality they are more reminiscent of the 1950s-style roadside motels that were designed as "Indian teepees." But they are neat, roomy, and comfortable bungalows, each named to honor various African and African-American leaders such as Malcolm X and Harriet Tubman, and are impressive by any standard.

As part of its mission, One Africa conducts tours of the Cape Coast and Elmina Castles, supplementing the slave trade history provided at the castles by conducting tours of its own.

"We try to be the best example we can to the brothers and sisters that are coming [to Africa] or who are thinking about coming," explains the dreadlocked Okofo. "This is our homeland, the land of our inheritance, according to Isaiah. And we've just come home to claim our inheritance to the best of our abilities."

Today, under a thatch canopy and with the sound of waves crashing against the beach, One Africa is hosting a meeting for about twenty members of the African American Association of

Ghana. A mix of newly retired social workers, teachers, and executives, all fellowship with young families looking for a new start in this land of their ancestors.

As new arrivals to this land, African Americans find that they have to define themselves. Some abandon their English surnames and adopt African names instead. Others keep their surnames, but integrate themselves into Ghanaian society. But regardless, everyone who decides to come to Ghana must come to terms with how others, especially Ghanaians, will see him or her.

Even the African American Association has called into question its very name. Does this group, by the nature of its name, exclude those from the Caribbean? Can an Afro-Canadian join the association? Would *black* be a better term for those inside the group?

"We have, after much discussion, ratified our constitution," says Annie Hall, vice president of the African American Association. Hall is a retired teacher from Seattle, Washington.

"One of the items that we had discussion about was membership," she continues. "Membership is open to Americans of African descent, that is, by virtue of birth in the U.S.A., its territories, and possessions. And African-American parentage, with one or both parents, and naturalization is accepted."

"Now, on the other hand, are we all agreeing to call [February] African-American history month?" she asks.

"We had a consensus a few years ago that we grew out of 'black,' " says Okofu. "But we don't call it African-American History Month, we just call it African History Month. Because a lot of African history is related to our history in America."

"I think that on the flipside, we can call it African Diasporan History Month," Janet Butler says. Butler is a business consultant in Ghana. "It's important, because one of the problems that we had early on with our association is that it eliminated our brothers and sisters from the Diaspora. If they were not born in America, they couldn't meet with us. So for us it was difficult because we had families who came from the Diaspora but not from America [in Ghana], and there were not enough of us who were born in America for us to come together to form any kind of coalition. And it was kind of separating us. So we said Diaspora. If you were born on the other side [of the Atlantic] then you have a right to be a part of our organization. We want to leave the door open for our Diasporan brothers and sisters."

"In the process of getting ourselves together, we must reach out [to others]," commented Hall.

This reaching out to others and redefinition of who and what African Americans are in this new land is part of the "de-obruning" process. To a lot of African Americans, this new land is not only their ideal, but also a culmination of their lifelong dreams. Among African-American expatriates, the word *paradise* is used time and time again. After many years of searching, Africa, and Ghana in particular, has become their own Shangri-la to those seeking a refuge from America.

"I came here to Ghana because I had never been to this part of Africa before," says one retiree at the meeting. "It is one of the best things that has ever happened to me. I'm retired. I retired three years ago, and when I retired I sold all of my things. I'm a farmer and contractor, dealing with heavy equipment. I sold all of my equipment the day I retired. It took me four months to sell everything that I had. I didn't want to have anything left because I didn't want to have anything to draw me back. What did Caesar say when he crossed the Rubicon? 'The die is cast!' There's nothing over there for me, and when I came here there was nothing left. When I go back to visit, I have to stay with my relatives. I have no place to stay. Ghana is paradise."

"I arrived here in Africa in 1999 and I have longed to be here my entire life, since I was a small boy," said John Childs, another retiree. "Now that I'm here, I'm one of the happiest human beings on the planet."

And for many African Americans who choose to stay in Ghana, it does represent paradise. A dream finally realized and no longer deferred. But even in paradise, there are some realities that have to be dealt with. African Americans, no matter how well they are accepted in their local communities, are still immigrants and noncitizens. As such, laws that govern everything including restrictive land rights, travel and visa requirements and business ownership are geared against the noncitizen. For example, Ghanaian law requires a foreigner either to go into business with a Ghanaian partner or pay a substantially higher fee to the government in order to run a business alone.

Also, for many years African Americans in Ghana have been hoping for a recognized citizenship status within Ghana. Former Ghanaian president Flight Lieutenant Jerry Rawlings had proposed dual citizenship for African Americans in a meeting with former President Bill Clinton, but to date, the measure had stalled in the Ghanaian legislature. However, at this meeting, Janet Butler's husband, Masao Meroe, reports on new laws that have just been passed by the Ghanaian legislature.

"In February 2000, [the Ghanaian legislature] had passed what is popularly known as the Immigration Ancestor Citizenship Bill," explains Meroe. "There were, in fact, two separate bills, one dealing with citizenship and the other dealing with immigration. The legislation was passed by Parliament, and then it could not take place until the enabling legislation was added. And they worked on that for a long time. When that legislation was finished, it was presented before Parliament again. It had to sit for twenty-one days, and if there were no major objections, then it automatically became law. About a month ago, the act became law."

The act is broken into two parts, dealing with citizenship and immigration. The citizenship section of the bill is mainly aimed at Ghanaians, in that it allows Ghanaians to have dual citizenship without renouncing the citizenship of their new residence or their Ghanaian homeland. However, African Americans who are married to Ghanaians find a change in their status.

"If you are married to a Ghanaian, then you have a right to Ghanaian citizenship," Meroe explains. "All you have to do is apply, because there are no language requirements."

In the immigration part of the bill, there are two things that affect the African-American community: one is the status of indefinite residents, and a person's right of abode. According to the new law, if a person has lived five out of seven years in Ghana, he or she qualifies for indefinite residence status.

In the right-of-abode legislation, Africans in the Diaspora have a right to apply for a right of abode, no matter how long they have lived in Ghana. This allows African Americans to live in Ghana without having to constantly apply for a visa. It also allows African Americans to work in Ghana without a work permit, and, more important, they don't have to set up a company in order to work. They can take any job that is available to any Ghanaian.

"This legislation that passed is absolutely historical," he continues. "Particularly in respect to Africans in the Diaspora. The rights that this immigration law gives are probably more than we could have possibly thought of, and it is more [rights] than any other African country is willing to give us."

Amid cheers and clapping, the members of association decided to submit all of their applications at the same time in order to show their support for the legislation. This would also allow them to track the speed with which the government processes their applications.

As the waves crashed against the beach, and African fishermen off in the distance began hauling in their catch, these very different members of the African-American community in Ghana were beginning to become that much closer to being full-fledged citizens of Ghana. And with the looks on their faces, it was easy to see that Ghana was truly becoming home.

27

Exchanging Cultures

Legon, Ghana

Throw your dreams into space like a kite, and you do not know what it will bring back, a new life, a new friend, a new love, a new country.

—Anais Nin

The alabaster walls of the University of Ghana, in the Accra suburb of Legon, glisten in the midday sunlight. The university, like most universities around the world, has students walking to and fro between classes. Each, it seems, has been supplied with a perfectly square white handkerchief designed to wipe the perspiration from their foreheads. To the back of the campus sits a building that holds the Council for International Exchange, and holding office hours today is Dr. Michael Williams, the resident director.

Dr. Williams is the point man for exchange students from throughout the world who choose to study in Ghana. A former associate professor of sociology and director of Africana studies at Simmons College in Massachusetts, Dr. Williams moved to Ghana in 1994 and has lived here permanently since that time. For him, it was the manifestation of a dream.

"In the U.S., I grew up in Washington D.C. but spent my entire academic adult life at different schools in the U.S.," he says, as he leans in his chair behind his desk. "I first came to Africa in 1979, when I was on a cultural African program. It was a smaller version of the Peace Corps, and it came out of the Kennedy era [idea] of reaching out to different peoples."

"In 1979 I visited Sierre Leone when Sierre Leone was fine, perfect, wonderful, and beautiful," he continues. "I traveled to Senegal for a while and I ended up in Liberia. I just fell in love with Africa. Even before coming to Africa, I knew that this was home and this was where I needed to be. But you know, I was married to my first wife, we were having children, and it wasn't easy to get back. I didn't get back to Africa until 1988. I was trying to find out how I was going to get here permanently. Theoretically, I was already here [mentally] before coming. When I first smelled, tasted Africa, I knew that it was for me. I just didn't know how to do it financially."

In order to make it to Africa, the opportunities of research and profession had to merge at the right time. That began in 1988, when his research on Ghana's first president, Kwame Nkrumah, began.

"I came [to Ghana] doing research, because I had been doing research on Nkrumah for a while. I came in 1988 to Ghana for the first time, then 1990, and then 1992 on some research projects. I started at Simmons College in 1990, and we were trying to develop an exchange program, on which I served as a consultant, because they didn't have any programs in Africa. So I set this program up in 1993, and then they offered me the job [in Ghana]. I wasn't expecting it, but I took the job and I've lived here since 1994.

"My French was good and I had an opportunity to go to Senegal. The women in Senegal are the most beautiful," he laughs. "But my connection [to Ghana] was Kwame Nkrumah. I had been doing research on Nkrumah for a long time, so I came here for some primary data. Although I think that West Africa is different culturally, you can see a lot of commonality with Africans from throughout the Diaspora. So as long as [Ghana] was relatively stable, I was willing to come."

When you talk with Dr. Williams, a casually intense man, you get the feeling that he has not looked back at living in the United States since he arrived in Ghana. His manner is that of a person who has stopped traveling and searching but has finally found his destination, whether that is professional or personal.

The Council on International Education provides opportunities for students in the U.S. and everywhere to study in different parts of the world. The university needs someone to care for these students while they are here, so Dr. Williams provides this.

"My position is really administrative, even though I'm in an academic setting. I'm in academic studies, but I don't teach, in fact, I'm trying to write fiction now. I really don't have any academic challenges. I'm tired of academia," he says with a frown. "I spent fifteen years teaching at universities in the U.S. and I didn't enjoy it. I started out at Fisk and really enjoyed it there, but after that it was all downhill. I liked the interaction with students, but correcting exams and going to all of the meetings [was tiring]."

After a divorce, Dr. Williams eventually married a Ghanaian and now raises his daughters in Accra. Contrary to a lot of African Americans living in Ghana, he chooses to cut most ties to the African-American expat community, preferring instead to integrate himself directly into Ghanaian society.

"As far as the [African-American] enclave thing, I want to stay away from that as far as possible," he says with a half laugh. " 'Cause I could live in the South Side of Chicago if I wanted that, and I didn't come here for that.

"A chief gave some land to a brother who wants to create an African-American community. I'm not going to cast a negative light on that, but it wouldn't be for me. It helps if you try to integrate in Ghanaian society. It helps that I'm married to a Ghanaian. There is a growing [African-American] community in the Cape Coast, but I'm not trying to hang out with [African Americans]. When I see folks, I'm polite and all that, but I'm too busy really to be hanging out. So the [African American] Association will always be without me because I don't need it. I guess if you need it, it's fine. It's kind of like church: for members it serves a kind of spiritual and social value. But I don't honestly need it. I have six daughters who are here with me. With my wife and my work, where is there time to go to meetings?"

Dr. Williams tries to impart this philosophy of integrating

within Ghanaian culture to his American students, particularly his African-American students. But he finds that African-American students tend to have a hard time adjusting to the cultural aspects of Ghanaian society, which sometimes don't meet their expectations.

"[African-American] students come with preconceived notions that are not accurate. They're really surprised when they see women straightening their hair. All kinds of white Jesuses [paintings], and the general kinds of inferiority complexes and self-hatred that we had in the Diaspora, I mean we weren't expecting them here. Africa is home and it retains its culture, but the Europeanization of our people is very strong here. And where we had a Civil Rights and a Black Power movement, they haven't had it here. And so part of the notions that we held about white people in the 1940s are still here in Ghana now.

"Typically, Ghanaians show favoritism toward white people and light-skinned people. Go to a restaurant, man, and you can wait five or ten minutes before they serve you. They'll serve the white customers before they serve you. So that's difficult in terms of transition for African Americans. I wasn't surprised, because I had read so much about colonialism and neocolonialism and its effect, I mean, all over the world, people have been exploited and that's what had happened to our people. I think older Diasporans can appreciate Africa more than the young ones. The younger ones have a great time, but generally they concentrate on the negative.

"[African-American students ask] 'Why they do this? Why they do that?' and they forget about what has happened [to Ghanaians]. And they forget about all of the pathologies in the U.S. One of the most pathological things in the United States [among African Americans] is fratricide. We are killing each other, and [the United States] has created a significant industry from our pathology. But young people come over here and forget all of that. But they've got the rest of their life ahead of them, and when they are thirty, forty, fifty, and are tired of all that [in the United States] and come to Ghana, it will be like a heaven to them because it's less stress.

Education is the center of the exchange experience, but Dr. Williams finds that both the exchange students and Ghanaians tend to be shortchanged, not only by the process, but also by the quality.

"The education that the students receive here is very British, and the [American] students generally don't find it challenging," Dr. Williams said. "Probably because the educational system reflects Ghana's underdevelopment, so it is a lot of rote memory. And this is a real problem. So we try to develop community service internships for the students in order to augment the things they should be learning in class. Actually, because of the influx of students coming from abroad, the academic culture is changing some. Lecturers are feeling compelled to engage their students more, because that's what African-American students are used to. And even when there are two or three students in the class, their presence can be felt."

Beyond the cultural and educational differences, African-American students, in Dr. Williams's view, are worn down by just the day-to-day life in Ghana, which as a developing country sometimes doesn't have the luxuries that the students are used to in the West.

"It may be issues of the underdevelopment in Africa, because I don't think that they are prepared for how underdeveloped the continent is. It's just that since the U.S. is such a developed nation when you compare it to Ghana, there is no comparison. Here the water goes out, the power goes out, and all of the different aspects of being an underdeveloped country kind of get to them."

But according to Dr. Williams, the phone calls that he receives after African-American students return to the United States make him think that they begin to have fond memories of Africa.

"Yes, I'm convinced of it. As they sit back and digest all of the tension and stress of this lifestyle, I think [they have positive feelings about Africa]. But I'm generalizing. There are some young African Americans that genuinely love it [here] and cry when it's time to leave.

"The female experience is generally a different experience here. Females generally have a difficult time because they are harassed a lot. Guys are looking to get married and get their visa. I haven't been able to put my finger on it, but it seems that the white students can handle Africa better, and it really confounds everybody."

Dr. Williams finds that white American students have an easier time adjusting to Ghanaian life, partly because they are not emotionally invested in Africa, as African-American students tend to be. There lies the irony.

"[The white students] enjoy it. Actually, they seem to handle Ghana better than the African-American students. I don't know how to account for that, but they really do. I think for African Americans it's kind of a homecoming that gets spoiled along the way. [The trip] doesn't unfold like they expect it, so the experience kind of turns negative for them. The white people who come to Ghana, they find everything fascinating. They're more tolerant."

And while African-American students may be disappointed in certain aspects of Ghanaian and African life, this is a two-way street. Ghanaians sometimes look at African Americans as being a negative influence in their country.

"[African-American students] confirm the values and norms that the Ghanaians are receiving through the media [about African Americans]," Dr. Williams says sternly. "One channel over here, which is kind of a BET, plays nothing but gangsta rap, and women are talked about as hoes and bitches. So some of the students come in and reaffirm that image by their talk and their dress. So in general, I think that the influence is not positive. Especially through the films that come here: we don't get the nice films, and the real negative hip-hop is very powerful.

"I think that our image gradually changed [from the positive to the negative], but it changed before I got here. It has to do with the influence of American capital. American culture is the dominant culture, so it is natural that an African community would feel closer to the African-American community than any other. That's probably our most powerful export, American culture. I mean, local musicians have to go abroad because they can't make a living here. People are buying [American] music, because Sony and the other companies can make sure that their artists are the major artists."

Dr. Williams wishes that Ghanaians, particularly Ghanaian youth, were able to use some of the benefits of American citizenship; however, he worries about the values that would be transmitted along with those benefits.

"If Ghanaian children went to America, they would at least be able to get the basic skills they may be lacking here, such as reading, writing, and arithmetic. But I'd be concerned with the values that they would pick up in America. Ghanaian children are very respectful of seniority, position, and their elders. But even that is changing, unfortunately, to the negative, but I'm so happy that my children were raised here [in Ghana]."

In 1995, United States President Bill Clinton, and Ghanaian President Jerry Rawlings met in Harlem. It was there that Rawlings announced that the Ghanaian government was working on legislation that would allow African Americans dual citizenship with the country of Ghana.

"We are moving quickly to develop a legal framework whereby every American of African descent will be eligible for dual citizenship, both African and American," said Rawlings to a Harlem audience. "You must interact with our people more intensively and bring your talents and resources to Africa's march to progress and fulfillment."

"That was just Rawlings grandstanding," says Williams disdainfully. "They have a new law where spouses of Ghanaians can get something akin to permanent residence. I'm really happy about that because I won't have to go every year to get my residency renewed. That's now available. This whole idea of dual citizenship may be in the Parliament, but I haven't heard anything about it.

"Actually, I saw an interview with Clinton and Rawlings, and Clinton was very supportive of it. Rawlings kept trying to cut him off because he thought that Clinton was going to be against it, but Clinton said no, it could serve both you and me.

But again, because of the political education of Ghanaians, there may be some opposition to it. They see us as brothers in some way, but a lot of people, especially the politicians, see us as potential investors. And in one way that's fine if we come as investors, but we should be able to come because it is our ancestral home. We want to raise a family and not necessarily bring a huge amount of money. We just want to live a life."

Dr. Williams takes a short phone call and then continues.

"I don't think that it will come off. There are groups of people that are pushing for it. But you have to have commitment from both sides of the world. It would be a great thing. When a Jew steps in Israel, he's automatically an Israeli citizen. But there is a lot of politics because these countries are externally indebted, and so their creditors wouldn't be happy. They've got to unfortunately take that into consideration."

John Agyekum Kufuor replaced Rawlings as Ghanaian president through a peaceful democratic election in 2001. Dr. Williams thinks that Kufuor is trying to lead the country in the right direction. But the external factors and corruption have traditionally been a hindrance to positive development in many African countries.

"I think that the new president is trying. To a certain degree I think that he's not politically naive. I think he's more honest. I didn't care for Rawlings much. A lot of people in his government were very corrupt. I don't think that he really had any type of vision. He had the equivalent of a junior high education, and you know, when we left junior high we weren't ready to run anything. Ghana suffers from a paucity of leaders. His intentions may have been good at the beginning, but you can have the best intentions in the world but nothing can happen if people are corrupt. It was just twenty years of marking time. So Kufuor, I think, is trying. He has zero tolerance for corruption, and it's made an impact. And he's brought more sanity to the government, and people have a little more faith, and people are trying. But honestly, the debt is no joke."

Even though Dr. Williams looks at Ghana and Africa through a pragmatist's eye, it is not to say that he is pessimistic about either Ghana or Africa. To the contrary, he is very optimistic about Ghana. To him, there are just some realities that are best dealt with straight-on, instead of by trying to hide them underneath false sentiment.

"Ghana is in a better condition than a whole lot of countries [in Africa]. The whole sub-Saharan Africa is just a mess. But even with saying that, it's hard to describe why I need to be here. It's just a certain feeling. I can walk into any community in Ghana, whether it's Accra or anywhere else, for that matter, and feel safe. I'm not really worried about somebody pulling out a handgun and blowing me away. I have great relations with my neighbors, and Ghanaians are very friendly. I get so much respect here that I wouldn't in America because of the gray hair. Children come up and call you Daddy. So these are some of the quality-of-life issues that make it worthwhile. Even with all of the underdevelopment, the bad leadership, there is something here [in Ghana] that they retain here, and that we lost."

Dr. Williams leans back for a final time and sums up why Ghana is home for him.

"It's more human here. You can bump into somebody, and they'll apologize."

28

Frankies for Lunch

Osu, Ghana

When you make the finding yourself—even if you're the last person on Earth to see the light—you'll never forget it.

—Carl Sagan

Frankies is a Lebanese-owned restaurant in Osu, a suburb of Accra. In America, it would be just another takeout joint, but in Accra, it is a pretty expensive diner. Serving fried chicken, shawarma, and some of the best Italian ice cream in the city; it's located close to all of the foreign embassies and caters to moneyed Ghanaians and Americans. Linda Horton and Ayaba Akofa Adaobi Logan, two African-American exchange students from Northern Illinois University and Spelman College respectively, are having lunch this warm afternoon.

"I am originally from Chicago," says Horton as she nibbles on her chicken. "I'm forty-four years old, and I'm a sociology major. What really made me come to Africa had to do with my church, Trinity United Church of Christ. However, I learned that my school offered a program to Africa, and I was the first student to attend this program. I have a lot of information that I have to take back to my school. I've learned a lot about myself as well as my people here in Africa. I've been here since August 25, 2001."

"Mainly, I came to Ghana because I wanted to understand my name," says Logan. "What tribe, what region, what area it originates from, and everything that I could find out about my name. So that was first and foremost. Because my father was so Afrocentric, he named all four of his children some sort of African name, and that was definitely my biggest push on coming.

"And then, I just wanted to be in Africa so that I could understand how the connection is between Africans in America and Africans here. How much have we lost? How much have we gained? What's better, what's worse about our relationship. Basically, I wanted to know the total package."

Two women, both from different experiences, have come to Ghana to explore not only an African society but also themselves. Horton had been struggling to come to Africa for many years and really didn't know what she would find once she got to the continent.

"I've been trying to get to Africa for five years," Horton says. "I did no research before coming here. Zero research. My expectations were not high or low because I didn't know what I was stepping into. I was really overwhelmed with a lot of things. First of all was the lifestyle, and the babies carried on the backs. I mean, that was just shocking to me.

"What I want to get out of this [exchange] program is to see how Africa connects with me as an African American, as well as getting an understanding of where they're at. I want to know whether our history has been taught to them, because I was never taught this part of my history. This was cut out of my whole schooling. I don't know if it is taught today in schools, but I do say this: I will make sure that my nieces and nephews would know about this part of their history. I told them that we are going to have African history day once a week in my house."

Logan received that African history from her parents, since they had traveled through the continent extensively. Their tales of diverse African peoples captivated Logan, and her African-derived name provided a daily reminder of her ancestry.

"My mother and father were involved in a lot of Pan-African things in New York, more so my father than my mother," Logan recalls.

Logan's father was a blacksmith who was intrigued with Africa and its connection to African Americans. He spent years building relationships with Africans from different countries.

"Through that [work], the president of Tanzania or Zambia invited my father, I can't remember which country specifically, to come to Africa. So then they visited Egypt, Kenya, Tanzania, and Zambia. They stayed with families and saw the countryside. I saw pictures of Africa, and they were all gorgeous. So I thought Africa was the best place to be on Earth. No problems at all. I always had positive images of Africa and Africans before coming here. As well, my name is West African, so that was a big part in me coming here as well."

Even though both women come from different backgrounds, they have drawn some of the same conclusions about Ghana and Africa. Their pride in things African, and their Afrocentric view of the world, make some of the things that they see in Ghana shocking to their long-held beliefs about Africa.

"I think that the most disappointing thing about Africa was that when we landed in Accra, it was not the picture of what I grew up with," says Logan. "It was ugly, it was dirty, and I didn't like the billboards for perms everywhere, the European this and that. Also, along with the look of Accra being disappointing, I've found that talking with Ghanaians, or any Africans in general, has been disappointing. Because I think, for me, I always looked to Africa and Africans as being, this is what our goal is [for African Americans to be like Africans]."

This disappointment in her initial impressions of Africa extends to her meeting with Ghanaians. In an ironic twist, Logan uses language when describing Ghanaians that is reminiscent of language used by whites when describing African Americans.

"Compared to educated African Americans in the U.S., here the Africans appear to be more childlike, as though they are waiting for somebody to tell or show them 'This is how you do this or that,' " Logan reflects. "And then, not just to show them, but somebody *European* to show them. Or somebody with light-skinned complexion, or somebody with white skin to show them. In terms of thought and mentality and ways of life [it] tends to be more Eurocentric than what I was expecting."

One incident sticks out in the minds of Logan and Horton. In Ghana, it is common to see images of Jesus and the baby Jesus on cars, vans, and posters. Logan and Horton decided to question the fact that almost all of those images of Jesus were of a white man.

"Linda and I were sitting in a car and a guy was selling Jesus posters," says Logan. "We told him that Jesus was black, and he was like, 'No, he's not; he's white.' So it's kind of like that we are just people to them just like Europeans, except that our opinion is less than Western opinion, and I have to [blame] colonialism.

"On the one hand, I didn't know how colonialism had played out here in Ghana, or even in Francophone countries. I had no clue. Whereas I think that African Americans like me always thought that this was a place of knowledge and this is where we should look back toward in order to gain that knowledge. And I think that this is both of our faults. If this is what I had always expected, and I had this great view of Africa in my head, [meaning that] it's beautiful, the people are highly intelligent, and they don't look to white people for anything, and then getting here, and [realizing] that they don't do that. They don't look to us for anything, and they don't even view us sometimes as their brother and sister, or their lost child or anything of that nature. We're more like stepchildren to them."

"Half of the Ghanaians I meet don't know who I am until I open my mouth," Horton says. Her close-shaved head often has Ghanaians mistaking her for a Ghanaian.

"But once I open my mouth, they know I'm an American. It was a while before I saw the difference, but I noticed that they do see me as different [from Ghanaian women]. And I get angry; I get really angry when I see that."

Her anger stems from her belief that Ghanaian women are not treated as equals in Ghana. As an African American, Horton thinks that her nationality can lead to exploitation by Ghanaian men.

"Now the men, for the most part, have yet to disrespect me," she says. "But I do feel that they want to have either a personal relationship with me or some connection with me. I've been told that this is because they want to come to the United States. Now, I'm not to say that that is what they are trying to get from me, because I don't know. And I [just] tell them please don't treat me any different than the sisters here in Ghana. Of course, they say they don't, but I feel they do.

"I came here to bond with my sisters, more so than with the men. But the sisters are very laid-back, so you have to take all of the initiative. I can walk up to a sister and say, 'That's a bad outfit you've got on!' They don't know what to do. A compliment is not in their vocabulary."

Horton is living with a Ghanaian family during her time in Africa. As part of this immersion into Ghanaian society, she is trying to learn about typical Ghanaian life while at the same time bringing American values to the family, particularly in how the daughter is respected by the family.

"I stay with a Ghanaian family and I share that with the family, [particularly] with the father of the household," she says. "He has a daughter that is twenty-two years old, and he feels that I can work with his daughter on some issues. [I told him] that he needs to start complimenting her. He needs to say, 'Oh, the dinner you cooked tonight was fabulous!' whether it was or not. Start building up her self-esteem. I asked him first of all, did he know what self-esteem was? Of course, he told me no, he did not. So I had to define that for him."

"I don't think that African Americans have as much influence in Ghana as Europeans, or the United States in general," Logan said disappointedly. "The music, they love. Hip-hop is everywhere. But in terms of getting your education and learning [about African Americans] in books, I don't think that we influence them in that manner. For example, I have tried to find every bookstore in Ghana that is possible, and the books that they get here are all Eurocentric. They don't seem to get African-American books. They don't get fiction or nonfiction in African-American literature at all. I think the best African-American book I found here was *Africana,* even though DuBois stayed here [in Ghana]. So I don't think that African Americans have as much influence as I thought African Americans would have here, as opposed to the Western view and Eurocentric view.

"Some Ghanaians, the highly educated ones even though it is not necessarily through book learning, ask African Americans 'How do you look at the world?' 'We are looking to you for answers.' While others feel that 'you're not my brother and I don't need to look to you. You're nobody.' "

While both Logan and Horton point out the negatives of their African experience, they both still have seen the good of Africa in their brief time on the continent. In their eyes, not all of the advances African Americans have made in America have been positive either, and they note that even though Africans may have fewer resources than African Americans, they may be richer in a number of ways that escape the African-American experience.

"African Americans have lost a lot," Horton explains. "We say that we care about each other, but I don't feel that we do care about each other. Or we care only if we know each other. We care only if we have some sort of interactive relationship with each other. But I think that we have lost how to care for people. I share with them [Ghanaians] that we have a lot more material things, but they have everything else, whether you are talking about family, tradition, or culture. I just see a whole lot of love here. And if it is imitation love, well they have fooled me!

"What I love about Ghana is how they interact as people. They more or less address each other by name. From the small child to the older person, they really focus on your name, and they will recall that a couple of days ago that you weren't feeling well. Their memory is incredible."

What has inspired Logan are the connections she did find between the two cultures.

"I've found that we as African Americans in the U.S. have not lost the root of what is African, the specific African personality. It's one of those things that I have trouble describing, but it is just one of those things," Logan tries to explain. "Even though we don't speak the same language, we can laugh at the same things. We know about each other's thinking. We have that friendliness, that welcoming spirit that says, 'Oh, come into my home; here are some drinks and some food for you.' It is the basic nature of us.

"However I think that we have lost the basic traditions of Ghanaian culture, or Senegal, or Cote d'Ivoire culture," she continues. "We have lost how to cook fu-fu, or how the African men interact with African women, and how men interact with men. Through my observations here in Ghana, at least on the university campus, it seems that men and women don't interact socially. Like you'll see one man and woman walking together. Or you'll see two men and two women walking together. But you'll rarely see a group of men and a group of women going somewhere together. So you kind of see male bonding and female bonding done separately. I don't think that this is a good or bad dichotomy at all. It is just different from the African-American experience."

But it is just that African experience that has Horton planning to stay in Ghana permanently. She recognizes the positives and negatives of both lands, and for now, chooses Ghana.

"My major adjustment [when I first arrived in Ghana] was trying to adapt to their way of living," she said. "Going to the market, for example, or, let's say, the food. Let's deal with the food. I was brought up on soul food. However, soul food is not heard of over here. Eating fu-fu wasn't pleasing. And the hygiene is one problem here. Outdoors, you see flies all over your food, and no one appears to be washing their hands.

"But in Chicago, we don't know how to treat each other. We're angry with ourselves as well as our neighbors. Here I find there is a little bit more compassion and sympathy. There's a little bit more understanding. I was here two weeks and I fell down one day, and Ghanaians were apologizing to me for my fall. I was like, 'Why are you sorry? I'm the one that fell!' In the United States, they would have been laughing at my fall!"

Her bittersweet laugh, thinking of the laughing faces, doesn't mask her feeling that America holds no new promises for her. She is willing to put up with the lack of hygiene and other inconveniences to be closer to what she feels is her real home.

"I think that I've learned from being here that I don't need as many material things to survive in this world," she reflects on her time in Ghana.

"Living in Chicago, I see the lifestyle that it has to offer, and I'm tired of that lifestyle. I'm just so at ease here. No drive-by shootings. No drug addicts. You know, it's just laid-back. The only thing that is making me go home is my mother and my church. If it weren't for those two, I'd get rid of that ticket.

"I'm treated as a sister here, and as a matter of fact, as soon as I got off the plane, someone said, 'Welcome home, sister, welcome home.' I knew that I was home then. I felt at home on day one, yes I did, and I still feel at home. As a matter of fact, I don't want to go home. I want to stay here permanently."

But before Horton makes that decision, she's going to take the advice of African Americans who have made that decision before her.

"One person suggests that I stay a year [in Ghana] and see how things go. But one of the [people] told me that as an African-American sister, not yet married, it would be harder for me to survive over here versus me marrying or going back to the United States, because if I come here, my role as a female would change. I would be expected to do the fu-fu. I would be expected to do all of the traditional women things. And so that scared me. I'm beginning to have a reality check, and I wonder, can I swing it? Can I pull it off? But I'm going to find some more American sisters and get their perspective [before I make a decision]."

For Logan, Africa had always been seen through the words of her parents, and in some ways, their real-life experiences had become a dreamlike experience for her. Only after she created her own African experience was she able to reconcile the two.

"I don't think that for anyone with a dream of Africa, that I can explain Ghana to them via my understanding," Logan said. "I would have just had to say that you have to visit it yourself. Because no matter if you look at my pictures, hearing my stories, you're never going to get the full flavor of Ghana or West Africa unless you come and see it for yourself and create your own understanding. This has definitely been a pilgrimage to me, and I think that most African Americans need to make the journey here to see the connection for themselves, or not see the connection for themselves.

"I don't have a favorite part of Ghana because I think that all of the good parts in coming here, that make up the best part of me, begin here. I think that meeting people here and just experiencing Ghana for what Ghana is, is the best thing definitely."

And what about her name? Was she ever able to find out what it truly meant?

"My mother always told me that my name meant 'girl baby born on Thursday bring quick-filling happiness.' But I wanted to make sure that she was correct in remembering. She was," Logan said, smiling.

29

In Search of E.

Birmingham, Alabama

Just As I Am *helped me to resolve my own questions of faith and sexuality. It was through writing that novel that I learned that the God I believe in loved me no matter what, that there were no degrees of sins.*

—E. Lynn Harris

E. Lynn Harris sits with a friend at the hotel bar, sipping a glass of white wine. It is a brief stolen moment, one that will quickly pass after the guests arrive in the next half hour. Harris is the guest of honor and keynote speaker at a three-day black writers' conference, and the usual author personal appearance drill of photos, handshakes, and book signings awaits.

"I never write my speeches," Harris says, sipping his wine. "I like to let the words come to me. I say what I feel."

A couple of women walk into the lobby and instantly make their way toward Harris.

"Did you see the article in the newspaper?" asks one. She is a local Birmingham journalist.

"No," says Harris as he rises from the bar. "Did you bring one with you?"

"Well, I'll go get it for you," she says eagerly. "There should be a newsstand right outside."

But before she leaves to get the article, she and her friend ask if they can take pictures. Of course he obliges, and soon photos from various angles and with different members are being taken. More people enter the hotel lobby, see what is going on, come over, and then there are more photos. Harris begins to scan the ceiling of the hotel, as though looking for a magical door through which to escape. None appears. Suddenly, it's ten minutes before the event, and finally Harris is able to beg off other photo requests until after the dinner.

"With the public persona, these people are my fans, and they have supported me, so I should treat them with a great deal of respect," Harris says, catching his breath before his speech.

"In my own private life, I've been fortunate that I have friends that have been my friends for years, and I wouldn't feel obligated to go to dinner if I didn't feel like it. My friends understand me. But I realize that when I go out there, I have to be on. With fans, I have to make sure that they don't cross the line.

"Fame isn't a burden, it is a blessing," he reiterates. "I don't really buy into the whole fame thing. There are people that I have met that are famous. I meet them and then I move on. With other celebrities, it's almost as though I became a member of a celebrity club. Other celebrities are more willing to give me their home number versus if I was a regular fan. I think that they think that I know what they go through. On a real level, I really don't. I've become friendly with Janet Jackson, but I have no clue to what her life is like. But I do know that her life is not like mine. But I do find her to be very comfortable around me, but I know that she can't walk the streets like I can.

"When I walk the streets, sometimes I wear sunglasses and people recognize me so they'll smile. But I do know that people hold me in high regard. I went to a Broadway play, and the girl at the concession stand began shaking. She asked, 'Are you a writer?' and I said yes. She knew who I was. Someone called me from Federal Express, and after she did what she was supposed to do, she asked if I was the person she thought I was."

The waiters announce that the dinner is ready, and people now begin gathering in the ballroom. Aspiring writers, beginning writers, self-published writers, best-selling writers have all gathered this weekend to learn more about the craft of writing, and this dinner is the payoff for their hard work. The group of three hundred consists, like most of Harris's readers, of African-American women.

"My most loyal readers have always been African-American women," notes Harris. "They bring their men as fans when the men read their wives' or girlfriends' copies of my book."

After a brief introduction, the host of the conference gets up to introduce Harris. She reads his bio, and at one point, Harris looks up from his food to note something she has said. She finishes and, to a warm welcome, Harris rises and makes his way to the podium.

"I was saying earlier that I don't normally mention my fraternity affiliation," he says with a smile. "That's private information. I've got to change that bio."

E. Lynn Harris and his three younger sisters were raised by their single mother, who worked in an AT&T factory in Little Rock, Arkansas. He was fourteen when he first met his father, who was killed the following year.

Graduating from the University of Arkansas in 1977, Harris went to work as a sales executive for IBM. His first novel, *Invisible Life,* referring to Ralph Ellison's *Invisible Man,* was self-published. Harris sold the book to African-American bookstores, beauty shops, and book fairs, traveling whenever and wherever he needed to go in order get new readers for his book.

"When I would go to conferences like these," Harris says, "I would ask the people if they could guarantee that I would sell all of my books at the event. Because sometimes the book sales were the funds I needed to get back home."

In less than a year, he'd exhausted the 10,000-copy first printing and handed over vending duties to Doubleday, which reissued it.

The Chicago-and-New York-based writer has written seven best-selling novels to date: *Invisible Life, Just As I Am,* and the *New York Times* best-sellers *And This Too Shall Pass, If This World Were Mine, Abide with Me, Not a Day Goes By, Any Way The Wind Blows* and *A Love of My Own. If This World Were Mine* won the James Baldwin Award for Literary Excellence. *Abide with Me* was a finalist for the NAACP Image Award. In 1999, Harris was awarded the Distinguished Alumni Award from the University of Arkansas, at Fayetteville. Harris has been excerpted in *Essence* and featured in publications from *Newsweek* to the *Los Angeles Times.* He's now the best-selling African-American male author in the book industry today.

"If you have one of the first copies of *Invisible Life,* I probably sold it to you," he laughs humbly.

He's come a long way from his modest beginnings, and as a best-selling author, Harris should be contented. But after spending time with Harris, you can't help but notice a sense of weariness. There's almost sadness to his demeanor. It could be that he's weary of yet another personal appearance. It could be that he's weary from myriad reasons, none of them deeper than just being tired from traveling from Atlanta to Birmingham. But for whatever reason, it is clear that the E. Lynn Harris you get is determined by the "E. Lynn Harris" that E. Lynn Harris wants to project to you. No more, and no less.

It is easy to see that he protects himself from the public via varying degrees of shields. For example, he refuses to let people know what the *E* in E. Lynn Harris stands for, because he wants to retain certain aspects of his personal life and keep them personal.

Tonight, he will wear sunglasses during his speech. He'll tell the audience that he is sensitive to flashing lights, but you still get the feeling that he is protecting himself, as just one more barrier between his personal space and the public space.

But the sadness is a sadness that says, to paraphrase a lyric from a U2 song, that he still hasn't found what he's looking for. Outwardly, he says that he is happy with his life and that fame hasn't been a problem; however, the sadness in Harris could be rooted in the painful memories of his writing beginnings.

"I really started to write out of pain in my own life. I was not happy doing the computer sales jobs for thirteen or fourteen years. In 1990, I started to lose a lot of friends to AIDS, and I didn't see where my career was going anywhere. I was just really, really miserable."

This depression resulted in Harris's running away from his friends and community. But his life changed when he went to visit a friend dying of AIDS.

"There was a friend of mine, Richard Coleman, who was like a big brother to me. When he was sick, I used to write letters to him, and he used to tell me how much the letters meant to him. He said that I had a knack for writing. He knew that I wasn't happy doing the corporate thing."

It was then that Harris gained the courage to strike out and find his true calling. In some ways, a dying friend had provided new life in him. He became comfortable about who he was as a gay man, and in terms of his profession. Harris said he fretted about his looks and lied about his sexuality for years before he was inspired to write about his experiences.

"It became a part of my therapy, if you will. I'd finally found something that I enjoyed doing, even though I wasn't making any money at it, because I had no book contract. Writing became my life, became my job, and it was something I just absolutely loved doing. I needed to have some sort of focus in life, and when I started writing, some of the cloudiness began to leave."

Harris's stories about black gay and bisexual men and their journeys to find themselves are rooted in common human themes of love and conflict.

"Friendship and family, plus faith, are some of the themes that run through my books," he says.

The spirituality that runs through his books also runs through his own life.

"It is the most important thing in my life," he says. "But not necessarily organized religion, just my abiding faith in Jesus Christ, who has seen me through some really tough times, and who I thank every day for this wonderful life I now have. Actually being able, as clichéd as it sounds, to look yourself in the mirror and say 'I like you' or 'I love you.' Realizing that you're the only one of you. That God didn't make any mistakes. Doesn't mean you're not going to go through turmoil or be tested, but that you have the fortitude to go through anything.

"I don't consider myself a gay writer," he continues. "I'm an African-American writer who is gay. If people were only interested just in the gay experience, then they would have left after the first two books. They don't need to come back for eight or nine books to feel the gay experience. They come back because of the stories. The gay aspect becomes just one more part of a character.

"I want to write novels that will make people think. Whatever that's about. I've covered the issue of sexuality, and I've touched on the issue of class. But there are so many others. If I come up with something I have a prejudice about, I try and tackle it, and think I'm not the only one. One of the things I'm concerned with now is changing classes. The success of my books has put me into a new financial category. I want to be sure the lessons I learned as a very poor writer will be lessons I can apply in my new life. What I try to do is sit down and tell a story like you're the only one who's going to read it."

What attracts a lot of readers to Harris's books are the colorful characters within. One of Harris's most popular characters is Basil Henderson, a bisexual African-American ex-jock, who runs through most of Harris's books. Most of his readers want to know if his characters are based on people that he knows, but he adamantly denies this. At best, they are composites of people Harris has known briefly.

"I wouldn't do that to my friends," he says seriously. "But I have met people like Basil. I love all of my characters, but Basil is my most complex character. I've had Basil in my life. But I wouldn't say that this person is specifically like my Basil. What happens when I say a character is based on someone, it is usually a chance meeting, not someone I know intimately and well. I just wouldn't do that with close friends. Basil might be someone I had a two- or three-month affair with, not someone I've been in contact with since."

His readers' loyalty to his characters could pose problems, but Harris says that regardless of how attached people may get to certain ones, they remain his to do with what he wants.

"I'm in control, so I can do whatever to the characters. I just feel a certain degree of loyalty to my readers. But if a character no longer has a purpose to carry the story, then I wouldn't think twice about eliminating that character. One of my most popular characters in my first two books, Kyle, was killed off. People still ask me about that but they get over it."

During his speech, Harris speaks about the fact that his gay themes sometimes proved too much for some readers.

"I had one sister, an older sister, say that she began reading my book but had to put it down when she got to the sex scene," Harris says, and the audience laughs.

"She prayed on it and then continued to read," he says as he smiles. She is now one of Harris's most loyal fans.

Harris also recounts how another loyal fan decided that she was going to make dinner for him, no matter what.

"She kept coming to my book signings, saying that I just had to come over to her house so she could cook for me," he recalls. "Finally, after I had kept declining the invitations, she just decided to bring the dinner to me at a signing. It was in Tupperware, so I took it up to my hotel room and put it on the desk. It began to smell good. In the car, my escort, an older white lady, asked if I was going to eat. She thought that it could have been poisoned. But it smelled so good that I called the hotel front desk and asked them to send up a plate, a fork, and a bottle of wine. And let me tell you, that meal was great!"

Harris is clearly a crowd pleaser. His speech is more inspirational conversation than traditional lecture. Traditional African-American call-and-response carries the day as he tells stories about his experiences. He encourages the writers in the audience to persevere while getting better at their craft.

An African-American gay man writing about relationships, sex, faith, and family is bound to have his critics, especially in the African-American community, where even talk about homosexuality is often suppressed or discouraged. But Harris says that he has relatively few critics, and certainly not in this audience.

"I haven't gotten any backlash, or none worth mentioning," he says.

After a brief game where Harris asks the audience to identify certain characteristics within his books, it is on to the book signing. The queue extends the length of the ballroom. Each person requires not just a signature but also eye contact, a listening ear, and possibly just one more photo with the reader. Harris sits behind the table set up for him, and with a deep breath, gets ready for the onslaught. He will obligingly sign books for over an hour.

"I was raised by a single mom," he says afterward. "We were taught the basic things about respect, but I think more than anything I remember my mom telling me to treat people the way I want to be treated. That's kind of my mantra. I think if that's what you live by, the rest of the stuff falls into place. Anytime I think of doing something disrespectful, I put myself in their position and I'm very sensitive. If people are making general comments about someone that aren't very flattering, I feel I can remove myself from that."

In addition to his fiction, Harris is contemplating writing nonfiction in the near future. He has already written a book for teenagers and hopes to expand soon. He also has plans to write his autobiography.

"I'm going to write my memoir and I'm going to write some social commentary, even though I don't know why writers should be held in esteem for their opinions."

For his next book, *A Love of My Own,* Harris will sequester himself in his Chicago home overlooking Lake Michigan and let the muse come to him. He doesn't necessarily know how each book develops, because he literally sits at his computer waiting for inspiration.

"I sit down and I don't know who is going to visit when I write. Yes, I have to write because I'm on deadline, but I don't know which character is going to show up or what situation is going to come about. I don't write in sequence. I write what comes up, and when it is all done, I try to figure out a way for it to work."

After his literary journey is finished, Harris says that he has a simple request once people review his body of work.

"I want people to say that I tried to change people's minds," he says with a smile.

Suddenly, another group of fans approaches asking for a photo. It looks as though his night will end in the same manner as it began.

30

Gifted Unlimited Rhymes Universal

Midtown Manhattan, New York

There is no more difficult art to acquire than the art of observation, and for some men it is quite as difficult to record an observation in brief and plain language.

—William Osler

The contemporary musician is always more interesting behind the scenes, rather than when he is onstage. His stage persona builds an artificial biography for the concertgoer, but backstage provides a closer vision of who the onstage persona truly is. This is why people will sacrifice their right arm for a backstage pass at a concert. And a simple word from the musician, a small conversation, or a nod of acknowledgment all means that this nobody is suddenly a somebody in this famous person's life, even though it may only last for a quick second. That said, the musician's story lies even deeper, into the contradictions that the publicists want to mask, and that the artist doesn't even realize exist. It is there that you find the motivation and vision for their work, and their reason for longevity.

Keith Elam is a name that wouldn't resonate in most circles, even among his longtime fans. But if you call him by his hip-hop moniker of Guru, then most hip-hop fans would instantly recognize him as part of the groundbreaking duo, along with DJ Premier, called Gang Starr.

"I went to the department store yesterday, and I was standing in line with some clothes to buy," Guru recounted. "The sister at the counter became excited and asked me for my autograph. I began signing and this woman behind me asked me who I was. I said 'Guru,' and she huffed that she'd never heard of me. I continued signing the autograph when she decided to say that maybe she hadn't heard of me because she was forty-two. I then told her that I was forty, and people know me worldwide. She then knew that she had fucked up."

We are sitting in the smoke-filled D&D music studio, just down the street from Times Square. Located in a dingy New York office building, D&D has the unmistakable atmosphere of coolness. You get off the rickety elevator and you immediately are in a small black-light hallway with a red-light glow. You say the magic words to the brother behind the glass partition, and then you're buzzed in. Ten steps to the left and you instantly walk into the hip-hop version of a clubhouse. In the front, there's a sofa-filled lounge with a big-screen television playing music videos continuously. The walls are lined with the photos and album art of the artists who have done work in the studio. A video game console and a vending machine complete the look. In back of the lounge sits a solitary pool table.

"I like working at D&D because we have been here for a long time," says Guru, settling into the couch. "We did half of our *Step in the Arena* album here in 1990, and since then, we've done all of our work here. It's great because we can use the same people, like the same engineer, every time we come here. Plus, all our boys have used D&D, whether you are talking about Frankie Knuckles, Biggie, or Jay-Z.

Various people enter the lounge, all giving Guru his props. A professional skateboarder who's using Gang Starr's music in a video says hello and promises to get Guru to ride the skateboard in the next week. Rappers, some of whom are just beginning their careers, hang out. Some are there to work, while others want to soak up the scene. All notice that Guru is dressed rather formally this evening.

"I had to go to court today as a character witness for one of my boys," Guru says somewhat apologetically.

His boy, he explains, had been accused of robbery.

Guru is at D&D to lay down final vocals to Gang Starr's new album, *The Ownerz*. DJ Premier, his long time collaborator, is coming in later to listen and give his opinion. Meanwhile, Guru has a few errands to do before work.

"My girl and little boy are downstairs in the car, so I'm going to shoot them home first," he says, getting up from the sofa. "We can talk on the way."

Guru's journey to hip-hop begins in Boston, where he is the son of Harry and Barbara Elam. Married for fifty-one years, Harry was one of the first African-American judges in Boston, while Barbara received her Ph.D. in library science, and ran the Boston Public Library system before retiring. The educational résumés of the Elam children are sprinkled with graduation from such schools as Harvard, Northeastern Law, and Stanford.

"When you hear my background, you think middle class, but the thing about my dad, he was a community leader," explains Guru. "He was always either working in the church, helping the elderly or the young people. I remember that when I would go into his office, I would be amazed by all of the plaques. Whether it was 'Man of the Year' or 'Father of the Year,' and it was through that work that he became a judge, as he was voted in."

But whether Keith was going to follow in the footsteps of his parents and siblings was touch and go. He was more attracted to the school of the street than academics.

"I was rebellious because we grew up in a private area right across the streets from the projects, and I felt that my father didn't know what I had to go through in order to get my respect on the street. I was actually more close to my two uncles than my father, because my father was so strict. But now, I understand what he was trying to do. But at that time, I thought that he wanted me to be just like him.

"And having an older brother that was doing all of the right things, that made me even worse. [My brother] was president of the student body in high school and then he went to Harvard.

Meanwhile I was just hanging out," laughs Guru. "Even before crack came out, I was hanging out with the dope dealers and was watching them cook up the freebase. I mean it was wild. But the Boston streets definitely prepared me for the New York streets.

"I was doing shit just to be doing shit. All of this rebelling came from my mind, which said that my father wanted me to be like him, when in reality, he just wanted me to be all that I could be, and to find myself.

But Guru's rebelliousness also pointed him in the right direction, as he ended up attending prestigious Morehouse College in Atlanta, in some ways to spite his father.

"One reason I went to Morehouse was because my father used to tell me that I wasn't going to do shit," said Guru. "He used to say I was going to be a bum. And if you hang out with nine broke niggas, you'd just be the tenth one. So I felt okay, I'm going to go on a high school trip of black colleges. At first, I just went so that I could fuck with the girls, but I got to Atlanta and really started liking it. So I applied to Morehouse and got in. And those were some of the best years of my life."

At Morehouse, Guru was exposed to young black men from throughout the country. He began deejaying on campus, and hip-hop became a focal point. He had formed a group while in Boston, with fellow rapper Big Shug, and they participated in various talent shows. He formed Gang Starr with a beat box guy and a deejay, and they put out demos.

After graduating from Morehouse in 1983 with a business degree, he moved back to Boston. He worked in myriad jobs, from construction to substitute teaching to advising youth in the juvenile court. But Guru wasn't satisfied. He wasn't doing what he truly wanted to do.

"Hip-hop was something that I was immediately attracted to," says Guru. Even coming from Boston, we used to come down to New York and go to the clubs. I saw everybody from back in the day. From Kool Herc and Flash to Chuck Chill Out and Red Alert, I was exposed to that early. And I said to myself, I want to do that!"

"Hip-hop really saved my life because it allowed me to get all of the tension and things that were on my mind out there. But in order to do that, we needed to go to New York. So I got my money together and made my way to New York."

So, packing everything that he had into a duffle bag, Guru drove to New York in a $500 Volvo, which promptly broke down right outside a Connecticut tollbooth, in a driving snowstorm. He hitchhiked his way to New York, and his hip-hop career began.

"I did some demos in Boston, but when I got to New York, I knew that I had to do my shit over," says Guru. "People weren't responding to them. I went over to the Fever nightclub for a talent show and they gonged me before I even got started, even though most of the people who were judges say that they don't remember doing that."

Guru continued to work at his craft, eventually dropping his Gang Starr partners to go it alone. Later, he hooked up with DJ Premier, a deejay who was rocking the Prairie View University campus with his innovative beats. Premier eventually moved to New York, and they became the new Gang Starr.

"Premier moved in as my roommate because he didn't want to live with his father because he was mad strict," Guru remembers. "So he comes rolling up in a Nissan truck, full of all his records. The brother didn't have any clothes, just crates of records! Wait, he did have one pair of slacks that I used to borrow, because I didn't have any, and I needed to wear them for my counseling job. But the records took up the whole apartment, and my most vivid memory is coming home from work with him cutting up and his head bobbin', and then I'd start free-styling, and that's where we really started coming together."

The combination of Guru's flow and Premier's genius of finding obscure beats made an unbeatable combination. They signed a deal with Wild Pitch records and then hit big with *No More Mister Nice Guy,* their first album. After that, they came to the attention of director Spike Lee, who chose Gang Starr and

Branford Marsalis to collaborate on "Jazz Thing," the signature song in Lee's movie *Mo' Better Blues.*

"Spike didn't really even know that we knew that much about him," laughs Guru. "I mean, we both went to Morehouse, and he didn't know that we knew about Branford.

"The next thing you know, people in Europe wanted to hear us. Other record companies began asking about us, and we got a better lawyer and new management.

"So then Digible Planet and US3 come out, and boom boom, they start to clump us in with other people doing jazz, just like it happened later in gangster rap. And it was offensive to me because Gang Starr is not just about that. We are street knowledge, intellect, and spirituality, so we could take the sounds of a toilet flushing, or a cell phone ringing, and sample that to make a song."

Guru, which stands for Gifted Unlimited Rhymes Universal, was influenced by multiple people in his life, and his lyrics reflect a spirituality that is too often missing from today's hedonistic hip-hop artists. He can battle on the mike as well as any emcee, but he can also talk about issues that are important to the black community.

"I had influences from a bunch of people. My sister is a Buddhist, my parents are Christian, and I had two female cousins that lived with us, one that went to Boston University and the other to Harvard, and they were in the Nation of Islam, and before that, the Black Panthers. And they got through to me when my parents couldn't. So all of this allowed me to come up with not only the entertainment aspect, but the educational aspect also.

"I listened to artists like Melle Mel, who wrote "The Message," which took hip-hop to the next level. My mother had always stressed creative writing, and I used to hate that. But it came in handy when I began writing rhymes with concepts."

The success of "Jazz Thing" got Guru thinking about what else could be done with hip-hop and jazz, and how he and Gang

Starr could distinguish themselves from the pack of other artists fusing jazz and hip-hop.

"To protect Gang Starr and to also say that we are pioneers of that jazz hip-hop era, we came up with the *Jazzmatazz* album."

Since 1993, *Jazzmatazz* has been a three-album jazz-hip-hop-R & B fusion that has attempted to expand the hip-hop genre beyond the James Brown/Funkadelic beats used by many artists. It is experimental, and for many Gang Starr fans, it is different from anything they've listened to before. Jazz artists Donald Byrd, Roy Ayers, and Lonnie Liston Smith contributed, as have R & B stars N'Dea Davenport and Amel Larrieux.

"I like the fact that I'm able to cross over. People come to a show and they may be a *Jazzmatazz* fan or GangStarr fan," he said.

"I was influenced by the example of Donald Byrd, who was on my first Jazzmatazz album. He walked into the music department at Howard with a James Brown album and an idea to fuse jazz and R & B, and they turned him down."

Organized in 1974 at Howard University by jazz trumpeter and educator Donald Byrd and named after *Black Byrd*, his hit fusion album of the previous year, the Blackbyrds provided their mentor and producer with a pop outlet for his multifaceted imagination. The group struck pay dirt in 1975 with the wonderfully buoyant "Walking in Rhythm," a number four R&B, number six pop smash, and again the next year with the number three R & B, number nineteen pop "Happy Music." Those two classics, along with such others as the funky "Do It, Fluid" and the smooth, jazzy "Summer Love," showcase the versatility of a brilliant young band that was clearly ahead of its time.

Guru has been talking as we've traveled from Manhattan to New Jersey and back. We're a block away from D&D, but it's time to buy a little Hennessey for the boys back at the studio.

"I'm trying to stop drinking beer because of the belly," smiles Guru, patting his stomach.

As we walk to the studio, Guru talks about what it takes to stay in the hip-hop game.

"There are a few things that you have to do in order to stay in the game as an old-school rapper. One is that you've got to have a rep, where brothers on the street recognize and respect you. Whether it is hip-hop with a message or gangster, it has to be what you started with. If you sold 200,000 records earlier in your career doing one thing, then stick with that, or slight variations of your specialty. You just can't go to the left all of the sudden."

"I performed in Cancun last weekend. The promoter flew me out, and when I got there, not a lot of people had arrived. He wanted me to perform on old-school night, and I had to tell him no. You see, I'm not trying to date myself. Much respect to Dougie Fresh and Big Daddy Kane, who is my idol, but the reason we didn't call our Gang Starr *Full Clip* album a greatest-hits album, was because we didn't want to date ourselves by referring to the length of our careers.

"What we do is adapt to the times. Premier continues to innovate with his beats, and mad deejays are taking his beats and using them for their own music. Me, I try to peep what's going on in the biz, and I adapt it to my old flows and come up with my new flows. And critical to my whole flow is my voice. But if I had this voice and my flow was corny, then no one would listen. I don't do a whole bunch of metaphors and punch lines. I do a little of that. I'll tell you about experiences that may make you cry, because these things may have happened to me or happened to you. My shit is militant without being a gimmick."

We get to the front of D&D and there are a couple of NYPD patrol cars just down the street. It seems that one of the rappers has been caught with ten bags of weed.

"Man, I can't deal with this right now," says Guru to Black Jesus, one of the rappers on Guru's label, Ill Kid Records. "I'll deal with it later."

It's back to the D&D lounge, and blunts are being passed around. Guru takes a deep draw and passes it around.

"In this game, you've got to be smart," says Guru. "That's where I'm glad that I have a business degree. I own my own publishing, and I don't take the publishing of the people on my Ill Kid Records. I just don't think that it's right.

He takes another hit of the blunt and looks to his boys on the other couch.

"Be true to the music and the people around you, and you'll have a long career," he concludes.

With that, he walks into the studio to go over the lyrics with Premier.

31

Frank Ski on V-103

Atlanta, Georgia

Humor is perhaps a sense of intellectual perspective: an awareness that some things are really important, others not; and that the two kinds are most oddly jumbled in everyday affairs.

—Christopher Morley

The object of the Morning Zoo radio show concept has to be a uniquely American one, because only Americans could think of this. This is the formula: take a personable deejay, add wacky characters, stir with news and sports, and wham, you've got your morning zoo. But it's not as simple as it sounds. Add a comedian, but if your listeners don't find her funny, then watch your ratings fall faster than Gary Coleman's career. If there's not a natural chemistry among all of the members, then the funny Morning Zoo turns into a mitigated disaster.

The coffee has just started brewing at V-103 when Frank Ski gets on the microphone. He walks into the studio, turns on the television for the morning news, reviews his E-mail, and waits as the associate producer sets out pretaped cassettes. Gospel music gently wafts throughout the room, and Frank begins to record an inspirational message for his awakening listeners. It's 6:30 A.M., and the rest of Frank Ski's morning crew hasn't arrived yet.

Frank Ski came to Atlanta from Baltimore, Maryland, in November 1998. A veteran of radio, television, and music production, Frank's very successful broadcasting career spans over fifteen years. He was the evening-shift deejay for Baltimore's

V-103 and had record-breaking numbers in every age category, crediting him as one of the top air personalities in the nation.

In 1994, V-103 management decided to try his on-air talents in the very important Morning Drive shift. In just six months, Frank Ski took the *Frank & Jean Morning Show* to number one with record-breaking Arbitron numbers. In 1996 Frank Ski joined Radio One's 92Q FM in Baltimore, where he was instrumental in bringing credibility to the new underdog radio station. In just one ratings period, Frank Ski's audience made the switch from V-103 to 92Q and once again propelled the *Frank Ski Morning Show* to number one.

Within one year, Frank has built another team at Atlanta's V-103 with his morning team of comedian Wanda Smith, producer Tara Thomas, and former Atlanta Falcon Chuck Smith, and he is now syndicated in both Atlanta and Baltimore. He again is number one in his market.

"I think that the way you build an audience is to stay in the know for our community," Frank says. "What is the lifeblood and what are the interests of our audience? We then become a part of the community. And then, once we become a part of it, we become part of the people who are shaping the things in the community. Then others in our market become followers to what we do because you are immersed in the community. And then, it becomes natural for people to listen to us.

"Atlanta is unlike other cities. Other cities will march or have a picket, and black folks will get all upset. Atlanta will shut you down. If black folks here get mad enough, they will shut you down. I remember when the Concerned Black Clergy were outside of Grady Hospital picketing because Grady wanted to charge a dollar for prescriptions for poor people. Up to that point, they had been getting their prescriptions for free. The Concerned Black Clergy were saying that poor people couldn't afford the dollar fee because as it was, they had to take the bus to and from Grady. And I thought to myself that these brothers are NOT out here for just a dollar. But sure enough, after a week of picketing, Grady said that they wouldn't raise the fee. That's the difference with Atlanta. Atlanta has black economic power and influence, socially and politically. Other cities have black communities, but Atlanta's black community dictates to the mainstream."

Tara Thomas enters and takes over. She is a ceaseless ball of energy, constantly shuffling new cassettes in order, checking lists, and keeping Frank Ski on track.

"That's that seven o'clock wakeup workout! Hello, who is this?" asks Frank as he opens a phone line.

"Hi, Frank?" the caller asks.

"Yes, who is this?"

"Frank, do you know that I almost lost my job listening to the morning show?" the caller replies.

"What? You know that you've got to have some type of self-control, now!" says Frank, for the moment giving up on getting the caller's name.

The caller laughs and suddenly finds that she has nothing more to say. A brief awkward moment ensues.

"Let me play a song for you. What song would you like?" Frank asks.

"Well, I'm old-school, so play anything old-school."

"Okay, honey, talk to you later!"

"In November, we will have been in Atlanta for four years," says Thomas after the call. "I've worked with Frank for eight or nine years, and out of all the morning shows we've worked together on, this is the strongest because there is a healthy mix of people. We all come from different backgrounds, so we all bring different elements into the show. I think that it makes for excellent dialogue. And a lot of people that work on shows like this aren't genuine about their friendship. They come to work and don't see each other beyond work, while here, I know everyone's kids and we really like each other. I think that comes across over the air, and when we're angry with each other, that comes across."

Wanda arrives, greets everyone, and takes her position behind the mike. Tara, who doubles as an on-air personality, sits down and takes her position. It's now time for the zoo to begin. Today's topic is living large, or, in the parlance of the hip-hop culture, big-ballin'.

"Hey y'all, let me tell you something," Frank begins. "Russell Simmons? He's not a baller. Jermaine Dupree? He's not a baller. All of these rappers? They are not ballers."

"Well, then, who is a baller?" says Wanda.

"From this point on, I have a different perspective of what it means to be well-to-do or well-off after this weekend. I have to admit, I had the opportunity to hang out with the Russell Simmons of the world, and they are worth three to four hundred million. But they aren't balling. I missed the *60 Minutes* special on this man. I missed the *Ebony* article on this man. But I went to the [Holyfield vs. Rahman] fight with attorney Willie Gary. And Wanda, girl, hold on!"

"Say it!" says Wanda.

"From migrant worker parents to having his initials on the back of a 737," Frank continues. "We're not talking Lear Jet or small plane. We're talking big plane. The limo drives through the gate and goes straight to the airplane."

"Like the mayor of Atlanta?" says Wanda.

"Wanda, even the mayor don't ball like this!" laughs Frank.

"You walk onto the plane and it's like you walked into the Ritz-Carlton!"

"Get out!" says Wanda.

"There's mahogany everywhere with gold fixtures. A panel moves back and there's plasma television."

"Umm, umm, umm!"says Wanda.

"He turns it on, and what movie do you think he played?"

"Scarface?"

"No! This brother is old-school! I turned on the Temptations. Including the man who flew back with us, Evander Holyfield!"

"You flew back with the champ?" exclaims Thomas.

"Evander was singing Temptations and Whispers songs.

"The plane was ridiculous!" replies Frank.

"Now, the question is, what do Tara and I have to do to get on this plane?" Wanda asks.

"You've got to sleep with a lot of people to get on that plane."

"Okay, where does he live?" laughs Wanda.

And so it went. Frank was describing his weekend in the company of Willie Gary, a multimillionaire African-American lawyer who's been labeled "The Giant Killer." For years, Willie Gary has represented little-known clients against major corporations, and he has won some of the biggest jury awards in U.S. history. He has also won more than 150 cases valued well in excess of a million dollars each.

Willie Gary's amazing success in the courtroom has earned him national recognition as a leading trial attorney. *Forbes* magazine has listed him as one of the top fifty attorneys in the United States. Willie Gary has been featured by nearly every national media print publication, such as: The *New York Times,* The *Chicago Tribune,* the *Boston Globe, Ebony, Jet, People,* and *Black Law Journal.* His remarkable career and his tireless work on behalf of his clients have also been well documented by prominent broadcasters like Morley Safer, who featured Willie Gary on CBS's *60 Minutes.* He has also been profiled as Person of the Week on ABC's *World News Tonight with Peter Jennings,* featured on *Lifestyles of the Rich and Famous,* made a guest appearance on the *Oprah Winfrey Show,* and appeared on a CBS evening news *Eye on America* segment with Dan Rather.

Last night, Frank Ski went to Atlantic City as part of Willie Gary's entourage to watch former heavyweight champion Evander Holyfield fight Haseem Rahman. Holyfield, who will appear on the show later this morning, won his fight. But Ski is more fascinated with the wealth of Gary than anything else. Now he asks his cohosts to come up with a list of who's a true baller and who's a fake baller.

"Donald Trump is a true baller," says Frank as he recounts meeting Trump in an elevator in Atlantic City.

"He shook my hand and I haven't washed my hand yet!" laughs Frank. "Also, Paul Allen is a big-baller!"

"Yes!" exclaims Tara. "We went to the Super Bowl, and we saw his boat. We could not stop staring at his boat. When we first got there, there was a little boat that we thought was the bomb, but then a little down the way was Paul Allen's boat. I've never seen anything like this in my life. I forget how much they said that it cost; I think that it was like a $120 million. It was beautiful.

"The whole front of the boat is glass. It had a place for a helicopter. We were staring at the boat like groupies. And it was cold, too. And then a black dude got off and we were like oh man! We thought he was the owner! He was like, it's my friend's boat. I just wanted to ask if we could just go inside," laughs Tara.

"Who do you think is really ballin', Wanda?"

"My person is Magic Johnson."

"He's a baller."

"What about you, Chuck?"

"I vote for Russell Simmons."

"He's a baller."

"Okay. Tara?"

"I say Oprah Winfrey. She is ballin' out of control."

"She's the billion-dollar woman! Definitely a baller."

"Do you have another one, Wanda?"

"I'm going to have to go with Bishop T. D. Jakes!"

"He can't be a baller; he's a bishop!"

"Well, then, he's a baller in Jesus' name!"

"And with that, we need to take a break."

The crew goes to break and starts laughing at each other.

The hour is flying by. Frank preps a few segments off the air. Now they go back on air, and it is time to name all of the people who are "fake ballers."

"Okay, guys, who is a fake baller? Wanda, who do you have as a fake baller?"

"Kirk Franklin! Kirk Franklin is a fake baller!"

The crew falls out of their chairs laughing.

"I'm ready to go home! Can I please go home?" laughs Frank.

"Franklin tries so hard, he's M. C. Hammer! He's pimpin' the Family!"

"Who do you have, Chuck?"

"Dawn Robinson from *En Vogue!*"

The staff outside the studio is now laughing. Apparently, Robinson left quite an impression on them during a previous visit.

The crew continues for the next hour, discussing and arguing about more fake and real ballers. All of a sudden, it's ten o'clock and the show is nearing its end.

Frank ends the show almost how he began it, with an inspirational message from the bible. Tara, continuing her double duty as on-air personality and producer, runs back and forth through the studio. As the show signs off, Frank takes off his headphones and reflects on where he wants to go in the future.

"I would like to add more markets to our syndication. My vision is more so than adding one hundred stations nationwide. I would like to add maybe ten stations nationwide and then some overseas," says Frank.

"Our aim, in no particular order, is to uplift folks, make them feel good, enlighten by opening their minds and educating, and be entertaining so that they have a good time. And we've been able to transform our community, and I think that if we were able to do that in other world markets, we would be able to transform how people see African Americans. Because the only place that they see us is on television, but they don't really know us. They just look at black folks by whatever television show they last watched. If they were able to hear us on the air, then they would know what we are concerned about, and who we really are. I'd like to syndicate to South Africa, so that they would know that we are really concerned with Africa. And I'd like to syndicate in Brazil and Europe, and any other place where there is a large black population. I would love a show running in Japan, because there they love black things, but they don't love black people. I want them to love black people."

32

A Woman in Search of a Country

Kingston, Jamaica

The observation of others is coloured by our inability to observe ourselves impartially. We can never be impartial about anything until we can be impartial about our own organism.

—A. R. Orage

Grace Cameron is a woman without a country. She is a Jamaican who grew up in Canada, yet has come back to Jamaica, and now she's desperately trying to leave this country to go back to Canada.

"I think a lot of people look at me and can't figure out why the hell I'm here. Why would you come back here to live?" She smiles. "There's that prevailing view of how Jamaicans see themselves. On the one hand, people are all proud to be Jamaicans, but on the other hand, they don't think well of their environment."

Cameron sits poolside at a Kingston hotel, sipping Ting, a local Jamaican soda, while her son plays a computer game a few yards away. Cameron works as a community reporter and editor for the Kingston edition of the *Jamaican Gleaner,* a newspaper located in both Kingston and Montego Bay.

Her intimate yet distant relationship with Jamaica and Jamaican people allows her to form very strong opinions about what it means to be Jamaican, and also what it feels not to be looked at as Jamaican. And although her Jamaican patois comes through in every word she speaks, she seems more Canadian than Jamaican, even by her own reckoning.

"I think that there is ambivalence about Jamaicans who return to the island," Cameron says as she sips on her Ting soda. "I think that there is a little bit of resentment, especially if you are coming back to stay, not if you are visiting. There are a number of reasons. If you are not particularly secure in yourself and who you are, then you feel threatened by other people. People will say that 'Oh, you went away and now you're back and so you think you're better than me.' So there is some resentment in some quarters. Also because there is the thought that if you come back then you are taking the job of a Jamaican. But that being said, some people still do welcome us.

"I was born in Kingston, but I left Kingston when I was in my early teens. I went to Toronto and grew up there. I went to high school in Toronto and then I went to university. I began working there. I actually, in the early eighties, came back to Jamaica and worked for two years. And then I went back to Toronto and worked there for quite a while, and then moved to Vancouver. I went to journalism school, and I've been writing since then. I've been back in Jamaica now for the past four years."

Arawak Indians from South America had settled in Jamaica prior to Christopher Columbus's first arrival to the island in 1494. During Spain's occupation of the island, starting in 1510, the Arawak were exterminated by disease, slavery, and war. Spain brought the first African slaves to Jamaica in 1517.

In 1655, British forces seized the island, and in 1670, Great Britain gained formal possession. Sugar and slavery made Jamaica one of the most valuable possessions in the world for more than 150 years. The British Parliament abolished slavery as of August 1, 1834.

After a long period of direct British colonial rule, Jamaica gained a degree of local political control in the late 1930s, and held its first election under full universal adult suffrage in 1944. Jamaica joined nine other U.K. territories in the West Indies

Federation in 1958, but withdrew after Jamaican voters rejected membership in 1961. Jamaica gained independence in 1962, remaining a member of the Commonwealth.

Historically, Jamaican emigration has been heavy. Since the United Kingdom restricted emigration in 1967, the major flow has been to the United States and Canada. About 20,000 Jamaicans immigrate to the United States each year; another 200,000 visit annually. New York, Miami, Chicago, and Hartford are among the U.S. cities with significant Jamaican populations. Remittances from the expatriate communities in the United States, United Kingdom, and Canada make increasingly significant contributions to Jamaica's economy.

"One of the biggest reasons that Jamaicans decided to go to Canada, and not just Canada but elsewhere, like the U.S. and the U.K., is because of economics for the most part, plain and simple," Cameron explains. "They also go abroad because they feel safer somewhere else. Jamaica is a very violent society. So they feel safer somewhere else. They also want to get away from the political tribalism. And they go away for an education."

"I decided to come back to Jamaica for many, many different reasons. I decided to come back because I thought that I would find more of a sense of community here," she remarks. "I also wanted my son to grow up in a place where he would see people that looked like him, in charge of running things. I also came back here because I hate winter, even though I can deal with it if I have to. So there are many different reasons all mixed up in there.

"I also left because there were some projects [in Canada] that fell through, and I found myself working really, really hard. And I thought that if I was going to work that hard, then I should come back to somewhere it might make some impact."

But things have been rocky for Cameron ever since she returned to Jamaica. In some ways, she is looked at as an outsider, a person without true Jamaican heritage.

"When you live away from Jamaica for a while, people call you a foreigner. They say, 'She from foreign.' And so if you have a new accent, you are definitely 'from foreign,'" she laughs. "So you're a Jamaican, but you're still foreign. It's another way of differentiating you from other Jamaicans.

"And they will excuse some things that you may do. Say, for example, that you come back to Jamaica with ideas or beliefs that are not traditional in Jamaica; then they will say, 'Oh, well, she grew up a foreign anyway, so no wonder!' Jamaicans always say about those Jamaicans that went to England that they come back strange and eccentric. One Jamaican saying is that the 'cold got up into their head!' "

Life for a Jamaican expatriate in Canada is different. Besides getting used to the decidedly different weather, they also begin to see themselves as both Jamaican and as being black. This can be disconcerting for these new émigrés.

"I think that once Jamaicans actually get to there [to Canada], they are pretty ambivalent about it. They like the orderliness of being in Canada, but it's still not their country. So you do have that feeling of being in a strange place. You have to cope with things like race, and then there is the climate, which is totally different."

Race can be something new to a Jamaican who has always looked toward nationality. Ironically, the expatriate Jamaicans who may never have associated with one another on the island can be forced to coalesce around race.

"I think for a lot of Jamaicans that move to Canada or the U.S., the idea of being black is different," Cameron comments. "Because I know that growing up in Canada, especially in Vancouver, a lot of people felt that they had to claim being black, whereas I think for Jamaicans on the most part, the color thing, meaning that you identify with being black and saying that you are black, is not such a big thing. It's more a national identity.

"I mean, there is a color hierarchy here in Jamaica, but it is not really the same. Here in Jamaica, if you are white then you are on top of the scale, and the darker you get, the further down you are. The ones that are lighter-skinned, and have been thinking of themselves as 'brownies,' as they call it here, are shocked that [Canadians] call them black. All of a sudden, they are lumped in this thing that they never thought they were a part of. And that is a supreme insult, and they don't know how to deal with it. For those of us who are dark skinned, it's a little bit more acceptable. But all would rather identify with being Jamaican, and [to a lesser degree] would identify as being from the Caribbean."

While the debate among African Americans throughout their history has been the connection to Africa, Cameron believes that with the exception of Garveyites and Rastafarians, most Jamaicans don't believe in a strong connection between their island and the continent of Africa.

"I think many Jamaicans know about Africa, but I think that many haven't thought about the [connection]. And those that do think of Africa reject Africa, because I think that Africa has been so painted in such a negative picture. To Jamaicans, Africa is way over there, while Miami is just an hour away. And when I was in school, we weren't taught about any African history.

"There's just not a consciousness here. You find it on an individual level, but no, not overall. People get upset with you if you tell them that they are from Africa. I mean, if you hold them to it they will admit that way back when, but God, no! If you tell them now, 'They think they come from monkey!' "

She laughs again, but it's a bittersweet laugh from Cameron. She doesn't say it, but you get the feeling that being called 'from foreign' has left an indelible mark on Cameron during her time in Jamaica. She loves this island, but her personal experience makes some things completely clear to her.

"I think that once people get to Canada, they become very protective of their Jamaican identity and of Jamaica. Many times they feel more pride in Jamaica away from Jamaica than when they are actually here. Because one, I think there is a feeling of protecting something, but Jamaicans tend to be very patriotic anyway.

"However, I think that when some people go away, they become very embarrassed and don't want anything to do with Jamaica," she continues. Some people go to the other extreme, where everything about Jamaica is bad, and it is so terrible. In their eyes, Jamaicans are bad; black people in general are bad, but black Jamaicans especially are bad. And so they don't want anything to do with the island if possible.

"Even though we have a reputation of being bad, I think that there's almost a perverse pleasure in being bad. So there's that. The joke from people from other islands is that when they were dropping off the slaves, they dropped the worst-behaving ones off in Jamaica," she laughs. "But I think that most people feel very protective of Jamaica. And even though we may know that there are bad things in Jamaica, we just don't want other people to say it, because people outside of Jamaica will put a very twisted interpretation on our situation."

That "bad" reputation about Jamaica comes from a number of reasons. Jamaica has a history of political violence, dating back to the 1970s and the formation of armed gangs with political affiliations. The Jamaica Labour Party and the People's National Party, formed by Norman Manley and Sir Alexander Bustamante respectively, divides the Jamaican populus virtually into armed camps. In 2001, over 900 people were killed in political violence.

"It seems to me, for the most part, the political parties will do anything to get in power, including using the people, and turning people against each other. And the whole gun culture, it has been said, can be traced back to these parties."

Cameron shakes her head in disgust. However, there is one newly formed political party that has Cameron a little optimistic.

Antoinette Haughton-Cardenas formed the United People's Party in 2001 as an alternative to the two entrenched political parties. Its driving philosophy is a new nationalism influenced by Garveyism, Christianity, and the vision of People's National Party founder Norman Manley.

The UPP declared the critical issue of crime and violence as one of its major priorities, and following its media launch in Kingston, the party has been presenting its "vision and objectives" to Jamaicans around the island in small community meetings, inviting citizens to join in the shaping of the party's development, recruiting candidates, and providing vocal leadership on important national issues. And also, the party has begun mining the large expatriate communities in New York for votes. But their road will be hard.

"I like Antoinette Haughton, and the fact that she's had the courage to get up and form her own party, and wants to make a difference. She's very passionate, and very emotional. And she doesn't come from the old labor movement, power-hungry-men kind of base. I mean that I like her well enough that if I was going to hang around, I think I would want to join her."

The Jamaican economy remains stagnant; however, the Jamaican people are known as being incredibly resourceful. As with most black countries, external debt continues to inhibit the growth of the island. Even though Jamaica is independent, they are nominally reliant upon their former colonial protectors, the United Kingdom and its neighbor to the north, the United States. Cameron has a simple solution for change in Jamaica.

"If I could wave that magic wand, I wish people in Jamaica would think about putting Jamaica first, rather than themselves," she says with resignation.

"All of these people who are so power-hungry and are so eager to grab this or that, I wish they would truly think of Jamaica first, as opposed to their own ambitions. Because it would seem to me that throughout our entire history that it has always been people who have come here, taken out, and then left. You're talking about slavery. You're talking about the colonial period. You know all of those people in England didn't live here. They reaped [the benefits] of all the things that left Jamaica and went elsewhere. And you still have it.

"A lot of professionals, new professional and old professionals, have their savings in U.S. dollars, and I can't blame them. They don't trust [the Jamaican government]. Our money goes out of the country, all to service our debt. So there's an enormous amount of capital [leaving Jamaica]. The economic situation in Jamaica is pretty bad. I really don't know how regular Jamaicans survive. I find the cost of living to be very high because there are very few bargains to be had. The cost of services is high, yet the labor is cheap."

Yet, even though their own country is not able to get out from under the grip of the abuses of power and a stagnant economy, Cameron believes that many Jamaicans just don't understand why African Americans in particular are in the state that they find themselves.

"I think that Jamaicans are puzzled by African Americans, because they don't understand how you can live in the land of the rich and not be rich and kick butt," laughs Cameron. "Jamaicans are very ambitious, and I think that a lot of the thinking is 'Boy, how can they live there and complain about racism? Yeah, there may be all that, but you should be able to pull yourself up by your bootstraps and get a good education.' Some people think that African Americans are just spoiled. The Jamaicans that have traveled and have been in contact with African Americans know that things are more complex than that."

It is finally time for Cameron to go. Her son is becoming antsy, and in a way she has become antsy also. From her words, it is clear that Jamaica holds nothing for her. She truly has become 'gone foreign,' both in the eyes of Jamaicans on the island and in her own eyes. And it is too late to change either fact.

"When you live away from Jamaica for a time, you sometimes find the way things are done here a little confounding. It's not necessarily right or wrong, just different. There are good people here like anywhere else. There are good things happening here like anywhere else," she concludes.

33

Basketball as a Metaphor for Life

Phoenix, Arizona

Good leaders make people feel that they're at the very heart of things, not at the periphery. Everyone feels that he or she makes a difference to the success of the organization. When that happens people feel centered and that gives their work meaning.

—Warren Bennis

The press guide says that Rob Evans's job is Arizona State University head basketball coach, but if that press guide were being truthful, it really should say that his job is multifaceted. At different points in the year, he is a teacher, marriage counselor, father figure, talent evaluator, psychologist, doctor, administrator, and friend to sixteen young men under his tutelage. This is a year-round job, and even when it is time to take a vacation, Evans can't bring himself to relax.

"When you are a college basketball coach, you get about a week to crash after the season is over, and then you have to get back recruiting," laments Evans. "What happens to you in coaching is that you get through in April and then you finish recruiting in May. In June, we have four weeks of basketball camp. We'll have two thousand kids in here for four weeks. And then in July, that's the only time that the NCAA allows you go to different camps and see recruits. Then, for only three weeks in August, right before school starts, that's when you can try to get some type of vacation. My wife, Carolyn, and I used to go on vacation, but I just can't vacation. Even when I'm on vacation, I have a feeling that there is something that I should be doing. So finally, Carolyn told me, 'Rob, I think that they can get along [without you].' "

It's two o'clock on a Thursday afternoon, and Rob Evans is standing on the sidelines of the Wells Fargo Arena, watching his assistant run through practice. This evening's game is against Pacific Ten Conference rival UCLA, and the players are sweating through various plays they will run. Every so often, an assistant coach stops them and, like a director blocking actors, moves the athletes to their correct positions. And then they run their plays, again and again. Periodically, Evans quietly barks out some instruction, and the players run to accomplish it, even if it is as simple as having them huddle together.

"One of my assistant coaches scouts the opposing team, and he will go over the scouting report with the team before the game. And the other coach will look at game film for Saturday's game against USC. I let those guys talk to the team. First of all, I don't have time to sit and look at a lot of tape and they do. It also teaches them to be head coaches. It allows them to learn more, and they are actually out here demonstrating things [to the players]. Now, a lot of head coaches don't allow that because they feel threatened by assistant coaches. These head coaches want to be in on everything and be out there in the public and let everybody know that they are out there doing all of the coaching. My objective is to win. So I'm going to designate certain things for my assistant coaches to do.

"During the games, there is one assistant that does the match-ups while another assistant does the substitutions. I make all decisions about what we are going to do, but I may tell the assistant to draw up the plays. So that's the way that I do it."

The players continue to work on plays, and about an hour into the session, Evans ends practice. The players meet at midcourt for final instructions from Evans and his assistants before their pregame meal. As they begin walking out toward the tunnel, Evans walks in the opposite direction.

"Now today, what we do is generally have a pregame meal, and at the pregame meal, we go over the scouting report again on the overhead. I generally go, but I missed one pregame meal earlier in the season because I was sick, and we've been undefeated at home ever since. So now the players just ask during the huddle, 'You're not going to the pregame, are you?' because they're superstitious," he laughs. It may be humorous, and the players may be needlessly superstitious, but Evans isn't going against their wishes. Whatever it takes, so there's no team pregame meal for him this evening.

Basketball has been in Evans's blood since he was a star at New Mexico State in 1967. A multipurpose athlete who was drafted by three different pro teams in three separate sports, Evans immediately walked into coaching after his collegiate basketball career was over in 1968.

"The whole time that I was at New Mexico State, I was watching guys I played with taking classes that the coaches picked. I never let them do that to me. I looked in the book and said, 'I'm majoring in English and these are the classes I'm supposed to be taking, so these are the classes that I'm going to take.' But the rest of the players would just take what the coaches gave them, hook, line, and sinker. So these players would be at school for four years and still three years from graduating. I thought to myself that they are putting these guys in BS courses and that isn't right. So I knew that I had to get involved in coaching, because I could see a lot of inequities in college basketball, and I had to be a part of change. So that's one of the reasons I'm a coach, because I'm all about being a part of positive change."

His first coaching stint was at his alma mater, and then he moved to Texas Tech for the next decade and a half. After another two years at Oklahoma State under Coach Eddie Sutton, Evans received his first head coaching job at the University of Mississippi in 1992.

"I was at Texas Tech for fifteen years because I wanted to be there," says Evans. "If I had been in a higher-profile situation I might have moved quicker, but my family was important to me. My kids were doing well in school and my wife, Carolyn, was completing her degree. I'm a pretty patient person, and you have to be if you are an assistant for twenty-four years. But I never blamed anybody for being an assistant that long. It has become a positive as a head coach. I've seen a lot of things over the years, things to do and things not to do."

His stint at the University of Mississippi saw his vast experience produce long-term results. Former Arizona State athletic director Dr. Kevin White said that Evans didn't rebuild the University of Mississippi program because Mississippi never really had a top-flight basketball program to begin with. In all respects, Evans took the Ole Miss programs to unknown heights, winning the Southeastern Conference in both 1996-1997 and 1997-1998. He won SEC Coach of the Year in the 1996 season.

But life wasn't all peaches and cream at the University of Mississippi. The university has had a long, historic struggle with race. The school's nickname is the Rebels, and until quite recently, Confederate Rebel flags were a constant presence at sporting events. The school song is "Dixie," and even the shortened name for the university, Ole Miss, refers to how African-American slaves allegedly addressed their white masters. Into this cauldron walked Evans, who was the University of Mississippi's first African-American head coach. And with his arrival, changes began to happen, some through gentle lobbying, and others through behind-the-scenes maneuvering.

"To a point, I'm still trying to fulfill a dream. During the Freedom Rides, I wanted to go down south and get involved in that, but my mother wouldn't let me do it. So I never felt that I fulfilled what I wanted to fulfill.

"I had spent a lot of time recruiting in the South during the sixties, when it was dangerous. But I was smart enough to know that I was down there for a reason. But every year I would go to the South and see a little bit of change. I could see change in Arkansas, change in Alabama, change in Louisiana, but I never saw enough change in Mississippi. So when the Mississippi job came up, I felt that I was being called. So when I got the job, we began to make some positive change."

Recruiting African-American students for his basketball was extremely difficult because of the traditional antipathy African Americans had for the university.

"I had recruits that lived only a few short miles from the university that had never set foot on campus," says Evans. " I had one mother who lived in Oxford her whole life, but whose first step on campus was when I recruited her son. I would get close to recruits, but they just couldn't pull the trigger. What would happen to them is that they would visit, feel good about everything, but go back to their neighborhood and people would say, 'How can you go to that school?'

"The way I changed things was working with the football coach, Tommy Tuberville. He is a white coach, and I would let him be in the forefront and I would work in the background. If I were to get out there in the public, they would crucify me. But I would do the dirty work underneath, but he was the guy out there speaking. And also the president was working to change a lot of things, and a lot of the old guard didn't like it.

"But I also worked on the community. We went to a mixed church, and there was a white guy who owned a trophy shop. Well, my assistant Russ Parnell, who is with me at the University of Mississippi and here, said, 'Coach, we should change our jerseys from "Ole Mis" to the "University of Mississippi." Because when we go to Los Angeles, they don't know who we are.' "

Well, the guy who owned the trophy shop sent me a letter. He said that he was a brother in Christ, and how could I change the jersey from 'Ole Miss' to the 'University of Mississippi'? So I went by the shop. I told him that we needed to go in the back of the shop because of the conversation we were going to have. I told him that my basketball program is like my house, and I do what I want within my house. Just like this shop here, you do what you want to. Now you have Confederate flags in here. I shop here, and I buy trophies from you, but I haven't said one word to you about your flags. He immediately said, 'Oh, I sell them, but I don't wave them.' So I told him that in other words, you sell the dope but you don't smoke it. He then said that he didn't have an idea that these flags offended me. I told him that they highly offended me. So what happened is that he got rid of those flags. He wrote me a letter saying that he now understood. So I converted him. And that's what you had to do. You had to convert them one by one."

Evans has made his way to his desert home, where his wife is playing host to family and friends. Three of Evans's teachers from New Mexico have made their way to Phoenix for the UCLA game. He'll relax a bit here before making his way back to the arena for the game. His pregame meal will consist of a quick Whataburger and some fries.

At Arizona State, his task has been to rebuild a program that was a complete shambles before he arrived. Former players had been indicted for point shaving, and the former coach had been forced to resign. So for Evans, it's back to rebuilding a program, and that means going back on the recruiting trail. It's all about finding diamonds in the rough.

"I've been coaching basketball for so long that I can look at a high-school player and project what he's going to be like one, two, or three years from now. But that is only if his work habits are good, and you don't know that. It's an inexact science because you see a kid that is very talented and is really good, but he doesn't get any better because he has poor work habits. But the way that you find out how much a kid should really be playing is that once you get him here, you put him in your workouts and you can kind of tell where he is, how much he can help you, and his maturity. But that comes with experience.

"During a typical visit, I would talk to the parent about their kid and why he should consider Arizona State. Basically, you've got to sell yourself first, because all of the schools tell you the same thing. Their tradition may be a little different than our tradition, but a lot of kids aren't worried about tradition; they just want to know if they will get a chance to play. Also they want to know if they are going to get on television; will they get some exposure? So, you've got to let the parent know that I'm going to be with the kid after basketball. I want a family atmosphere. I want people to feel at home with me. But basically, the players that you already have on your team are your best recruiters. If they don't like it here, then they will tell recruits that they shouldn't come here. But I had one former player tell recruits that if there is a school to go to, then you must go to Arizona

State. The former player won't BS you. So those are your best recruiters."

College basketball is big business, and the influences and expectations go beyond the coach and the player. Often, many people are hitching their cart to a horse that may be a future star. Hence at an early age, some basketball players feel as though they are owed things in life, and that it is not necessary for them to work hard.

"[In terms of a sense of privilege] what you have now are AAU programs that are vying for these kids. We have two in this area, one run by Nike and the other run by Adidas. So when these kids are ten years old, they'll have Air Jordans, and warm-ups, and so they get to a point where they start thinking that they are special. So I tell them that it is a privilege to play this game of college basketball. And with those privileges come responsibilities. And therefore, if a kid misses class, then not only does he come out at five in the morning, but he also misses practice. During practice time, we set up a tutor for the player. And in my system, if you don't practice, you don't play.

"If you miss a class, I'm going to get you up at five in the morning and you're running five miles. That's the first thing. And so what happens is that they don't miss classes. They'd much rather get up at eight o'clock than five o'clock. And if they have to be there at five o'clock, they know that they have to get up at four in the morning, so they are not going to miss. I also make them sit up in the first two rows of class, because if you sit up there, by osmosis you're going to get something. And you can't go to sleep. So I put all of those parameters on them and so I've had a lot of success with kids graduating. You know, athletes are pretty competitive people. When they are not successful in the classroom, it tends to be because they don't go. When they don't go, they get behind and frustrated, because when they do go, they're lost and then they can never catch up. So I don't allow them to not go to class.

"What I tell these guys is that we all have some deficiencies. And if you can't read, it's not a sin to not be able to read, but it is a sin if you continue to not be able to read with the opportunities you have. It used to be that kids, when I first started coaching, that they didn't want to be branded as dumb. I tell them that it is when you are fifty years old and can't read—that's when you have problems. If we have a kid that has trouble reading, we are going to have him in a reading program.

"Parents can also be an obstacle to success. A lot of parents are living through their skilled children, with many willing to overlook their children's deficiencies for short-term success.

"I deal with parents honestly. We have a kid on our team that was ranked the thirty-third best high school basketball player in the country. But he hasn't blossomed because of his work ethic. On this level, you've to be tough, and he's not tough. For example, he's got to go out there and guard UCLA's Jason Kapono tonight, and Kapono is going to try to take your heart. And if you aren't tough enough, he's going to eat you up. The kid has a lot of ability, but his toughness is lacking. Well, his dad called me on the phone during his first year and asked if he could come by and visit with me. I told him yes.

"So he comes by and says that when I recruited his son, that I was going to build a program around him. I said that we are and I intend to, but he's not ready for that right now. So he went on and on talking about that I could have played him more, and I told him that he was going to get more time when he earned it. I told him that he couldn't get his son more time, and that the son was the only one that could get him more time. We talked some more and the father said, 'Well, it's kind of embarrassing to me around town,' and I said, 'Whoa! Now it's about you!' Now the truth of the visit was coming out. I told him that when I recruited his son, he had trusted me. I told him to now get out of my way and let me handle him with no strings attached. And so with two or three sessions like that with parents, you can clear things up. But if you ever waver, then you've got problems. So the dad knows where I stand. And so he sits down with the kid and tells him, 'It's on you and you've got to get it done.' But the kid wasn't complaining, because he knew that he wasn't doing what he needed to get it done. And so the dad would get tricked.

The dad raised his son by himself, and I told him that he did a great job raising his son. But he appears to be one of those kids that laid on the couch while everybody else was going to work. The kid was watching TV with the remote control and telling you, 'Dad, bring me a hamburger and coke.' I said that the bottom line is that he's spoiled. Now it's my job to toughen him up because you didn't."

Evans is now back at Wells Fargo Arena, only a couple of hours before the game. In the Arizona State locker room, about six televisions are showing various college basketball games from throughout the country. The assistant coaches have already arrived, and a couple of former University of Mississippi players have arrived to visit Coach Evans and see the game.

Each of the sixteen players on the Arizona State squad presents challenges, but the biggest challenge so far was presented when a player transferred to his current squad with a litany of issues to deal with. But it is Evans's job to help him get through those issues.

"I've got a kid that is learning-disabled, has an attention deficit, and is bipolar. It's really a strange story because of how the kid was raised. His mother was a police officer, but she didn't raise him because he was in trouble with gangs in Chicago when he was a young kid. And his younger brother just got out of prison.

"He was playing baseball and his baseball coach, who is a white guy, decided to adopt him. He signed right out of high school for the University of Tennessee but didn't qualify, so he had to go to prep school. Out of prep school, he went to the University of Illinois. But he played there for only one year. My friend Lon Kruger, who was the coach at Illinois before he went to the pros, told me about him and said that he needed some special attention, but he didn't tell me how much attention. So we took him. Now I spend 90 percent of my time with him.

"I think that he was abused somewhere in his background, because of the way he acts. He has to take medicine every day for his attention deficit. And sometimes he wouldn't take the medicine because it would break him out and he didn't want to look bad. I finally had to get to a point where I told him that he had to take the medicine in front of the trainer, because if he didn't take the medicine, he'd go off. Well, that embarrassed him, because he's twenty-three years old and he's asking why he's got to take this in front of this guy.

"I could tell him something tonight [at the game] during a timeout and he could go out on the floor and instantly forget it. And then if you get on him about it, he'll get more frustrated, but I think that I'm the only person that he respects. And he'll tell you that. I'm honest with him, but I'm firm with him. I tell him that I refuse to believe that he can't remember what I tell him. I refuse to believe that, because he can go home every day, so why can't you remember what I tell you?

"He really tries to do everything I say, but he sometimes can't help what he does. I suspended him for the Oregon State game because during the Oregon game, he had swung at a kid. You can tell him that he can't do things like that and he'll say 'What?' And then you show him the tape of the game and he'll bow his head.

"But I can't fail him. As a head coach, if I fail, then that kid fails. I've got to do right by him. My assistant coaches told me that I said that the next time that he took a swing at someone that I would suspend him. I told my assistant coaches that I had to make sure that the intent was there. In this case, you're talking about a kid's life and psyche. In this situation, he got tangled up with another guy, and as he tried to shake the guy off of him, it seemed like a natural reaction. And when this kid can't deal with something, he's going to strike back. Whether or not it is verbally or physically, he's going to strike back. And I don't think that this was intentional. So I wrestled with this all night. Should I or should I not suspend this kid? Well, my mind went back to number one; I don't want to lose the rest of the kids, because they know what I said. I don't want to lose my staff, because they know what I said. Yet I still don't think that it was intentional, but I still have an obligation to suspend him. When I suspended him, he went nuts. He didn't say anything but it really got to him, but he took it. And the next day, he worked very hard."

The locker room is quiet now. Five managers stand at the ready in the trophy room while the basketball players are sitting on benches, taping up ankles, listening to the assistant coaches go over the game plan. Evans stands to the side, listening. All, including Evans, now have mentally transformed themselves into people with a single-minded focus: winning a game. In other words, everyone in the room has his game face on. Evans brings them together.

"I want you to play hard and remember what we have told you," says Evans. "Let's go."

And with that, the managers open the door to the hallway leading to the court, and the basketball team rushes out, shouting encouragement to each other as they run. Evans stays behind, erasing the white board that has been used to diagram priorities.

The arena is packed, the band is playing, and their opponents, the UCLA Bruins, are already warming up at one end of the court. UCLA coach Steve Lavin walks to center court to shake hands with Evans, and they exchange greetings. Each knows what the other is going to try to do, and it is now up to their players to execute the game plan.

"Most coaches don't go outside of their comfort zone. Basically, they are going to do the same thing every time. If a guy is a man-to-man coach, he's pretty much going to remain a man-to-man coach. He might do a little zone, but he's not going to do much. If a guy is like Lavin, who likes to press, then he's going to press. Whether he's home or on the road, he's going to press. He'll change defenses on you. What Lavin does is junk [the game] up. He has great talent, so what he's saying is that he wants to confuse you a little bit and let his talent override. All he wants you to do is to turn the ball over, and if he can get more possessions than you, then he's going to win. Conversely, we have to take care of the basketball and just get as many possessions as we can, and shoot the basketball well."

The game begins and Arizona State doesn't get a good start. They miss thirteen of their first sixteen shots, but they make up an early eight-point deficit and eventually lead the UCLA Bruins 29-28 before falling behind at halftime with a score of 36-31.

At halftime, the players and the coaches run to the locker room. The coaches drink water while waiting for the statistical report to come in from the managers. The players go to another room, drinking fluids and talking among themselves. There is no ranting or raving, just a calm. Finally, the reports come and the assistants in unison lament the shooting statistics. Evans quietly tells the assistants what he wants to emphasize to the players.

They move to where the players are, and Evans, for the first time, raises his voice.

"You can't go out there and just play for yourself," Evans says. "You've got to play hard and be tough."

The players sit in rapt attention. After Evans finishes, the players repeat the same energy they had before the game and again storm out of the locker room.

And again, UCLA begins the half with a scoring run, leading Arizona State 50-39. But three-pointers by the Sun Devils bring the team within five points. In a game of scoring runs, UCLA widens the game to a thirteen-point lead, with about nine minutes left in the game. But Arizona State rallies, creeping within four points with only thirty-nine seconds left in the game. But this is when the referees make a controversial call. It is a technical foul call assessed on the Arizona State bench.

Early in the game, the referees warned Arizona State that the crowd had been throwing things on the court. Now, with the game on the line, the referees call a technical foul on the Sun Devils when some fans throw coins onto the court. That proves to be the difference, as the technical foul shots spread the lead to eight. After a furious rally, Arizona State's last-second three-point shot falls short and UCLA wins, 82-79.

There are no moral victories in the Arizona State locker room. Defeat means that all of the hard work has not been rewarded, and the deflated faces both of the players and coaches reflect that fact. Evans first addresses the team, noting what they have done in the game but also being honest about what it is going to take to win in the future.

Now it is time for the postgame interviews. One is for the cameras, while the other is for the Arizona State radio show.

"We always expect a tough game with a Rob Evans coached team," UCLA coach Steve Lavin remarks after the game. "The shoes are always squeaking when we come in here. We were fortunate."

The cameras and reporters are waiting for Evans and he sits in front of an Arizona State banner. He answers the reporters' questions carefully and succinctly, making sure to maintain his composure throughout. He knows what his role is and what they are trying to do. That's why he has a simple philosophy about dealing with the media.

"I don't read the newspapers during the season because you are going to react to what you read. No matter who you are, you are going to react. If you see something in the newspaper that says, 'How can you not play a certain player,' then your mind goes to 'This reporter believes that I should play this player.' And if you're not careful, you'll get in a game situation and you'll start thinking about it. I'll read the *USA Today.* I'll read the *LA Times.* But I'm not going to read the local newspapers. Bottom line, those [reporters] really don't know what they're talking about. They don't come to practice, and they write what sensationalizes. They know that they are writing things that get letters to the editor. Plus, the reporter has the pen last."

"That technical shouldn't happen," Evans says during the press conference. "When the game is close, you let the players decide things. It was demoralizing when you work as hard as these kids worked."

His wife, Carolyn, who is off to the side lending her moral support, watches with a pained expression on her face. It soon becomes evident that not only the coach and players take losing hard, but the families do also.

Finally, both interviews are over. Evans gathers his family

and friends and moves back to the locker room. It's time to figure out where to go for a postgame dinner. Evans knows that it is a long season, and there is another game on Saturday.

"We'll get them next time," he says with a wry smile.

He's right. Arizona State beat UCLA in Los Angeles in the next month. It would be Arizona State's first victory over UCLA in Los Angeles in fifteen years.

34

Gearing Up for an Education

Washington, D.C.

Education is a companion, whom no misfortune can depress, no crime can destroy, no enemy can alienate, no despotism can enslave. At home, a friend, abroad, an introduction, in solitude a solace and in society an ornament. It chastens vice, it guides virtue, and it gives at once grace and government to genius. Without it, what is man? A splendid slave, a reasoning savage.

—Joseph Addison

The Longworth House Office Building just like all of the other government buildings in Washington, D.C., after the terrorist attacks of September 11, had to be cleared because of the deadly anthrax letters. No one knew who had sent the letters, but the government did know that people had died because of exposure, so they were taking no chances. Congressman Chaka Fattah's office was no exception. But the offices are clean now, and the only thing that would let you know that people hadn't been in their offices recently was all of the out-of-date magazines still on the shelf.

About eight staffers share this office space, some cloistered in corners, while others have cubby holes. Offices of varying degrees of luxury are guarded and cherished within the building and can be allocated and withdrawn depending on political whims.

Jerome Murray is Congressman Fattah's office assistant. He makes the coffee, answers the phones, and is the first person you see when you walk into the congressman's office. He wants to be a public servant, and this is how you pay your dues.

"I had a fascination with politics, but the reason that I came to D.C. was because I got into law school at Howard University," says Murray as he settles behind the desk. "I didn't know which route I wanted to take to get into politics. I'm from Massachusetts, and most politicians there become attorneys and then they get into the political field. So I thought that maybe I'll try that law thing, but I never wanted to work for a firm. I never wanted to make the big money or the high salary, but I just wanted to do the public service. And after my first year, it just wasn't cutting it for me. It just wasn't what I wanted to do. So now, I had a chance to come here on the Hill.

"I'd interned originally for my congressman from my district back in 1997. My mother was a longtime staffer for a congressman from Massachusetts, so I kind of grew up around it. And so I said to myself, let me look at the public service and public administration route."

He turns on all of the televisions in the office; they are constantly overhead, either on C-Span I or II, or one of the news channels. Harking back to an earlier age, there are buzzers and lights within each office that signal when the congressman is needed for a vote. On any given day, the congressman may go back and forth ten times during the day. The traffic is so much that House guards will stop automobile traffic as the representatives crisscross the street.

Congressman Fattah arrives at the office about ten A.M. His office, filled with commendations and trophies, is comfortable. It is obvious that Representative Fattah is a golf enthusiast, as he has a portable golf putting green sitting next to the wall.

As he settles behind his desk, his first calls are from his son and daughter. They're checking in, reporting their test results, and letting him know their progress. It's all good news.

The first meeting of the day deals with Washington, D.C., and staffers assigned to research are meeting with Fattah in order to go over final instructions for a project.

"I think that we should look at how capitals are treated, especially by our counterparts, and then we can walk back from that to see how we can work in the District," he instructs them.

Washington, D.C., has always suffered from a dearth of funding, since its budget is determined by Congress. Fattah, as a member of the committee responsible for Washington's budget allocation, wants to see how other nations treat their capitals.

"If you look at world-class capitals, places where people are excited to go to, like Paris and London, then we can find out if there has been a significant interaction with the national governments in order to make those cities thrive. And we just want to see if we can quantify what is the actual situation between the items of support provided by national government and what the decisions are. We noticed that in these other capitals, people retain their voting rights. And when we look at the contributions of the national government to those cities, such as London, it almost seemed to be the reverse of what we have here in Washington. What we allocate for local spending is what their national government usually spends."

Fattah smiles and tells them that visiting all of these cities is not required. They laugh, asking if there is any way that it could be budgeted. Meeting over.

Chaka Fattah was elected to Congress in 1994 to the Second Congressional District, representing the city of Philadelphia. In a year of unprecedented Republican gains in Congress, Fattah won 85 percent of the vote in his district. He's a liberal Democrat elected during a conservative-Republican takeover of Congress. With seventy-three Republicans and only fourteen Democrats elected that year, 1994 was not the best of times for any Democrat, especially an African-American one.

"I got elected in 1994, which was a watershed election for the Congress in the sense that the Republicans took the majority for the first time in forty years. So there were about eighty new members of Congress, and I was one of a handful of new Democrats."

Nevertheless, he is viewed as an independent thinker who is willing to listen to any serious discussion of the issues. At age twenty-two, the unknown Fattah ran for his first office, a Philadelphia city commissioner position, and came in fourth in a citywide election featuring twenty-four Democrats. It was only discovered after the election, and after Fattah had received endorsement from two major Philadelphia newspapers, that at twenty-two, he was two years too young to serve on the board.

But even though he lost, this grassroots campaign would be the impetus for future campaigns, and by the time Fattah challenged the Democratic incumbent for retiring Congressman William Gray's old congressional seat, his Philadelphia political machine was set.

Subsequently elected as a Pennsylvania state representative and later a state senator, in the 1994 election, he defeated popular Democrat Lucien Blackwell without many Democratic endorsements. Therefore, even within his own party, Fattah is considered something of a maverick, and ambitious, rubbing some party members the wrong way.

After his election to Congress, Fattah told the *Philadelphia Inquirer* magazine, "Ambition can be a cross or a crown, and more often than not it's both things. Yeah, I'm ambitious. I think there's nobody in politics that is not ambitious. . . . The question is, what has my ambition and other positive and negative attributes been able to produce in terms of results?" He added, "It's funny how people admire ambition in most professional circumstances. People who are ambitious in business create companies, and in journalism they win Pulitzer Prizes. In politics we win elections.

"I'm not at all in awe of the Republican majority," he told the *Philadelphia Inquirer,* right after his election. "I believe that the only majority that counts is the majority of American people who want change." Elsewhere in the *Philadelphia Inquirer* he concluded: "I would like to be in the majority, but I don't feel handcuffed in terms of my ability to do anything because I'm in the minority. . . . Hey, I've been a minority all my life. Let's get it on."

Today, Fattah says that ego is really not what drives him. He's gotten over that and is more interested in creating a long legacy of legislation that remains after he leaves Congress.

In Congress, Fattah wants to be a shaper of urban public policy. To that end, Congressman Fattah scored a legislative victory when his first major education initiative, GEAR UP, was passed in 1998. GEAR UP (Gaining Early Awareness and Readiness for Undergraduate Programs) partners students from low-income schools with colleges and universities to help build an education pipeline for students to realize their college dreams. Including this fiscal year, there are 251 university partnerships and 28 state programs serving nearly 1.3 million students. Policy experts point to GEAR UP as one of the most innovative educational programs.

The William H. Gray College Completion Grant is another Fattah legislative achievement designed to help nearly 18,000 low-income minority students successfully complete college. This program aims to retain college students by offering resources to help them complete college and be fully prepared for success in the workforce or in graduate school. To date, GEAR UP and the College Completion Grant have received nearly $700 million in total combined funding.

"I think that in terms of empowerment, I think that education is unparalleled in terms of its ability to deal with adverse circumstances. It's a natural because it's a linchpin to everything else to the degree that if you can deal with education, people can deal with all of the other issues with which they are confronted."

Every congressman has the ability to do two things: work for his district and work for national legislation. Each has to make a choice, and Fattah chooses to balance the two, but with an emphasis on national legislation.

"There are about forty of us here who are African American and we're the only ones that can introduce policy. With forty million black people in this country, there are only forty of us who can do what we do. And so we should spend some part of our time doing legislation versus doing other things. At every point, every legislator has to make a decision about how much time they are going to spend on legislation and what types of issues. You have all kinds of pressures. I have 640,000 people in my district who like to see me, like to be able to talk to me, want to meet with me, and want to hear more about things that are more relevant to their immediate issues.

"You can focus on constituent services as your priority and you can focus on the potholes. Senator D'Amato's famous quote was that people didn't really care about what he did in Washington as long as he was responsive to his district. So what we have are certain members that make their districts their primary emphasis. We had one member from Philadelphia that went back to Philadelphia every single day that he was in Congress. And he was here for twenty years. He had a simple policy, which was that if you were in his district and you were in his office, no matter how many people that were in his office when he arrived back from Washington, he would see each and every one of them. Now, he never introduced any legislation in Washington, but he couldn't care about what was going on. That was just his way of doing things.

"You have members that are principally involved in how they can represent their district by how people in the district vote. They take polls and try to find out what are the issues within the district. Sometimes you are involved in all of these things to some degree or another. It's just something takes more of a priority than something else.

"I put together a quality staff in the district, and it is their principal job to deal with people in the District. Now if someone wants to see me, they get to see me. Now the reality is that if they need a passport, someone in the District is probably in a much better position to help them than I am. Because they are going to know much more about things than I'm going to know. But you can't tell some people that. But they first get offered real help for their difficulties," he laughs.

"You kind of work through it and I have to make some judgments. Now I have had a very successful political career, and I have a very good political operation in Philadelphia. So I'm not sweating every vote, because in the next election, I'm not going to be challenged in any significant way. So I have some luxury to be able to go over the wording of bills fifty different times so I can give the bill the focus and nuance that it is supposed to have."

Fattah's emphasis on making national legislation has been made difficult by the fact he is part of the Democrat minority within the House. Education, on the federal level, has long been a target of the Republican Party for dismantling, particularly among the Republican class of 1994, which pledged via its Contract With America that this and other departments would be eliminated. But Fattah has been able to work with them, he thinks partly because Republicans now realize that education is, along with Social Security, another third rail of politics.

"Republicans have always argued that there isn't a federal role for education," Fattah explained. "The conservatives argue that in the U.S. Constitution, education is not mentioned. If you take their argument to the extreme, the most right-wing Republican view is that the most the federal government should do is national defense. Things other than that, they see as the formation of a strong central government that was not intended by the drafters of the Constitution. Now, I don't agree with that at all, but that's their position. And then you have people like myself: that to promote the general welfare and provide for national defense has to include transportation, education, health care, and affordable housing, and so on. We get these two varying views, and depending who's in the White House, who's in the majority, and where the politics are at the moment, you get somewhere close to the middle.

"The Republicans, who took over in 1994, wanted to get rid of the Department of Energy, the Department of Education, Department of Commerce, because this was all a part of their Contract With America," he continued. "Then when the public began figuring some of this stuff out, they thought that they were crazy. You can't take a poll that doesn't say that education is not the number one issue in this country. So they literally had to back off. If you look at the Republican Congress up to Bush, meaning from Clinton to Bush, the Department of Education budget has doubled. So with all of that rhetoric that they wanted to get rid of it, they had to mold their reality to the will of the country. But even if you double the budget, it is still a tiny part of the total budget. Education is only two pennies out of every dollar of tax that you pay. It is still a drop in the bucket."

So if federal education programs are your bread and butter, yet you are a minority in a minority party, how do you get things done?

"Being in the minority makes it more difficult. I've never had the luxury of being in the majority. You are in a situation where you can't control the agenda. You can introduce bills, but you can't control the committees that the bills are referred to. You can't control whether the bill is ever brought up to discussion. So then you're left to trying to orchestrate things on the floor. We've been working for the past couple of years on equity in educational resources from the K-through-twelve level. But it's impossible to get a voting committee. So I have to go through other mechanisms to get legislation.

"Also, being an African-American member, you are in a minority caucus within a minority part. The Congressional Black Caucus, even though it is significant, is less significant in a Republican Congress when all of our members are in the Democratic caucus. So you have a number of different dynamics going on. However, having said that, I've been very successful in terms of getting things done, and I think that part of that is, there is a minority of members that are guiding the legislative debate. A large part of the membership on any particular issue play a very passive role, but there are a small group of Congressmen who are guiding the process. They're the ones offering the ideas and shaping the legislation as to if you are for or against the legislation. What I try to do is ingrain myself in the legislative process. We've been successful in spite of our circumstances, but I guess that's the case with most black people," he laughs.

"There are a number of ways to try to deal with passing legislation. For example, with my GEAR UP program, I introduced the bill and first off I needed to get one hundred Democrats behind the bill. We have 435 members of Congress, and 100 is the magic number in order to see if the idea has merit. And then to show that it has some reach beyond the Democratic Party, we try to round up about twenty Republican members of Congress to cosponsor. And that was an important mark to get President Clinton on board. So once we got the administration on board, we then began to work on how we could get a vote from the committee.

"The chairman of the committee, Republican William Goodling, was opposed to the idea, and the Republican Party was opposed to any new national educational initiative. That was one of their positions. They had a number of positions. One is that they wanted to dismantle the Department of Education at that time. And two, their legislative position was that they didn't want any more national education legislation. They wanted a consolidation of what they said were hundreds of education programs that, if consolidated, would be more effective. They wanted to consolidate and eliminate the targeting within the legislation, which says that funds should be used for low income neighborhoods, etc. They wanted to get rid of all of that, lump the money together, and then give the money to the states. So we come along with another national program that is specifically targeted to middle school children who are impoverished, which immediately goes to about three thousand middle schools in this country. This targets African Americans, Hispanics, and some rural school districts. And it's new and has never been done before. It basically promises these young people financial aid if they go on to college. That was the sizzle. The meat of it is that the middle school had to change its curriculum and do a whole bunch of things. They had to create a partnership with a college over six years, and you couldn't pull out kids with potential and leave the rest behind. Whatever you were offering, you had to offer to all of the kids. It was a much different approach than any federal effort in the past."

One of the people that Fattah convinced to support the bill was conservative Republican Mark Souder of Indiana. Souder noted that there is a shift on both sides of the House as members are beginning to realize that it is possible to work together on issues with common resonance.

"There are a group of young African-American leaders who

are willing to work with Republicans and focus on economic opportunities rather than just do finger-pointing."

"Some of it is generational politics," says Representative Harold Ford of Tennessee, a fellow African-American congressman. "A lot of the new guys associated with the conservative wing of the Republican Party bring an approach to governing that it's all about what works."

"So as we got it out of the House, we identified problems in the Senate," Fattah continued. "But that's my job, to identify problems and fix them. We were able to find support in the Senate from the Republican chairman of the Education Committee there, with some minor modifications, which encompassed changing the name of the program to incorporating some efforts the chairman had worked on years ago. So it all began to work together. And it worked out quite well."

But one of the ironies of creating legislation that is targeted toward African-American communities is that oftentimes, the money is not allocated to as many African-American communities as possible, mainly because African Americans are not a part of the process of grant allocation.

"You have a structural problem [in the African-American community]," said Fattah. "A lot of our institutions, school districts, colleges, community organizations, fraternities, and sororities don't have a person or a group of people that seek the money. They don't have the necessary person or persons to look for what grants are out there that fit with what they are trying to do. Whether it is government grants, foundation grants, it doesn't matter; you've got to have someone going after it. If you're not after it, you're not going to get it. You got to know, what are the rounds of cycles, and when are the applications due? What does the application require? Like for Gear Up, we did technical-assistant workshops all across the country, and everybody could come and learn how to apply and what the legislature required, but it was a new program. This program requires a college, a middle school, and a community service organization, and anybody can take the lead. So that's number one. You've got to have a staff person or a grant writer chasing the dollars.

"Secondly, they've got to write quality proposals, because programs like GEAR UP are competitive programs. There's no one in the federal government that says this place gets the program and this one doesn't. It doesn't work like that. During the first year, we had five hundred applications and only one hundred were funded. There were three cycles of readers who go through the proposals. Now, anybody can volunteer to be a reader. There may be fifteen different grants, and you can volunteer to read about five. The reader reads through the proposals and then gives them a grade. And then they go to someone else, and they also give the proposal a grade. And the ones that go to the top through this mechanism are the ones that get funded. We don't have enough African Americans who volunteer to be readers. Do you follow me? We've got a network over here that is skewed against you. So it's hopeless, but it is a systematic problem at each level, with African Americans not reading about grants available, not reading the grants, and so we don't get the grants."

Fattah gets around this problem by writing language into the bill that naturally points the grants to poor communities, the great majority filled with African Americans and Hispanics.

"Now the majority of the grants go to minority communities because of how the bill is structured. The law requires that the middle school have sixty percent of the students at the poverty level or below. But if you ask what are the percent of African-American colleges that are participating, or African-American community organizations, the number is very low because they're not applying. And it's not just my program but a lot of programs.

"The key thing with legislation is that whatever is not written into the law is up for interpretation. And as a lawmaker, you're not going to get a chance to interpret. So when it is in your hands, you must be as specific as possible. You want the bill to be clear about who the target is, what the problem is, and GEAR UP is just one example. But in GEAR UP, we targeted middle schools with an aggregation of poverty. Not a school where just one or two kids are poor, but where there is a significant population of students at the working-class level or lower. Because obviously, you have a study that shows this population goes to college a lot less than the rest of the population. So that limits you to three thousand middle schools out of tens of thousands of middle schools that could be the center of that activity."

Fattah thinks that the involvement of colleges in the process makes the program work, as the middle school children that they work with are more enthusiastic about the prospect of attending college, versus the high school student who may have already given up on the thought.

"Colleges have traditionally never been involved in middle schools. To the degree that they are involved at all, they tend to work with high schools. They tend to be more mature, and there's a little bit of more gratification because the college wants the student to come to their college. So if they work with you in the eleventh grade or twelfth grade, then there is a more likelihood that you are going to come in their direction. If you work with a middle school kid, you don't know where they may end up. So now [for the colleges] it is more that you want them to go a college and not just go to our college."

Now that Gear Up has been passed, Fattah is trying to attack one of the central reasons why there is a disparity in education in America. School districts in the United States are funded by local property taxes, leaving rich neighborhoods with resource-filled schools, and poor neighborhoods with marginal schools.

"The Equal Protection School Finance Act uses federal leverage to encourage states to equalize per-student expenditure of state funds across school districts. Using the equal-protection clause of the Constitution as the legal foundation for the requirement, the legislation establishes this equalization as a precondition for the receipt of federal funds for education," says Fattah.

"Since 1971, 69 court cases have been filed in states across the nation testing the legality of school finance systems that deny children equal protection by generating inter-district financial disparities. Therefore, children from economically distressed districts are consigned to inferior education. Thus, creating unequal educational opportunities. The Equal Protection School Finance

Act will provide the legal basis for the swift resolution of pending cases so that the process of evolving a modern system of school finance that invests equally in the future of each child can begin."

It is now just after lunchtime. The phone is beginning to ring constantly as other representatives, students, and constituents are beginning to inquire, ask questions, bargain, and ask for help. Nothing seems too mundane. Even an irate Philadelphia teacher, who feels that the school district is out to get her, gets an ear. Now it is off to vote.

"The congressman's constituency loves him," says Murray, as the Congressman walks out the door. "Just the fact that the people that you represent love you that much speaks volumes. They love his gritty attitude and also his savvy. He's in a Republican Congress but he still gets things done. That speaks to you as a legislator, as you understand what is in the best interest of your district. He keeps their interest in mind and doesn't compromise his values. I think that they like that about him."

35

The Sage of Blacksburg

Blacksburg, Virgina

A poet is someone who is astonished by everything.

—Anonymous

Nestled in the Blue Ridge Mountains, the Warm Hearth Village retirement community in Blacksburg, Virginia, sits as a tranquil retreat, a respite from the frenetic highway construction happening only a mile away. Forest land and gently undulating hills house various facilities. Although about two hundred elderly residents live in the Warm Hearth Village complex, it doesn't feel like the typically sterile retirement home setting. On a typical day, you can see Warm Hearth Village residents jogging along rustic trails, walking through the forest, or just sitting on any one of the many benches.

According to the brochure, the Warm Hearth Village residents can enjoy a variety of activities such as line dancing, nature tours, flower classes, and arts and crafts, or they can integrate themselves with the Blacksburg community. But on this Wednesday morning, six women sit in a lobby, waiting patiently for something else, something not mentioned in the brochure. They are waiting for a Virginia Tech professor, a professor who for the past decade has been leading a writers' group at the Warm Hearth Village.

The elevator door opens to the third-floor lobby, and the professor smiles and greets the women assembled. To the stranger, there is an immediate contrast between the professor and the women. First, the women are all white, while the professor is a black woman. The women are all elderly, and the professor, while a little older, has a young attitude. The women look like they lived their lives close to the Norman Rockwell ethic, while the professor has a tattoo on her arm as a tribute to the late rapper Tupac Shakur. However, first impressions can be deceiving, as these women of different backgrounds do have something in common. They are writers, and as writers they find it important to tell their stories each week in a workshop. And leading that workshop is none other than Professor Nikki Giovanni.

"We represent an age that is passing," says Giovanni as she settles into her chair. "Storytelling has always been how human beings trained themselves, and it is being lost."

Nikki Giovanni is about five feet something and weighs about a buck and small change. In other words, she is not very tall or very big in physical stature. Yet she has an unmistakable presence when you are around her. Her hair is graying and styled in neat braids, à la Allen Iverson. She wears an oversized suit because, as she stated once, "Everybody I know who's powerful wears a tie, and I want to be powerful." Giovanni is her own woman.

The official biography says that Yolanda Cornelia "Nikki" Giovanni was born in Knoxville, Tennessee, and raised in Ohio. In 1960, she entered Fisk University, where she worked with the school's writers' workshop and edited the literary magazine. After receiving her bachelor of arts degree, she organized the Black Arts Festival in Cincinnati and then entered graduate school at the University of Pennsylvania. In her first two collections, *Black Feeling, Black Talk* (1968) and *Black Judgment* (1969), Giovanni reflects on the African-American identity. Recently, she has published *Blues For All the Changes: New Poems* (William Morrow & Company, 1999), *Love Poems* (1997), and *Selected Poems of Nikki Giovanni* (1996). Her honors include the NAACP Image Award for Literature, in 1998, and the Langston Hughes award for Distinguished Contributions to Arts and Letters, in 1996.

Several magazines have named Giovanni Woman of the Year, including *Essence, Mademoiselle,* and *Ladies Home Journal.* She is currently Professor of English and Gloria D. Smith Professor of Black Studies at Virginia Tech.

The ladies of the Warm Hearth Springs writers' workshop know all about Professor Giovanni's credentials and awards, but that's not what they are thinking about today. A local television crew has spotlighted the writers' workshop as a human-interest piece, and a workshop member has taped the segment for today's meeting.

"The tape is only about seven minutes long," one woman says, somewhat disappointedly, as the tape begins.

"Seven minutes on television is a long time," Giovanni gently informs her.

The tape begins, and all of the women groan slightly, as it seems the old adage that television adds ten pounds seems to be true. But all agree that the piece was a very flattering one, and it highlights not only Giovanni but also the work of the workshop. By the time the tape ends, all of the women have smiles and pleased looks on their faces. It's now time for the workshop to begin.

"This is a nonpressure writers' workshop," Giovanni explains as the microphone is set up. The microphone is for those workshop leaders who are hard of hearing.

"It is also a noncritical one. But everyone writes better [when they attend]. Over the years, you can hear how people are now telling their stories."

A few years back, Giovanni and various workshop members collected their stories to produce a compilation called *Appalachian Elders.* For most of the women, this was the first time that they had been published, and now it seems as though it has whetted their appetite for writing. Now they speak about collecting their memoirs and poetry for possible publication.

But first, there is the matter of the health check. Being advanced in age, the health status of individual members is not an idle interest, but in some cases a matter of life and death. This week, everyone is concerned with the health of Nadine, a workshop member who has suffered a fall and broken her wrist and hip. She's recuperating in a local hospital.

A short discussion commences about what flowers can be delivered to a hospital room (roses are okay, other flowers are not).

"Make sure to give me her information so I can send her a card," Giovanni tells the group.

With that, the group begins telling their stories. The writer's story is a simple one about a day in Blacksburg. She talks about a day of eating peach cobbler, the difference between city girls and country folk, and flat-foot dancing.

"I had never heard of flat-foot dancing before, but it goes a little like this," the writer says, before launching into a spirited demonstration.

"That reminds me of how women in the Holiness Church move when they catch the spirit," Giovanni remarks. "You see, they can't lift their feet when they move because that would be dancing. So they slide their feet."

Next is a poem about time and how the youth and the elderly view the same element, with drastically different meanings. Another speaks about growing up in Denver, Colorado, before most modern conveniences. Last, in a poignant reading, one writer recalls the funeral of her stepson. She notes how, as an LSU professor, he was able to be just as colorful in death as in life.

Giovanni's role in the workshop is not necessarily to critique the quality of each piece, but to somehow put it into some sort of context. The seniors are not professional writers, but that's not the point. They are introspective and are clear about who and what they are. But they still want to know what their words mean beyond the context of their own thoughts. How do others hear their words? Giovanni helps them by referring to different mediums, such as old movies, to continue to illustrate the words of the workshop members.

And just like that, as soon as the workshop began, it is over. An hour goes by quickly. Giovanni tells the group that she will miss the next meeting because of a commitment to a book event sponsored by Ethel Kennedy. But she promises to see them again soon. The good-byes are said, and soon Giovanni is on the elevator.

In 1967 Nikki Giovanni was actively involved in the Black Arts Movement, a coalition of African-American intellectuals who wrote radical poems to raise awareness of black rights and the struggle for racial equality. Her poetry is renowned for its call of urgency for black people to realize their identities and understand their surroundings as part of a white-controlled culture. In other works, Giovanni also focuses on her family and personal relationships. The rest of her Wednesday will encompass both of these elements.

When you spend even a little time around Giovanni, it becomes readily apparent that she has developed a lot of opinions about a number of subjects, and she expects that if you are in her presence, you'd better have thought about some of these things also. She's blunt and in your face, but not just for the hell of being blunt and in your face. She curses without apology, and expletives sprinkle her sentences like spicy seasoning. And she doesn't suffer fools. It's as though she's saying, "What are you made of? Do you agree with everything I say, or do you have the balls to have your own opinion and express it?" Time would tell.

But on the other hand, like most famous people, Giovanni doesn't live her day-to-day life as an icon, in this case a poetic icon. She doesn't walk through life spitting out deep verse to random strangers. Giovanni the regular sister plays a mean game of bid whist, loves to cook, shops at the local Barnes and Noble, and can recite dialogue from classic movies.

In some ways, Giovanni is a traditional Southern woman, even though technically she grew up in Cincinnati, Ohio, a Northern city. For most black folks, Cincinnati is an "up-south" city, more often influenced by nearby conservative Kentucky realities than adhering to any so-called liberal Northern sensibilities. So in Giovanni's life, the spirituality that comes with the African-American experience in the South is one of the connective tissues that tie all of her personal life and professional life together. Giovanni even created Virginia Tech's choir, the Hush

Harbor Choir, which demonstrates the power of the spirituals to the Blacksburg community.

"Slaves gathered in hush harbors—the fields or swamps away from the owner's house—to sing their spirituals. Such gatherings were illegal and punishable by whipping, being sold, or even being killed; but when the spirit moved the slaves to praise their Lord they snuck off to sing songs about their tribulations and their faith," Giovanni explains.

After the workshop, Giovanni begins the rest of her day. Her tasks range from the mundane, such as getting her rug cleaned and buying shoe polish, to the personal. Her beloved mother is anemic and not eating regularly, so she is meeting with her sister Gary and Giovanni's best friend and fellow Virginia Tech professor, Ginney Fowler, for lunch at an Indian restaurant. They feel that if they go to a restaurant, she'll eat more. After that, it is back to her Virginia Tech office for her final office hours of the semester, as school ended yesterday.

Giovanni tools her red Toyota around the streets of Blacksburg, and the conversation turns to Spike Lee. Lee has just appeared on the Virginia Tech campus, and per his usual, he made a number of controversial comments about Hollywood and certain actors. Giovanni took issue with his comments about Morgan Freeman's portrayal of the black chauffeur Hoke Coburn in *Driving Miss Daisy.* Lee had denigrated Freeman as being racially offensive.

"Lee is full of shit and I told him that to his face," Giovanni remarked. "I thought that Morgan Freeman deserved an Oscar for his performance. Here is a black man that loses his job and then finds a job that puts his daughter through school so that she earns a doctorate. And that is somehow wrong?"

"And what is it with Lee and women?" she continues. "I mean, did you see that scene in *Do The Right Thing* where Lee gets in bed with his sister? What the hell was that about? That's when I knew that something was wrong with him."

What is her opinion about Oprah Winfrey?

"My problem with Oprah is not that she is getting a billion dollars. My problem is that she is blocking others in order to get that billion. Anyone can say, 'Good morning.' But she thinks that she is uniquely qualified to do what she does."

And what does she think about Oprah's mentor and fellow poet Maya Angelou?

"I lost respect for her when she testified for Clarence Thomas," says Giovanni. "Not a lot of people know about that."

Giovanni drives on. The rug's dropped off (curbside service) and the red shoe polish ordered, a quick stop at the Barnes and Noble is required in order to autograph a copy of her book, *The Selected Poems of Nikki Giovanni.* As she enters the bookstore, she picks up an *Ishmael Reed Reader* that lies on the remainders table. It is a bargain at only five dollars.

Blacksburg is a relatively small town, and except for the large Virginia Tech campus, it could realistically fade into the rest of rural Virginia. One of the traditional aspects of small-town life is that people in town get to know each other. Giovanni is no exception. The rug guy greets her by name, while the shoe-polish store owner kids her about working so hard that her shoes are wearing out. To them, she is just another neighbor.

It is on to the restaurant. Standing outside are Ginney, Gary, and Ethel Giovanni, Nikki's mother. The place is packed with Virginia Tech students for the lunchtime buffet.

"Hello, Mommy," Giovanni greets her mother. She gives her a kiss and they all make their way to a table. Instantly, two of Giovanni's students greet her and talk about their impending graduation. They leave and now Giovanni's attention turns to her mother. Ethel is a slight woman, even tinier than Nikki, and even though she doesn't hear well, she has a hearing aid which causes people to have to speak directly to her ear—she lives life with a mischievous glint in her eye. She knows that her daughters are trying to get her to eat, and she's trying to fool them into thinking that she is going to eat.

"Mommy, what did you eat this morning?" asks Nikki.

"Gary made me some breakfast," she replies.

"Did you eat some grits?"

"No, I didn't."

"You should eat some grits."

Ethel smiles. She didn't eat grits this morning, and it doesn't seem that she is going to ever eat grits unless *she* decides that she wants grits. It is easy to see where Nikki gets her constitution. However, she is here at the restaurant; she does seem to have an interest in this food. She and the family have been here before and she likes the food. Today it will be soup.

As Ethel eats her soup, Nikki begins telling her mother the importance of eating regularly. Ethel looks up and points to a rather obese woman sitting at a distant table.

"See that woman right there?" she says with a wry smile, "you guys want me to look like her!"

They all laugh, but Gary and Nikki are truly worried about their mother. Their love for her means that as they leave the restaurant, although a little bit happier because they saw her eat a meal, they are still coordinating future meals for their mother.

With two out of three missions accomplished, it is now on to the Virginia Tech campus for final office hours of the semester. As we walk on the campus, Giovanni sees and greets fellow professors. On the sidewalk pathway to her office, there are noticeable white patches. It looks like the sidewalk has been scrubbed by a high-pressure hose, and it has.

"We had a 'Take Back the Night' march, and someone decided to spray-paint 'Stop Rape' on the sidewalks," Giovanni explained. "The university got angry and decided to confiscate the computers of the organizers. They wanted to figure out who was responsible. It was ridiculous. So as a protest, I don't use my computer in my office."

Giovanni gets to her office, and immediately students begin to stop by. The office, bedecked by a large framed poster of Tupac Shakur, is just like any typical English professor's office. Books, on top of other books, are everywhere. Class projects are stacked neatly.

About five students stop by the office to sit and have a quiet chat. One graduate student brings over his girlfriend because she has always wanted to meet Giovanni. Another is a student in Giovanni's class, and she is just saying good-bye for the summer. One other has brought a stack of Giovanni's books for autographs. And there's one more who is telling Giovanni about his graduate school plans.

The students in this office are a racial mix. In fact, only one of these students is African-American, demonstrating the appeal that Giovanni has among all of the Virginia Tech students.

The students go over their classes, future plans, and laugh at Giovanni's humor. Giovanni cracks them up by saying that she would love to have an honorary degree from Oxford University, because their robes are beautiful.

"I'm on the board and I keep dropping hints," she laughs.

Recently, Giovanni read Eric Schlosser's best-selling book, *Fast Food Nation. Fast Food Nation* tells the horror of America's obsession with fast food, and its impact on the world. Giovanni, who is adamantly against fast food, says that there is another unpleasant aspect to eating fast food.

"You know, there's a student that is always eating Burger King, and I swear that the office always stinks when he leaves the office," says Giovanni, to the laughter of the students.

After a bit, they all peel off, wishing Giovanni a nice summer. A final student enters. She's a dreadlocked sister who is a graduate art student. She's coming to Giovanni for some advice. She's worried that her art colleagues at Virginia Tech think that she's standoffish because she doesn't socialize with them. And she's wondering if this will affect her career.

"I am a person that is more interested in going to a poetry slam than going to slam beers," she says. "I'm trying to figure out whether or not I want to be an artist or an activist. People think that I'm antisocial."

After she goes on about another five minutes, Giovanni cuts to the chase.

"What does it matter if you are not social?" says Giovanni, staring her directly in the eyes. "You don't have to explain to the people in the department that you don't want to have a beer with them."

"I just know that I'm not friendly," she continues. "I had a revelation that in all of the time that I lived in New York, that I didn't have a lot of friends there. I had a lot of people that I worked with, and sometimes that is better. And I lived there eleven years.

"I don't see any particular reason to alienate people," she concludes. "You can say no, but there isn't a reason to be impolite. But people will make you crazy."

Both laugh, and it now seems that the sister has a better perspective on her problem. But Giovanni has one last piece of advice for the young woman.

"Don't get distracted by talking about what you want to do, and do what you want to do. I could spend my time arguing with Virginia Tech about teaching a course on the spirituals, or I could just teach a course on the spirituals. I don't care if people like it. I'm just going to do it."

There's an unspoken peace around Giovanni's aura. It is what attracts people to her. Beyond her blunt and honest nature lies a vulnerable person. But she's not vulnerable as in being weak. Giovanni has allowed herself to be vulnerable to letting her spirituality and love of God and family lead her in life. And through that, she has found the strength to survive cancer, raise a son, and become a success. Maybe that's why every conversation with her begins and ends with a smile. She doesn't have time to let things in this life get or keep her down, and whether she's working on her poetry, sitting with students, or leading elderly residents in a writers' workshop, she is happy with who and what she is.

"Ninety percent of happiness is job satisfaction. I get a great deal of satisfaction as a poet," she says.

Postscript

About African Americans and the Death Penalty

In 2000, 88 percent of all known executions took place in China, Iran, Saudi Arabia, and the U.S.A. In China, the limited and incomplete records available to Amnesty International at the end of the year indicated that at least 1,000 people were executed, but the true figure was believed to be much higher. In Saudi Arabia, 123 executions were reported, but the total may have been much higher. Eighty-five people were executed in the U.S.A. At least 75 executions were carried out in Iran. In addition, hundreds of executions were reported in Iraq, but many of them may have been extrajudicial.

Use of the death penalty in the United States dates back to colonial times, with the first recorded execution taking place in Jamestown in 1608. Although its use has always varied from state to state, it was practiced regularly throughout most of our history until 1967, when a temporary ban was instituted while the Supreme Court reviewed its constitutionality.

In 1972, in a 5–4 decision *(Furman* v. *Georgia)*, the Court ruled that the death penalty as practiced in Georgia was a violation of the Eighth Amendment, which bans cruel and unusual punishment. The ruling focused on unguided jury discretion and the resulting arbitrary and capricious sentencing that took place because of it. However, the court left open the possibility that the death penalty could be reinstated if it were redesigned to avoid these problems. In response, several states set about redrafting their sentencing laws, and in 1976 the Court reinstated the death penalty after a ten-year moratorium. The first execution took place on January 17, 1977, when Gary Gilmore was executed by a firing squad in Utah. Federal death penalty statutes were revised in 1988, 1994, and 1996. Since 1977 over 650 people have been executed.

Death penalty supporters argue that justice demands a death sentence in certain cases, and that the concept of "an eye for an eye" is based on the nation's shared religious values. They further argue that the death penalty can deter capital crimes and possibly save lives in the process. In addition to any deterrent effects, supporters argue that there is an additional incapacitation effect as executed offenders will never commit another capital offense. Opponents counter that there is no valid statistical evidence supporting the assertion that crimes are deterred by the death penalty, and that capital offenders can just as easily be prevented from committing further crimes by a life sentence with no possibility of parole.

Opponents argue that that high rates of error in the criminal justice system make it quite possible to execute someone who is innocent, making the state itself guilty of murder. Since 1973 at least 88 people on death row were released after evidence emerged indicating their innocence. Supporters counter that there is no evidence that any innocent individual has ever been executed since the death penalty was reinstated in 1977, and that releases of innocent individuals on death row since then were either due to legal technicalities or demonstrated that the system's checks and balances work.

Opponents argue that only a small percentage of those convicted of capital crimes actually receive the death penalty, and those who are executed are most notable for their lack of resources or poor legal representation. Race is often posited as a potential factor. For instance, while African Americans only make up about 13 percent of the U.S. population, they made up 43 percent of the inmates on death row in 1999, and a little more than a third of those actually executed that year. Supporters argue that African Americans are more likely to commit murders than whites, and that their victims are more often African Americans themselves, so racial issues cut in both directions.

About Pornography

An estimated $8–$10 billion is spent annually by Americans for pornography in all forms, and this exceeds the combined gross of ABC, CBS, and NBC, which is $6.2 billion. 200 million copies of *Hustler, Penthouse,* and *Playboy* are distributed in U.S. homes every year. The combined circulation of *Playboy* and *Penthouse* exceeds that of *Time* and *Newsweek.*

The average age at which men first see *Playboy* or a similar magazine is eleven. A pornographic film can be made for only $20,000 to $125,000 and can make up to $2 million in profit from retail sales.

Laboratory studies have shown that viewing violent pornographic films can increase aggression against women. In a 1985 study of 256 nonincarcerated perpetrators of sexual offenses who were undergoing treatment, 56 percent of rapists and 42 percent of women said they had been sexually abused by someone they knew, as a direct result of his use of pornography. A 1986 *Woman's Day* magazine survey of 6,000 readers found that 21 percent of women said they had been sexually abused by someone they knew, as a direct result of his use of pornography.

The actual making of pornography sometimes involves violence and sexual assault; actress Linda Marchiano testified that she had been held at gunpoint to perform in the movie *Deep Throat.* It is believed that 70 percent of women involved in pornography are survivors of incest or child sexual abuse.

About African Americans and Inner-City Schools

There are approximately 46 million students in about 16,000 separate public school districts, and of these, 16 percent are African American. 88 percent of public school teachers are white. The most intense school segregation happens in large Northern metropolitan areas surrounded by white suburbs. Students of color in rural areas and small towns are much more likely to attend integrated schools than those who live in large cities.

Big metropolitan areas maintain school segregation by having smaller school districts. The 1974 Supreme Court decision in *Milliken* v. *Bradley* forbids desegregation plans that cross school district lines, so if the suburb and the city have separate districts, their students won't be able to attend the same schools.

Schools in this country are both separate and profoundly unequal. White suburban schools have vastly more money than inner-city schools, whose students are often 90 to 100 percent children of color. That's because almost half of school funding comes from local property taxes. In New York State, the richest school district spent $38,572 per student in 1992. That's seven times what the poorest school district spent, which was $5,423. In Illinois, the ratio was eight to one. In Texas, per-student spending ranged from $3,098 to more than ten times as much, at $42,000.

In metropolitan Philadelphia, inner-city dropout rates are four times as high as those of suburban schools.

About Blacks in Canada

The first known black man to arrive in Canada was Matthieu DaCosta, in 1603. He acted as a translator between the Micmac Indians and the French with Champlain. Clearly, DaCosta had been in Canada some time previous to Champlain's voyage of discovery, since Micmac is neither a European nor an African language.

In 1628, the first known slave, Olivier LeJeune, is recorded. As a child of six, he had been captured in Africa and was later given the surname of one of his owners, a priest.

In 1779, with the hopes of winning the American Revolution, the British under Sir Henry Clinton invited all black men, women, and children to join the British side, and promised them their freedom for doing so. Ten percent of the Loyalists coming from the Maritimes are black. Later, in 1793, the Upper Canada Abolition Act, supported by Lieutenant Governor Simcoe, freed any slave who came into the province of Ontario, and stipulated that any child born of a slave mother should be free at the age of twenty-five.

The Cochrane Proclamation invited refugees of the War of 1812 to become British citizens through residence in British territory, including Canada. Black veterans of the War of 1812 established the settlement of Oro. In 1833, the British Imperial Act abolished slavery in the British Empire, including Canada.

Between 1800 and 1865, approximately 20,000 blacks found their way into Canada via the Underground Railroad. Harriet Tubman, one of the most famous "conductors" on the Underground Railroad, spirited several hundred fugitive slaves into Canada, despite a $40,000 reward for her capture, dead or alive.

The year 1905 marked the beginning of the "Black Trek," the migration of dissatisfied African Americans from Oklahoma to the Canadian prairies. That year, a group led by W. E. B. DuBois and Monroe Trotter met secretly in Niagara, Ontario, to organize resistance to U.S. racism.

But despite the lack of enthusiasm for slavery, and the progressive outlook of lawmakers in Canada, the social and economic conditions for black settlers were not very promising. Black settlers, most of whom were farmers, were easily squeezed out of the land by unfavorable, arbitrary terms for land and property rights. No laws protected them against abuse of rights to work and livelihood, or provided immediately attainable recourse to combat such injustices.

During the First World War, black Canadians joined combat units, despite opposition, and in 1916, a segregated unit, the Nova Scotia Number 2 Construction Battalion, was formed. In the Second World War, authorities again tried to keep blacks out of the armed forces, but blacks insisted on serving their country. Eventually, they joined all services.

The first black member of Parliament, Lincoln Alexander, was elected in 1968. In 1979, he became Canada's first black cabinet member, as the minister of labour in the federal government. In 1985, he became Ontario's first black lieutenant governor, and the first black to be appointed to a vice-regal position in Canada. In 1993, Jean Augustine was sworn in as Canada's first black member of Parliament.

Today, about 2 percent of 28.5 million Canadians identify themselves as black.

About African Americans and Book-Buying

African-American book buyers are heavy consumers of fiction, are usually making their purchase at a chain store, and are generally eschewing national best-seller lists in favor of personal recommendations. According to one study, 68 percent of African Americans surveyed said that they didn't use a best-sellers list for making purchasing decisions, but among those African-American book buyers who do use lists, black media are far and away the most influential factors.

In the same survey, 83 percent of African-American respondents said that they are more apt to have purchased a book from a chain store versus 9 percent from a black store.

About African Americans and the Automobile Industry

One of the major problems with the automobile industry has been their traditional reluctance to spend marketing dollars to woo the African-American and minority community. Also, although American car dealers have shown a commitment to marketing to these communities and opening minority-owned dealerships, strategic marketing and dealerships with import companies have been a rarity for African Americans.

African Americans are increasingly aggressive at flexing their muscle and targeting their spending dollars. When soliciting or being solicited for business, they are highly concerned about relationships with the African-American community. Many establish certain kinds of partnerships as conditions for doing business, including internships, scholarships, and other bridges to African-American participation. The prevalent position in the African-American community is that African-American dollars are commodities that are sought after and that must be used to leverage opportunities for African-American people.

Under pressure from Jesse Jackson's Rainbow Push and other civil rights organizations, the car industry has been creating new programs designed to address these issues.

Hyundai Motor America devoted 15 percent of its marketing budget to reach minorities, with an emphasis on Hispanics and blacks. In 2002, Hyundai would spend $21 million, up $12.6 million from the year before. The automaker hopes to reach consumers who have considered Hyundai in the past. About 7 percent of Hyundai buyers are African-American.

In 2002, American Honda and its upscale Acura division, which has 1,262 dealerships, had only 41 dealerships owned by minorities. In order to increase its minority dealerships, Honda has created a program that allows blacks, Hispanics, and Asians to buy dealerships with only 15 percent equity. Honda will finance the rest of the dealership. And after five to seven years, the minority dealer will be able to buy out the company.

Of the eight minority dealers who have been awarded franchises during Honda's 2002 fiscal year, which ended in March, two were awarded franchises under the investment program.

Compromising 13 percent of the U.S. population, African Americans have an annual income of approximately $500 billion per year. This earning level would be high enough to rank African Americans among the Summit of Eight nations; right alongside the Russian Federation, which has a total income of $331 billion.